PUBLIC RELATIONS DEMOCRACY

MANCHESTER
UNIVERSITY PRESS

PUBLIC RELATIONS DEMOCRACY

Public relations, politics and the mass media in Britain

AERON DAVIS

Manchester University Press
Manchester and New York

distributed exclusively in the USA by Palgrave

1/03

Published by Manchester University Press
Oxford Road, Manchester M13 9NR, UK
and Room 400, 175 Fifth Avenue, New York, NY 10010, USA
www.manchesteruniversitypress.co.uk

Distributed exclusively in the USA by
Palgrave, 175 Fifth Avenue, New York,
NY 10010, USA

Distributed exclusively in Canada by
UBC Press, University of British Columbia, 2029 West Mall,
Vancouver, BC, Canada V6T 1Z2

British Library Cataloguing-in-Publication Data
A catalogue record for this book is available from the British Library

Library of Congress Cataloging-in-Publication Data applied for

ISBN 0 7190 6068 0 *hardback*
      0 7190 6069 9 *paperback*

First published 2002

10 09 08 07 06 05 04 03 02   10 9 8 7 6 5 4 3 2 1

Typeset by
D R Bungay Associates, Burghfield, Berks

Printed in Great Britain
by Bookcraft (Bath) Ltd, Midsomer Norton

CONTENTS

LIST OF TABLES

List of figures

PREFACE AND ACKNOWLEDGEMENTS

This book is about the rise of professional public relations and its impact on the news media and political process in Britain. The public relations profession has expanded quite considerably over the last two decades. Its methods and personnel have been adopted by a wide range of institutions, businesses and interest groups. In the same period the shape of both the news media and the British political system have also shifted. Such shifts have left the media more vulnerable to the promotional efforts of political actors. They have also made the media more central to the setting of political and economic agendas and the decision-making processes that follow. In other words, the rise of public relations has contributed to a greater 'mediatisation' of the political process. The results have been the development of a sort of democracy by public relations.

In terms of theory and empirical content this book is fairly interdisciplinary, covering subject matter of interest to scholars and students of media studies, politics, sociology and public relations. Its primary target audience is, however, those with an interest in media sociology and political communications. For media sociologists it makes a strong case for putting the topic of public relations firmly on the research agenda. It also reiterates the case for looking more closely at the part played by the media in policy-making. For political communications the findings suggest that research needs to be expanded far beyond the narrow focus on general elections and party-political spin doctors that has hitherto guided the subject. For both subdisciplines it is also an attempt to merge two very separate sets of literature and data. The results are probably best described as a political sociology of the media, something that should also be of significant interest to political sociologists. Finally it should be stated that, although this book offers some interesting reading for public relations practitioners, it is not written specifically with them in mind. It is not a do-it-yourself guide to the subject nor does it really engage with the principle concerns of many in the profession.

There are several formal and informal acknowledgements which need to be made. Beginning with the formal, I must start by thanking the Economic and Social Research Council (R00429824372) for providing the funding needed to complete this work. Thanks are also due to Sage and Arnold for their permission to reproduce material that earlier appeared in the following articles: 'Public Relations, News Production and Changing Patterns of Source Access in the British National Press' in *Media, Culture and Society*, Vol. 22, No. 1; 'Public Relations, Business News and the Reproduction of Corporate Elite Power' in *Journalism: Theory, Practice and Criticism*, Vol. 1, No. 3; 'Public Relations Campaigning and News

Production: The Case of "New Unionism" in Britain' in J. Curran (ed.) *Media Organisations in Society*, London, Arnold, 2000. Thanks are also due to: the University of Michigan Press for permission to reproduce Table 3.1 which originally appeared in N. Mitchell, *The Conspicuous Corporation: Business, Publicity and Representative Democracy*, Ann Arbor, University of Michigan Press, 1997; and to Jon White and Laura Mazur for reproducing Table 4.2 which originally appeared in their book *Strategic Communications Management: Making Public Relations Work*, Wokingham, Addison-Wesley, 1995.

I would like to thank all those who agreed to be interviewed and who helped me find my way round numerous library collections and filing systems. Those who stand out for being especially helpful include staff at the Trades Union Congress (TUC), Public Relatons Consultants' Association (PRCA) and Institute of Public Relations (IPR) libraries, the Communication Workers' Union (CWU) union, Citigate, Group 4, the Prison Officers' Union (POA), and the Communications Group. Mike Power (TUC), Chris Hopson (Granada), Richard Power (RF Hotels), Alistair Defriez (the Takeover Panel), Stephen Farish (PR Week) and Tim Jackaman (Square Mile) were all extremely generous with their time.

For agreeing to take on this project and gambling on a relative newcomer I am very grateful to Tony Mason and Richard Delahunty of Manchester University Press. For useful insights, words of encouragement, supporting references and administrative help, amongst other things, I want to thank the following: James Dunkerley, Chris Taylor, Colin Leys, Dave Morley, Bill Schwarz, Gareth Stanton, Christine Geraghty, Angela McRobbie, Nick Couldrey, Peter Golding, Margaret Scammell, Herbert Pimlott, Jonathan Burstein, Sheila Sheehan, Colin Aggett, and Kay Shoesmith. For their continuing personal support, my love and thanks to Helen Davis, Neville Davis, Anne Solomon, Michael Neil, Roman Krznaric and Mike Kaye. Finally, I will always be grateful to James Curran, my guide and mentor during this project. A combination of thoughtful insights, kind words, tough deadlines, publishing advice, friendship and Wimbledon football tickets all played a part in getting me to the finish line.

LIST OF ACRONYMS AND ABBREVIATIONS

ABCC	Association of British Chambers of Commerce
ACAS	Arbitration and Conciliation Advisory Services
ACRE	Action with Rural Communities in England
AEEU	Association of Electrical Engineers' Union
AEU	Association of Electricians' Union
AFSC	American Friends Service Committee
AGM	annual general meeting
AMA	American Management Association
AMO	Association of Magistrates' Officers
ASLEF	Associated Society of Locomotive Engineers and Firemen
AUEW	Associated Union of Electrical Workers
BAA	British Airports Authority
BALPA	British Airline Pilots' Association
BBC	British Broadcasting Company
BFAWU	Bakers, Food and Allied Workers' Union
BFI	British Film Institute
BIFU	Banking, Insurance and Finance Union
BMA	British Medical Association
BP	British Petroleum
BT	British Telecom
CARMA	Computer Aided Research and Media Analysis
CBI	Confederation of British Industry
CD-ROM	Compact disk-read only memory
CEO	chief executive officer
CMA	Communication Managers' Association
COI	Central Office of Information
CRE	Commission for Racial Equality
CWU	Communication Workers' Union
DfES	Department for Education and Skills
DHSS	Department of Health and Social Security
DoE	Department of the Environment
DTI	Department of Trade and Industry
DVLA	Driver and Vehicle Licensing Authority
EAG	Economic Advisory Group
EFL	External Financing Limit
ERM	Exchange Rate Mechanism
EU	European Union
FCO	Foreign and Commonwealth Office
FDA	First Division Association of Civil Servants

FT	*Financial Times*
FTA	Financial Times Actuaries
FTSE	Financial Times Stock Exchange
GATT	General Agreement on Trades and Tariffs
GDP	gross domestic product
GICS	Government Information and Communication Services
GIS	Government Information Services
GLC	Greater London Council
GMB	General and Municipal Boilermakers' Union
GMWU	General Municipal Workers' Union
GUMG	Glasgow University Media Group
HCSA	Hospital Consultants and Specialists Association
HMSO	Her Majesty's Stationery Office
IoD	Institute of Directors
IPR	Institute of Public Relations
IRS	Investor Relations Society
ITC	Independent Television Commission
ITN	Independent Television News
ITV	Independent Television
LSE	London School of Economics
LWT	London Weekend Television
MAFF	Ministry of Agriculture, Food and Fisheries
MAM	Mercury Asset Management
MEAL	Media Expenditure Analysis Limited
MMC	Monopolies and Mergers Commission
MoD	Ministry of Defence
MORI	Market and Opinion Research Institute
MP	Member of Parliament
MSF	Manufacturing, Science and Finance Union
MU	Musicians' Union
MUA	Mail Users Association
NACRO	National Association for the Care and Resettlement of Offenders
NAFTA	North American Free Trade Agreement
NALGO	National Association of Local Government Officers
NAPO	National Association of Probation Officers
NATO	North Atlantic Treaty Organisation
NCB	National Coal Board
NCC	National Consumer Council
NCCC	National Council of the Churches of Christ
NCU	National Communications Union
NEDC	National Economic Development Council
NFSP	National Federation of Sub-Postmasters
NGA	National Graphical Association
NORWEB	North Western Electricity Board
NUJ	National Union of Journalists
NUM	National Union of Miners
NUR	National Union of Railwaymen
NUT	National Union of Teachers

OFT	Office of Fair Trading
OFTEL	Office of Telecommunications
OFWAT	Office of Water Services
PFI	private finance initiative
PKFA	Pannell Kerr Forster Associates
POA	Prison Officers' Association
POUC	Post Office Unions Council
POUNC	Post Office Users' National Council
PPA	Periodical Publishers' Association
PPS	Protect our Postal Services
PR	public relations
PRCA	Public Relations Consultants' Association
PRP	public relations practitioner
PSBR	Public Sector Borrowing Requirement
RADAR	Royal Association for Disability and Rehabitilation
RMT	Royal Maritime and Transport Workers' Union
RSPB	Royal Society for the Protection of Birds
SDP	Social Democratic Party
TGWU (T&G)	Transport and General Workers' Union
TUC	Trades Union Congress
UCW	Union of Communication Workers (old CWU)
UNISON	Public Services Union
USM	Unlisted Securities Market
VAT	value added tax

Part I

Introductory frameworks

1

INTRODUCTION

Public relations, politics and the mass media

This book documents the expansion of professional public relations in Britain over the last two decades – particularly in sectors outside institutional politics. It then attempts to evaluate the impact of this on national news production, patterns of news-source access and the political process more generally.

As chapter two will illustrate, the public relations (PR) profession has expanded significantly during this period, well beyond the confines of Westminster. A wide range of organisations have joined political parties and governments in adopting professional public relations as a means of achieving political and economic objectives. There are now over 2,400 separate PR consultancies registered in Britain (Hollis, 1998). The consultancy sector in the UK, which almost exclusively serves the corporate sector, rose by a factor of 31 (or elevenfold in real terms) between 1979 and 1998 (Miller and Dinan, 2000, p10). In the 1990s several other types of organisation, including unions, pressure groups, religious organisations, charities, local councils and other state institutions have followed suit. Organisations in all these sectors are not simply utilising PR to improve their image (or 'brand') with the public. They are employing professional communicators to achieve a number of more specific objectives, including: influencing policy-makers, raising share prices, winning industrial disputes, increasing income, and generating interest in particular issues and new cultural products. Thus, behind the current media interest in a few key 'spin doctors' a substantial layer of 'cultural intermediaries' has evolved with a significant impact on news production and decision-making processes. Politics has become further 'mediatised' as a form of public relations democracy has developed.

These trends appear to have been noted in many quarters, yet little serious investigation of their consequences has taken place. Journalists attempt to drag 'spin doctors' into the light and try to wrong-foot media-trained politicians. All the while public cynicism grows. However, despite much speculation there has been little focused research on the subject in the UK. What there is is dispersed amongst various sub-disciplines and practitioner accounts within public relations, journalism, media sociology and politics.

In the PR industry itself, and in the few university public relations departments that have recently emerged, research has generally been anecdotal and in an applied, rather than critical, form. The research has thus been aimed at practitioners and has had little engagement with the research interests of other social science subject areas (Newman, 1984, and L'Etang and Pieczka, 1996, being two rare exceptions). Journalists' accounts (e.g., Cockerell *et al.*, 1984, Cockerell, 1988, Jones, 1995, 1999, McSmith, 1996, Rosenbaum, 1997) have been rather more concerned with the influence of public relations practioners (PRPs) on news and politics but, once again, tended to offer anecdotal snapshots, with little in the way of rigorous empirical research or theoretical engagement.

Within departments of media studies and politics, the subject of public relations has generally only been considered as part of other research on, for example, media-source relations or party political communications. Political communications has focused rather narrowly on the PR involved in institutional politics – most especially on general elections. This interest has yet to filter through to political sociology, where there appears to be very little research on the PR activities and media relations of organisations acting in civil society. Media studies, having been guilty of the charge of being 'media-centric' for many years, has begun to explore this new subject under the research topic of 'sources' and 'media-source relations'. However, much of this research was conducted before the recent development of professional public relations within such organisations. Hence public relations per se was not the principal object of research. Thus, while the list of studies which devote attention to the subject of professional public relations is growing (see, for example, Franklin, 1994, Miller, 1994, Negrine, 1994, Crewe *et al.*, 1995, 1998, Kavanagh, 1995, McNair, 1995, Scammell, 1995, Manning, 1998, Norris *et al.*, 1999) several questions remain. Indeed there is still significant scope for focused research in this area – the results of which would serve to intervene in several evolving debates across media studies, politics and sociology.

Frameworks and debates

The research in this book, while focusing on Britain in the last two decades, is more generally concerned with the role of the mass media in modern democratic states. Simply put, in liberal democracies the national news media are expected to fulfil a number of 'ideal' functions (see Dahlgren and Sparks, 1991, Keane, 1991, Negrine, 1996, for discussions). These include providing a source of 'objective' information, widely available to all citizens and interest groups; a check ('watchdog role') on the activities of powerful institutions, organisations and individuals; an arena for rational debate on the issues and policies affecting society and the state; and access to a wide range of citizens and interest groups to put forward their views. For advocates of liberal democracy, although these ideals are not fully achievable, they are realised to an acceptable degree. For critics, certain institutions and groups have far too much power in the democratic process and that extends to power and influence over the mass media. Such debates about the media's ability to fulfil its ideal functions have continued in various forms and currently are most commonly discussed in terms of the Habermasian public sphere (Habermas, 1989 [1962], 1997).

With these ideals in mind the book explores the following questions:

1   How much has professional public relations expanded in the last two decades and in what sectors of society?

2   How and in what ways has this expanding profession influenced news production?

3   Which types of organisation and institution are benefiting most from using PR to influence media coverage and in what ways? Who is being included or excluded from participation in public discourse?

4   What part is being played by PR-inspired media coverage in setting political agendas and influencing elite decision-making processes?

Media sociology and the fourth estate media

The effect of public relations on news production naturally follows on from long-running debates between liberal pluralists and their critics over the functioning of the fourth estate media. Liberal pluralist studies of journalists at work have contributed to an account in which the media function as independent 'fourth estate' guardians acting in the public interest. They thus emphasise the neutral objectivity of the news production process that results from autonomous journalists reporting a plurality of competing interests and opinions. Professional values guide journalists towards neutral coverage of issues that are significant to the mass of consumers and, therefore, tend to act as a check on major concentrations of power (Tunstall, 1971, Gans, 1979, Alexander, 1981, Hetherington, 1985, Harrison, 1985, Tiffen, 1989, Schudson, 1996). Internal news formats, genres and agendas guide news values accordingly. Market-oriented pragmatism (Gans, 1979, Koss, 1984, Veljanovski, 1989, Sola Pool, 1983) ensures that consumers get what they want – news that is balanced and broadly reflective of the concerns of the mass of citizens. While the liberal ideals that underpin journalism (see above) can never be fully realised, the media still fulfil vital functions in democracies.

In contrast, radical media sociologists have argued that journalists cannot be independent because powerful interests – namely state and/or corporate elites – have continually managed to influence the news production process. This top-down influence has been maintained through conscious control of media organisations (e.g., ownership and management) and/or less conscious factors (e.g., economic and ideological). Ownership, whether by the state or private corporations, has brought with it the power to allocate resources, appoint senior staff and influence editorial agendas. Additionally, the state has also controlled news production with its ability to regulate the media through legislation on censorship, libel laws, licensing and media ownership. Corporate elites have extended their control through overlapping networks of shareholders and directorships, and through advertising – a principal source of media funding. As many accounts (Evans, 1983, Schlesinger *et al.*, 1983, Glasgow University Media Group, 1985, Hollingsworth, 1986, Herman and Chomsky, 1988, Schiller, 1989, 1992, Tunstall and Palmer, 1991) have documented, both states and private owners have frequently abused their control and sought to influence journalist employees and the political process for their own ends.

Radicals have also argued that independent journalism is affected by wider economic conditions; by the fact that news is a business operating in a capitalist system and is affected accordingly. Market pressures, to take advantage of economies of scale and greater advertising revenues, have encouraged production for mass audiences and a steady stream of concentration and conglomeration. The results have been a restriction on entry for alternative and critical news producers, cuts in costly news production and investigative journalism, and pressure to increase audiences through the creation of populist and apolitical 'newszak'. All such trends have been widely documented (e.g., Curran, 1978, 1986, Fishman, 1980, Murdock, 1982, Garnham, 1990, Gitlin, 1994) and have accordingly reduced the capacity of journalists to fulfil the media's fourth estate remit to an unacceptable level.

However, what was all too often absent in radical accounts, at least until the early 1990s, was a substantial focus on micro-level influences and individual agency. Advertising and ownership may arguably affect the shape of news but, critics ask, have radicals adequately demonstrated that such factors really undermine media autonomy and objectivity on a day-to-day basis? It is on this micro level that scholars in sociology and cultural studies have inadvertently joined journalists and liberal media sociologists in supporting the case for the fourth estate media. Thus, much cultural studies research (e.g., Morley, 1980, 1992, Ang, 1985, Fiske, 1989) has argued the line that journalists and media consumers have rather more autonomy and agency than radical political economists have hitherto assumed. Studies of post-Fordist managerial structures and independent producers (e.g., Piore and Sabel, 1984, Hall and Jaques, 1989, Veljanovski, 1989) have emphasised the fact that media production power has been significantly dispersed. Many of the other charges of such studies – that radical political economists are uniformly too 'functionalist', conspiratorial, overemphasise 'economic determinism' and assume consumers are 'cultural dupes' – have become recognised for the straw (wo)men that they are (see Curran, 1996, Golding and Murdock, 1996). But a critical core objection remains: that radical accounts of biased mass media have been too reliant on work that stresses macro and wider political and economic trends and have not adequately tested this thesis with micro-level empirical work that observes active agents. In effect, several bodies of work have reinforced the liberal media sociology case for the fourth estate media on grounds that radicals have been slow to counter.

There thus appears a need for radicals to supplement their macro-level arguments about the fourth estate media with arguments at the micro level. Work on sources and media-source relations (see below) has been one area of research at such a level. However, to date, this work has avoided coming to definitive conclusions on the matter of journalists' autonomy in their relations with sources. Up until the early 1990s, those media sociologists who addressed the question (Tunstall, 1971, Sigal, 1973, Gans, 1979, Fishman, 1980, Tiffen, 1989) tended to agree that the attempts of either side to manage the other were often superseded by the benefits of co-operation. Thus the two sides were actually engaged in a 'seesaw tug of war' in which, although sources were slightly stronger, neither side dominated for long. With increased interest in the subject (Ericson et al., 1989,

1991, Schlesinger, 1990, Deacon and Golding, 1994, Miller, 1994, Schlesinger and Tumber, 1994), pluralist themes have directed research agendas. As such, the reaction to earlier radical functionalist/structuralist accounts of media-source relations, coupled with an emphasis on exploring source competition in the media, has thus meant that the debate about journalistic autonomy has been sidestepped.

At the start of the twenty-first century, the debate over journalist autonomy is more important than ever. A growing body of evidence suggests that, after two decades of upheaval in the media industries, the independence of journalists is being further eroded (see, for example, Williams, 1996, Curran and Seaton, 1997, Bagdikian, 1997, Franklin, 1997, Herman and McChesney, 1997, Goldsmiths Media Group, 2000). Deregulation, concentration and conglomeration in the news media industries have proceeded apace. In the UK the media industry has played a leading role in fighting union recognition, the minimum wage, and the social chapter, in addition to reducing the security and rights of its own workforce. Over 40 per cent of national journalists are now employed on a freelance, temporary or part-time basis. Privately owned media organisations are now openly partisan in their coverage on issues such as Europe, taxation, crime and immigration. Political parties, in turn, try to woo media owners in an attempt to raise their 'brand' images and gain vital electoral support – the rewards include knighthoods, tax concessions and the relaxation of regulatory regimes. These observations are no longer simply put by radicals. They are being documented by many journalists and liberal media sociologists on both sides of the Atlantic (Kimball, 1994, Blumler and Gurevitch, 1995, Fallows, 1996, Seymour-Ure, 1996, Tunstall, 1996). Such works have clearly begun to acknowledge the patterns observed by radical political economists and to show concern at the developing 'crisis of public communication'.

The rapid expansion of public relations, coupled with other changes in the UK media and political environments (see below), has obvious ramifications for the debate on the autonomy of the fourth estate media – and at the micro level. Indeed, if public relations has expanded so dramatically and, according to all industry surveys (e.g., *PR Week* surveys, 27.5.93, 20.8.99), 'media relations' is the principal activity of its practitioners, then it would seem essential that the impact of PR on journalistic autonomy is researched. But, as already stated, with all these studies, public relations has not been the key focus. Several of the studies mentioned have noted the part played by public relations and the questions posed by its expansion (see also *Media, Culture and Society*, 1993, Vol. 15, No. 3). But no general study on the profession has since been published in the UK.

The study of professional public relations thus offers a potentially productive research area in which radical and liberal media sociologists may meet on micro-level territory. Of central concern is the question of whether the expansion of PR suggests a micro-level undermining of journalistic autonomy, or a boost to journalists doing their jobs? Are journalists significantly affected by powerful PR practitioners – consciously or unconsciously – or are they strong enough to maintain their professional independence? Is news becoming more of a tainted product constructed out of partial public relations outputs or, as the PR industry itself suggests (see, for example, Grunig and Hunt, 1984), does it simply facilitate a clearer and wider flow of two-way information between sources and their publics? These questions are addressed directly in chapter two and indirectly in each of the remaining chapters.

British politics and political communications

According to most accounts (e.g., Kavanagh and Seldon, 1989, Young, 1989, Middlemas, 1991, Letwin, 1992, Budge and McKay, 1993, Hutton, 1996) of British politics in the 1980s and 1990s there has been a strong shift to the right. The then new Thatcher government of 1979 decisively broke with the post-war tripartite consensus that had appeared to balance the interests of trade unions, the corporate sector and the state. The ideas of the Keynesian welfare state, that had under-pinned policy-making by successive governments, were rejected for a neo-liberal political and economic agenda. This agenda, which emphasised the market and entrepreneurship as the means for improving the wealth of the nation, also trans-formed the balance of power and the distribution of political and economic resources in British society. After four terms in office policies dictated by this agenda had resulted in (see, for example, Pollard, 1992, Lowe, 1993, Hills, 1996, Taylor, 1994, Hutton, 1996, Mitchell, 1997): greater concentrations of economic power in fewer companies; a crippling of union power, a steady casualisation of, and increased insecurity for, much of the work force; rising inequality, greater levels of poverty and homelessness; a decline in manufacturing industry while the service and financial sectors expanded; extensive privatisation and deregulation of indus-tries and the financial sector; the shift of the tax burden towards indirect taxation and away from top earners and corporations; and attacks on the welfare state and public spending.

In effect, government interventions in the economy have worked to support the interests of international capital accumulation (the interests of the City and multi-national corporations) at the expense of national wage labour (trade unions, manu-facturing industry and the welfare state) and the power of the state itself. According to Pollard (1992) the overall result of Conservative policies has been to put in motion 'a reverse Robin Hood programme'. While certain sectors of society have gained, the 'life chances' (Dahl, 1985) for many others have narrowed. Much of the Thatcher legacy continues to direct New Labour policy, including: income tax cuts and an increase in indirect taxation, tight control over public spending as a lever for controlling inflation, privatisation, attempts to maintain good relations with the City, and a tough stance on immigration and law and order issues. Similarly, the main beneficiaries continue to be large corporations and financial elites, and the targets continue to be single mothers, refugees, travellers, the disabled, the elderly and other welfare claimants.

How have successive governments managed to gain mass support for policies that, in effect, have significantly shifted power and resources towards a small, largely anonymous, rarely accountable, set of elites? What has been the role of mass communications in this transition? As several recent studies of political

communications have documented, part of the answer is to be found in the rise of professional public relations within government and political parties. A series of works
has thus emanated from politics (Crewe and Harrop, 1986, 1989, Crewe and
Gosschalk, 1995, Kavanagh, 1995, Scammell, 1995, Norris and Gavin, 1997, Crewe
et al., 1998, King, 1998, Norris et al., 1999) and media studies (Billig et al., 1993,
Franklin, 1994, Negrine, 1994, 1996, Blumler and Gurevitch, 1995, Gaber, 1995,
1998, McNair, 1995). These works variously document the 'Americanisation'/'professionalisation' of government and political party communications, the development of the 'public relations state' and the conflict between 'spin doctors' and
journalists.

This large collection of UK literature (there is rather more in the USA) would
suggest that ample research has been done on the means and ways political communication affects the political process. However, this is far from the case. To start
with, the different sub-disciplines rarely engage with the literature and empirical
material produced on other sides of the academic divide. So while media studies
scholars frequently omit vital literature in politics and policy-making, those in politics departments rarely refer to the research of media sociologists.

More importantly, mainstream political communications only concentrates on
select aspects of a story. Their focus, on political parties, government and, above all,
general elections, is based on a rather narrow view of the political process. It is a
view that has limited the scope of much of the research mentioned. First, the heavy
emphasis on elections and party campaign machines ignores the obvious fact that
elections are extremely unrepresentative periods. They account for a very small
period of time in the cycle of government. Second, and rather ironically, the vast
majority of the literature on elections has concluded that campaigns have very little
'effect' on voting behavior (e.g., Harrop, 1986, Curtice and Semetko, 1994,
Kavanagh, 1995, Kavanagh and Gosschalk, 1995, King, 1998, Norris et al., 1999).
As several of these studies also conclude, changes of voting behavior are due either
to other factors or to long-term media campaigns and influences.

Third, the focus on institutional politics ignores the activities of numerous
other groups and individuals acting in civil society and outside the nation state –
from businesses and business associations to pressure groups, unions and charities.
These actions clearly contribute to the development of party manifestos, the shape
and passage of legislation, the budget calculations of the Treasury and even to the
profiles of parties and governments themselves. Indeed, during the last two decades
the power of government and political parties has in many ways diminished. The
global economy, supranational bodies, transnational corporations, quangos and
large associations and pressure groups have gained more control over political and
economic resources (see, for instance, Held, 1995, Negrine, 1996, Grant, 2000). For
example, in the first year of Conservative power, in 1979/80, the equity value of the
London stock market was roughly 40 per cent of government income. By 1996/97,
the value of the stock market had risen to three and a half times government
income. The top chief executives and fund managers now preside over far larger
sets of funds than most cabinet ministers. Membership of political parties has

declined but increased in associations and pressure groups. Once again, the strongest unions and pressure groups, such as the Public Services Union (UNISON) and the Royal Society for the Protection of Birds (RSPB), have much larger memberships and annual expenditures than the main political parties. As this book will demonstrate, many of these groups spend significant funds on their public relations operations. In fact, all government and political party communications account for less than a sixth of total PR employment.

In effect, the majority of work on political communications (Negrine, 1994, 1996, being the main exception) has, to date, been both 'source-centric' and 'Westminster-centric'. Consequently a narrow definition of politics and political communications has resulted in a large research gap in the literature. The links between the media, public relations and the political decision-making process thus require further work. How do the requirements of public relations and the media influence the development of policies by political parties and governments? How are those policies affected by the public relations activities of businesses, pressure groups and other organisations? Which public relations operations are most effective in setting political and media agendas and under what conditions? Although this book does not focus directly on political parties and government communications, several chapters (two, three, six, seven, eight and nine) contribute in some depth to these questions.

From interest groups and political sociology to news sources and media-source relations

A focus on interest groups and their relations with the state is an alternative starting point for the study of politics and policy-making. At the risk of oversimplification, research in this area can also be divided into liberal pluralist and critical/neo-Marxist positions (if one neglects periodic excursions into elite theory and corporatism). On the one hand classic liberal pluralism, as presented by Truman (1951) and Dahl (1961), argues that the exercise of power is 'fragmented', 'non-cumulative' and is shared and competed over by numerous groups in society. Even though power is not equally distributed it is contested and largely representative of different social interests. This ideal picture has been challenged from a variety of critical perspectives. These include: the inability of large collective groups to act as effectively as small organised and powerful interests (Olson, 1965, Offe and Wiesenthal, 1985); the way in which decision-making regularly excludes the concerns of certain groups in society (Bachrach and Baratz, 1962); the role of the state in actively supporting the interests of the capitalist classes (Milliband, 1969, Poulantzas, 1975); and the need for the state to yield to the demands of business and established groups in order to sustain economic prosperity and therefore its own long-term survival (Lindblom, 1977, Offe, 1984). Thus, for a variety of reasons, business and other powerful interests have a much greater influence than others over the policy-making process.

Similar perspectives have likewise informed studies of pressure groups and 'policy communities/networks' in Britain. Once again, there are those who argue for the power of the corporate sector (Marsh and Locksley, 1983, Coates, 1984,

Hutton, 1996, Mitchell, 1997), because of the privileged access of business leaders to government decision-makers, the fact that economic power is highly concentrated in a small numbers of corporations and the strength of the financial sector – all factors of particular note in British politics. They are generally opposed by those (Richardson and Jordan, 1979, Abercrombie *et al.*, 1980, Jordan and Richardson, 1987, Grant, 1993, 1995) arguing that: economic power does not translate to political power, a wide range of anti-business groups have flourished, and political and ideological divisions amongst the business community ensure their power over policy-making remains contested and widely distributed.

However, like traditional studies of politics, the pressure group perspective has tended to ignore the part played by the mass media and political communications in decision-making (Mitchell, 1997, being one rare exception). Thus, once again, questions about the role of the media and public relations in policy-making are left unexplored. As stated above, all sorts of interest groups and institutions are now making use of public relations – including those 'insider groups' with privileged access to government. Clearly, the latest public debates over road building, the railways, agriculture, taxation and the environment, are all current examples of interest groups and the state arguing over public policy through the news media. Several questions therefore present themselves. Are the relations between interest groups and the state mirrored by the relations between interest groups and the media? How has PR affected the representative nature of pressure group politics? Which groups are more effective in their use of communications strategies? How much is news coverage affecting decision-making and, therefore, altering distributions of power and resources?

These questions have been tackled by media studies for some time – generally discussed under the subject of 'news sources' and 'media-source relations'. Like much of the literature on interest groups, media sociology has been divided between liberal pluralists and their critics. Liberal pluralists have always worked on the assumption that democracy thrives on a range of competing interests which balance each other out. Within this framework the news media give voice to a plurality of competing voices (McQuail, 1977, Alexander, 1981, Blumler and Gurevitch, 1986, Harrison, 1985); a plurality that is expanding with new technologies such as the Internet, cheap video equipment and new digital broadcasting (Negroponte, 1995, Pavlik, 1996). To date, liberal pluralists have rarely looked directly at sources, preferring instead to underpin their arguments with the observation of such things as journalists' routines and professional values.

However, pluralist assumptions concerning source access have been continually undermined by one repeated finding in media sociology. Studies, both liberal (Tunstall, 1971, Gans, 1979, Blumler and Gurevitch, 1986, 1995, and Tiffen, 1989, Hallin, 1994) and radical (Sigal, 1973, Glasgow University Media Group, 1976, 1980, Hall, *et al.*, 1978, Fishman, 1980, Gandy, 1980, Gitlin, 1980, Herman and Chomsky, 1988), have all confirmed that news has been consistently dominated by sources from government and established institutions. As a result, what literature there existed on sources was, for some time, dominated by radical thinking.

For the Glasgow University Media Group (1976, 1980, 1982), where unequal access between interest groups was not sufficiently accounted for by macroeconomic explanations, it was by the prevalence of 'dominant ideology'. This accounted for the dominance of corporate and state elite opinions and agendas in media texts because journalists were unconsciously guided by established elite norms and values. Hall *et al.*'s (1978) 'structural culturalist' alternative skilfully elaborated on these themes. They argued that journalists, in their search for 'objective' and 'authoritative' accounts, automatically sought out institutionalised sources which were already legitimised by their power, representativeness and expertise. The media's 'structured preferences' for the opinions of 'primary definers' meant that non-institutional sources, and journalists themselves, could only respond to those agendas and frameworks already determined.

However, the largest problem with this earlier work was that virtually none of it actually looked at the activities of interest groups and their communications. All work had been, in Schlesinger's words, 'media-centric'. In the time that elapsed between this early work, in the 1970s, and new research on sources, in the early 1990s, the research climate changed considerably. New work attempted to distance itself from earlier 'overly structuralist/functionalist' accounts. Schlesinger's (1990) critique of Hall *et al.* summed up the case most definitively: primary definers, being often in conflict, did not speak with one voice; neither did they retain the same levels of access over time, let alone possess equal amounts of access. Similarly, journalists and non-official sources were not always relegated to subordinate positions of counter-definition, but did on occasion challenge official accounts. In effect, the structural culturalist approach, like the radical functionalist one, gave an overly deterministic picture that did not account for change and the 'dynamic processes of contestation in a given field of discourse'.

The body of work on sources that followed has been either pluralist or radical-pluralist in nature. Much of it has focused on assessing the media strategies of pressure groups (Anderson, 1991, 1993, 1997, Cracknell, 1993, Hansen, 1993, Manning, 1998). In line with liberal work on journalism (Tiffen, 1989, Schudsen, 1996) these studies often explained away the dominance of elite sources as being a result of the organisational routines and values of news gatherers, i.e., for variable organisational, rather than structured ideological reasons. At the same time Hallin (1994) noted that although elite sources dominated news texts, those same sources were often in conflict. Thus it could be argued, in a more pluralist vein, that conflicts amongst primary definers are reflected in the media and act to cancel out other elite source advantages.

In a more radical-pluralist vein has come a series of studies comparing various types of source. These have been in the 'criminal justice arena' (Schlesinger and Tumber 1994), in the Northern Ireland conflict (Miller, 1993, 1994), in policy-making in the health sector (Miller and Williams, 1993, 1998) and during attempts to introduce the 'poll tax' (Deacon and Golding, 1994). Each of these studies (see also studies on pressure groups cited above) has both documented non-official source media strategies and demonstrated the potential means by which official sources occasionally fail to dominate media discourses. All therefore fleshed out a scenario where media access and the accumulation of media status (a form of 'cultural capital') are continually contested matters. Overall there seems to have developed quite an impressive body of literature on the subject of non-institutional sources – much of it resulting in an alternative radical–pluralist synthesis. Some of the work has also produced material relevant to the study of public relations in a variety of sectors.

However, many gaps and questions remain. While several studies observed state institutions at a time when professional public relations had already been established, the same cannot be said of other sectors in civil society. The business sector has been virtually ignored in media studies. This is a significant omission given that (a) this sector is by far the largest employer of public relations, and (b) policy-making has had a clear free-market pro-business slant over the last two decades. At the same time, all studies of 'outsider' and 'resource-poor' sources were based on research at the end of the 1980s and early 1990s and, as such, were completed before the recent and widespread adoption of professional PR practitioners and methods in those sectors. As a result, most (Miller, 1994 and Manning, 1998, being the main exceptions) have not been concerned with separating the practice of PR from its source ties. Professional PRPs themselves – those working outside formal politics – have largely been ignored. Public relations has simply been seen as an extension of the resources and media relations of an interest group or organisation. It is thus generally assumed that there exists a fairly accurate correlation between a source's economic, political and 'cultural' capital, and its media profile, and that the fluidity of contestation in the media waxes and wanes accordingly. Outsider sources can only make a temporary and limited impact, and only if they become institutionalised and/or dominant elites are in conflict. Similarly it is assumed that organisations relate to the media and have the same degree of access/influence as they do with government. Source-media relations closely mirror interest group–government relations.

With little focused research on public relations itself, these assumptions have not been tested. A few simple points about professional public relations and journalist–PRP relations reveal clear inconsistencies in such premises. First, the 'newsworthiness' of sources appears to be as much conditioned by a variety of internal journalist imperatives as by an external source's level of resources. So, for example, corporate sources, despite their high level of resources and expenditure on PR, have not gained comparable levels of access or positive coverage (see chapter three). Second, PR strategies, in themselves, can considerably affect the levels of cultural and political resources of sources and the news-gathering routines of journalists (see chapters seven and eight). Third, within the industry, public relations is considered to be most effective when acting invisibly. This not only means PRPs being invisible, it also means sources feeding information to journalists and other groups and setting agendas without themselves necessarily appearing in the media (see chapters five and eight). Fourth, as most PRPs are aware, general coverage and public opinion are often less important than influencing key audiences and decision-making processes (see chapter four).

All of which indicates that there is ample scope for a thorough investigation of how public relations has affected the ability of various types of source/interest group to impact upon the British media and public discourse. Clearly, if many types of source organisation are adopting public relations and media strategies as a means of obtaining their objectives, then it must be asked: are particular interests benefiting at the expense of others? Is public relations simply a means by which particular 'official', 'insider' and elite interests can further dominate access and manage media agendas? Or, does it enable 'non-official', 'outsider' and 'resource-poor' groups to gain media coverage that was previously denied to them? How much does coverage instigated by these different types of group/source manage to influence decision-makers? These are the central question that are discussed in different ways in chapters three to eight.

A few notes on theory and methods

Theoretical influences

There were many potential debates and theoretical frameworks with which to study the topic of public relations. One obvious route, spelled out by Baudrillard (in Poster, 1988) and applied by Wernick (1991) to 'promotional culture' generally, was to take public relations as an empirical focus for the advancement of post-modernity. However, as evidenced by the above discussions, my interest in the sub-ject was too 'modernist' to pursue this option. This book has a strong interest in relations of power and how material, political and cultural resources are contested and distributed. As will become obvious, public relations clearly contributes to many of the phenomena described in postmodern theory. But what also seems evi-dent is the way in which conscious agents use material and other resources to influ-ence cultural outputs in order to gain further control over material and other resources – not something best discussed within a framework of postmodern theory.

Another approach was to research the subject in terms of debates about the public sphere as set out by Habermas (1989 [1962]) and pursued by several sociolo-gists (see collections in, for example, Dahlgren and Sparks, 1991 and Calhoun, 1992). I do not do so for several reasons. First, discussions of how the media should function to fulfil the needs of the public sphere are not that different from longer-running debates in media sociology about the actual functioning of the mass media. The achievement or otherwise of liberal ideals are still at the heart of both debates. Second, the idealised public sphere of earlier centuries that Habermas describes was, like the Greek agora before it, based on mass exclusion and face-to-face dialogue – things that do not quite match up with mass communications (even when later addressed by Habermas, 1997). Third, theories of the public sphere assume rational debate and rational actions. While news sources and PR practition-ers may act with rational goals, public relations battles, and the public discourses that result, are far from rational. In many cases the establishment of rational norms and values are completely undermined by PR. Even without public relations I believe that a significant proportion of the understanding and framing of news stories is not rational – even if individual goals and reactions are.

Rather than concentrate on interpreting the rise of public relations within one particular theoretical framework it seemed more appropriate, at this stage, to generate empirical material for further debate. There are, however, certain theoretical influences guiding the research here.

First, my interests and sympathies lie with critical political economy. I am therefore concerned with questions about the contestation and distribution of political, economic and cultural resources. I also view that contestation and distribution, as well as media coverage, as being unequal in that they tend to favour, in one way or another, particular interests over others. At the same time my research avoids the excesses of some forms of political economy – particularly those which have an overreliance on functionalism, economic determinism and class conflict. Such approaches do not account for agency, dynamic processes of change and contestation, and the complexities of power relations – all of which also direct this research to some extent.

This research is, in fact, propelled by an interest in relating the actions of agents and the 'micro-physics of power' to more macro-level outcomes as they are observed in the political economy tradition. From this perspective power is more dispersed – although still cumulative. Similarly, unequal power relations and the distribution of resources are, to a significant extent, also related to numerous micro-level developments and conflicts. These are significant, not just at the level of government policy-making but across all parts of industry, civil society and other state institutions. At all levels 'policy networks' make decisions, develop interpretive frameworks and contribute to the formation of discourses in society. At each site, activity, alliances and frameworks change and exchanges of capital (cultural, social and economic) take place. And, increasingly, parts of the media have come to be involved in many of those discursive networks – both as spaces of conflict and facilitators for the exchange and transfer of alternative forms of capital. In these respects, Foucault (1975, 1980) and Bourdieu (1979, 1993) have contributed in part (and not without qualification) to shaping and adapting my political economy perspective. As is the case with both these thinkers, and the political economy tradition in general, empirical research and a sense of historical specificity focus the theory.

Research parameters and methods

The book therefore has clear empirical parameters. To start, the research is British based and covers the period 1979–99. Although much of the literature discussed is North American and European, the empirical work only engages with UK organisations and media. While collecting general data on the rise and use of public relations by a range of institutions and organisations, the more detailed research looks at corporations and pressure groups. These areas are then further narrowed down by looking at the financial public relations of large (Financial Times Stock Exchange (FTSE) top 150), publicly quoted companies and also at campaigning by

TUC-affiliated trade unions. At the centre of the research are two detailed case studies – one a big City takeover battle, the other a conflict over privatisation.

There are two further parameters. First, public relations in Britain has many sub-specialities and overlapping roles. Lobbying, marketing, advertising and internal staff communications are all conducted by PRPs as well as other communications specialists. At times this book does refer to such activities. However, its principal focus when referring to 'public relations' is 'media relations' work – the main activity of the industry. Second, all specific research referring to the news media has been confined to the national press – thus excluding regional and trade press and national and regional broadcasting.

This study adopted an eclectic range of both quantitative and qualitative methods. The intention was to relate the micro-activities of individual agents to more general macro outcomes. Small-scale actions were to be traced to larger political and economic trends, as opposed to inferring micro-activities from identifiable macro-patterns. It therefore seemed appropriate, on the one hand, to gather and generate qualitative data, in the form of interview material and qualitative content analyses of specific documents and media texts, in order to identify micro-level activity. On the other hand, this was to be matched with survey material, financial data sets, and quantitative content analyses of media texts – to establish macro-patterns. The micro-level activity of public relations and media-source relations could then be linked to more general outcomes. This research is relayed in chapters two, four and seven.

The case studies, in chapters five and eight, explore the findings of these earlier chapters in more detail. These studies, in a sense, might be described as short-term 'policy communities' in which the media have been heavily involved in the decision-making process. Both looked at conflicts in which rival organisations employed extensive PR campaigns to influence the media discourses which informed decision-making on specific issues. The impact of sources on news production was judged by taking source data and comparing it with media outputs. Public relations materials, policy documents and source interviews were correlated with media texts and interviews with journalists. Quantitative and interpretive content analysis of news texts was then used to assess the impacts of PR and the effectiveness of both corporate, institutional and union sources. Relevant news texts and campaign documents (public and private) were, in most cases, already compiled by the organisations involved. Logged articles and organisational profiles were then subjected to more sustained quantitative analysis by use of the *Financial Times* (*FT*) Profile database and CD-ROMs. A total of 867 articles were analysed for the two case studies.

During the research 103 interviews were conducted with a range of public relations practitioners, sources and journalists. About two-thirds of these were 'on the record', although parts of some interviews could only be reproduced anonymously. The interviewees are listed in the bibliography. Additionally a survey of TUC-affiliated unions took place and drew a 73 per cent return. The list of interviewees and references for additional survey material and other primary source documents are all reproduced in the bibliography. Tables from the survey can be found in appendix II. Further details of the methods used are listed in the footnotes of relevant chapters (see also Davis, 2000d)

Book outline

The book breaks down into eight chapters grouped into three parts. The first part (chapter two) details the rise of public relations in Britain, its profile and distribution. It then evaluates ongoing debates about the nature of working relationships between news sources, public relations practitioners and journalists. It concludes that what was once a 'tug of war' between sources and journalists has been replaced by an increased media dependency on the 'information subsidies' provided by PR. Public relations has therefore increased its influence, not as a result of powerful 'spin doctor' pressure, or media-source conspiracy, but because working news journalists have become increasingly stretched as a result of rising competition. Public relations professionals, with their rapidly increasing resources, have thus been ideally placed to make good the shortfall in news-producing industries.

Part II (chapters three, four and five) then focuses on the corporate sector. The corporate sector is not only the principal user of professional PR; it is regarded, along with the state, as the source which is most influential in media production. Chapter three thus asks: how, and in what ways, has corporate public relations benefited the corporate sector in Britain? The chapter concludes that, contrary to the conclusions of several critical studies in media sociology, corporate public relations has had limited success in promoting corporate agendas and ideals to the general public through national mainstream news. Instead, corporate PR has been more involved in specialist news sectors – most significantly in the area of City and financial public relations and business news.

Chapter four thus concentrates its investigations on financial PR activity. Although PR in this sector is promoted as a means of information dissemination for the perfect functioning of the market, and financial and business news is deemed to be a response to greater public interest, very different trends are in evidence. Rather, PR has developed more as a corporate tool, used to gain competitive advantage, in an era of increased conflict and competition between rival financial elites. It concludes that the consequences of the use of PR in this sector are that financial and business news has been 'captured' by financial elite news sources, and that non-financial elites have been excluded. The long-term results of such closed 'elite discourse networks' have been (a) a steady stream of corporate decision-making driven purely by market imperatives, and (b) a neo-liberal economic consensus being continually reaffirmed and exported to outside constituents. Chapter five documents all these aspects with a detailed case study involving Granada's takeover of Forte in 1995/96.

The question in part III (chapters six, seven and eight) reverses the perspective. It asks: can public relations be used successfully by 'outsider' and 'resource-poor' groups to secure and widen their media access and, therefore, gain access to 'elite discourse networks'? Its empirical focus is the British trade union movement. Chapter six begins by reassessing critical media sociology accounts of why such groups failed to get positive coverage in the 1970s and 1980s. It finds fault with the early explanations for the causes of media bias against outsider groups during the 1980s – suggesting, from a media-source relations perspective, that there is some scope for professional communications to improve coverage generally. Chapter seven goes on to document the extensive use of PR by unions in the 1990s and observes various means by which union communicators have overcome their resource deficits. It is thus demonstrated that 'outsider' groups are also capable of 'spinning' elite decision-makers and occasionally forcing significant changes. Chapter eight illustrates these findings in some detail with a case study of the Union of Communication Workers' (UCW's) successful PR campaign to halt Post Office privatisation in 1994 – the first privatisation successfully opposed by a union during the Conservative government.

The final chapter (nine) pulls together the conclusions of the previous chapters.

2

THE EXPANSION OF PUBLIC RELATIONS
AND ITS IMPACT ON NEWS PRODUCTION

The recent rise and dissemination of professional public relations

The profession of public relations is not new. As several accounts have recorded (Kelley, 1956, Tulloch, 1993, Cutlip *et al.*, 1994, Ewen, 1996, Rosenbaum, 1997, L'Etang, 1998) it has been employed by governments and large corporations for most of the twentieth century. The work of Edward Bernays and Ivy Lee, the 'grandfathers' of the industry, began with corporate expansion in the USA in the 1900s. The Democratic and Republican parties established their PR offices in 1928 and 1932 respectively. Government information services and propaganda operations grew tremendously during the First and Second World Wars. Indeed, the modern foundations of British public relations – the Central Office of Information (1945) and the Institute of Public Relations (1948) – were established with personnel from largely redundant government departments used formerly to administer the empire and promulgate government information in wartime (see Tulloch, 1993, L'Etang, 1998).

However two clear trends in the development of the profession in Britain are discernible after 1979. The first is its sudden growth. The second is its widescale adoption by a variety of different types of organisation. To date, most research has focused on the first trend within Westminster politics. As several accounts suggest (e.g., Ingham, 1991, Franklin, 1994, 1999, Jones, 1995, 1999, Kavanagh, 1995, Scammell, 1995, Rosenbaum, 1997), the Conservative Party initiated a new era in which political communications became increasingly prioritised by the main political parties. In 1978 the Conservatives opened their first full-time account with a professional advertising agency – Saatchi and Saatchi. For most of their time in office they were advised by the heads of several top-ten PR companies, including Tim Bell of Lowe-Bell and Peter Gummer of Shandwick. As Kavanagh observed (1995, pp56), 'Mrs Thatcher supplied a set of beliefs but used the latest public relations techniques to a greater degree than any of her predecessors'.

The other parties began to adopt similar communications personnel and approaches as the 1980s progressed. In 1981 the Social Democratic Party (SDP) was launched with massive PR support from Dewe-Rogerson – another top-ten PR company. The Labour Party had no such industry support, but also began revamping their communications operations internally shortly after their 1983 defeat. As many studies of British politics have documented (see also Crewe and

Harrop, 1989, Crewe and Gosschalk, 1995, Negrine, 1996, Jones, 1997, Norris and Gavin, 1997, Crewe *et al.*, 1998, King, 1998, Norris *et al.*, 1999) all the main political parties have now increased their spending on promotional matters and allocated greater control to their professional communicators. The influence of PR has thus become apparent in policy development, party and personality brand management and, most of all, during election campaigns. One indication of this growth of promotional work is in the increasing levels of election campaign expenditure by the main parties. According to Lord Neill's report (1998) in 1983 the Labour Party spent £4 million (at 1997 prices) and the Conservatives just over £6.5 million (see figure 2.1). By 1997 those figures had risen to £26 and £28.3 million respectively. In effect, communications expenditure for the two main parties (although not the Liberal Democrats) has increased by roughly two-thirds with each general election since 1983.

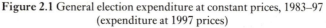

Figure 2.1 General election expenditure at constant prices, 1983–97 (expenditure at 1997 prices)

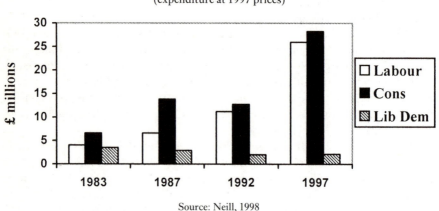

Source: Neill, 1998

Government communications expenditure also increased significantly during the period. In 1979, the Central Office of Information (COI) budget was £27 million and advertising expenditure was £44 million. By 1988 these figures had risen to £150 million and £85 million respectively (Scammell, 1995, pp204–6). The government frequently tops the table of annual advertisers in Britain. Similarly, employment of information officers (see table 2.1) has roughly doubled across Whitehall over the last two decades. Of the major government departments, maintained over the period 1979–97, only the Ministry of Defence (MoD) and Department of the Environment were smaller in 1997 than they were in 1979. The rise in in-house government communications was matched by a rise in the employment of PR consultancies to promote government policies (see chapter three).

Table 2.1 Changes in numbers of information officers employed in government departments and public institutions, 1979–99

	MAFF	MoD	DfEE	DoT	DoE	FCO	DHSS	Home Office	DTI
1979	22	58	23	13	65	19	24	27	38
1981	26	53	22	12	57	17	21	29	93
1983	23	34	22	18	37	17	18	25	77
1985	24	37	22	29	38	18	35	28	59[b]
1987	25	34	29	30	44	13	44	33	67
1989	34	35	38	33	40	16	55[a]	37	65
1991	41	36	78	33	34	20	57	37	62
1993	44	32	68	44	42	20	88	42	65
1995	40	36	54	40	44	22	108	43	69
1997	39	47	44	37	42	30	141	50	67
1979–97 % +/-	+77	-19	+91	+185	-35	+58	+488	+85	+76
1999	44	56	96[c]	–	97[d]	46	171	54	74
1997–99 % +/-	+13	+19	+118	–	+23	+53	+21	+8	+10

	Cabinet Office	PM's Office	Treasury	Buckingham Palace	CBI	Inland Revenue	Metropolitan Police	BBC	CRE
1979	–	6	12	3	8	5	6	5	5
1981	–	6	12	3	8	5	8	6	5
1983	–	6	12	3	10	4	8	9	6
1985	12	6	10	3	13	4	8	12	6
1987	11	6	13	4	19	8	12	12	6
1989	9	6	10	8	17	11	12	11	6
1991	10	6	9	9	16	13	53	12	6
1993	14	10	9	9	14	16	58	17	6
1995	13	10	13	12	18	18	61	35	8
1997	14	12	16	10	18	15	42	34	8
1979–97 % +/-	–	+100	+25	+233	+125	+200	+600	+580	+60
1999	23	14	20	13	19	18	51	32	7
1997–99 % +/-	+79	+17	+25	+30	+6	+20	+21	-6	-13

Source: Figures compiled from COI 1970–99. *The IPO Directory – Information and Press Officers in Government Departments and Public Corporations* (formerly the *Chief Public Relations, Information and Press Officers in Government Departments, Public Corporations, etc.*).

Notes: [a] Department of Health and Social Security (DHSS) was split into two. Figures from 1989 (inclusive) are the sum of the two departments
[b] Departments of Trade and Industry (DTI) were separate until this point. Figures before 1985 are the sum of the two departments
[c] Department of Employment becomes the Department of Education and Employment (DfEE)
[d] Department of the Environment (DoE) and Department of Transport (DoT) becomes the Department of Environment and Transport.

The government PR expansion has continued apace with the new Labour adminis-tration (see table 2.1). Most notably, the Cabinet Office has increased impressively – thus indicating a rise in the personal communications power of the Prime Minster. According to Franklin (1999b, p32) by the end of 1998 the number of ministerial special advisers, many of which had a public relations role, had more than doubled to seventy people – up from thirty-two. The government's desire to control the Government Information and Communications Services (GICS) had also resulted in twenty-five out of forty-four heads and deputy heads of information either resigning or being replaced by early 1999 (*ibid*).

Table 2.2 Distribution of IPR members in employment sectors, 1998

Sector	%
In-house central government	*0.7*
National government	0.5
Government information services	0.2
Other government	*15.9*
Local	6.7
Education	3.3
Health	3.0
Armed forces	0.6
Other government dept/agency	2.3
External	*45.2*
Consultancy	39.1
Advertising	0.8
Sole trader	5.3
In-house companies – industries and services	*20.2*
Manufacturing	6.1
Services	7.7
Finance	3.7
HQ/holding company	2.1
Nationalised industry	0.6
In-house companies – cultural industries	*2.8*
Tourism/leisure	1.6
Press/broadcasting	1.2
Arts/culture	0.1
In-house non profit/pressure group	*6.4*
Charities	3.2
Trade/prof bodies	3.0
Political organisations	0.1
Trade union	0.1
No Response	*8.8*

Source: IPR membership survey, 1998

However, the expansion of public relations has not been restricted to institutional politics. Looking at the distribution of IPR members (table 2.2) it becomes clear that central government and political parties currently employ only a few per cent of those in the profession. Even accounting for an obvious pro-business bias in the profile of IPR membership, it becomes apparent that the business sector employs the majority of PRPs. Twenty-three per cent of the IPR's 5,700 members work in-house for businesses and 45.2 per cent work for consultancies – 90 per cent of whose clientele is corporate (see PRCA annuals). In fact, it is in the corporate sector that the growth of the profession has been most impressive. Although the IPR (1948) and Public Relations Consultants Association (1969) had been in existence for some time, the corporate PR industry expanded at unprecedented rates in the 1980s.

Surveys by Carl Byoir and Associates (PRCA *Year Book*, 1986), reproduced in table 2.3, show that over a five-year period it became the norm rather than the exception for top companies to use PR. The numbers of consultancies and total consultancy income each rose accordingly (see figure 2.2). The PR consultancy industry grew at annual rates of 25–30 per cent during the 1980s and more consultancies were created during that period than in all the previous decades put together (BDO Stoy Hayward Management Consultants, 1994). *PR Week*, the industry's own trade journal, was launched in 1984. By 1990 a British-based company, Shandwick, had fought off the US competition (temporarily) to become the largest PR company in the world. By 1992, Saatchi and Saatchi, with related interests in PR, was similarly claiming to be the world's biggest advertising agency. In spite of the recession of the early 1990s the consultancy sector in the UK rose by a factor of 31 (or elevenfold in real terms) between 1979 and 1998 (Miller and Dinan, 2000, p. 10).

Table 2.3 The percentage of top companies (in *The Times 1000*)
using PR consultancies

	1979 %	1982 %	1984 %
UK top 50 companies	28	45	90
UK top 100 companies	25	45	85
UK top 500 companies	20	36	69

Source: Carl Byoir and Associates, in PRCA *Year Book*, 1986

During the 1990s, professional PR began to spread into many other sectors of British civil society. It instigated a substantial secondary industry of service suppliers, and prompted the development of a number of DIY guides, specialist reference books and educational courses. A range of organisations and individuals have accordingly shown interest in the adoption of corporate promotional strategies and expertise as a means to achieve their objectives. Fifteen per cent of IPR members (see table 2.2) work for local government and other state institutions outside central government, and 6.4 per cent work for pressure groups and charities. A survey of NUJ (National Union of Journalists) members (NUJ, 1998), with a clearly anti-corporate bias, put the figures higher. Out of the 24.4 per cent of members who

Figure 2.2 Growth in PRCA members' fee income, 1983–97

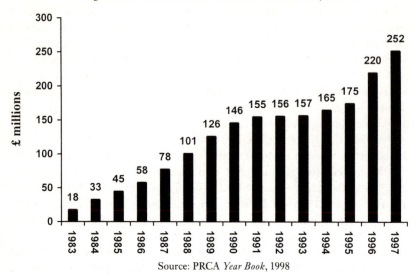

Source: PRCA *Year Book*, 1998

worked part- or full-time in PR, a third of these were employed by charities, societies and associations, and a fifth for unions and local government – equating to roughly 3,500 people.

The growth rate for public relations in local councils and other state institutions appeared to match that in central government. By 1994, according to Franklin (1994, p7, 1997), 90 per cent of metropolitan local authorities had established PR departments. Looking at the end of table 2.1, it is clear that institutions such as the British Broadcasting Company (BBC), Metropolitan Police and Buckingham Palace also expanded their public relations quite significantly. Such institutions, along with schools, universities (see Wernick, 1991) and health authorities (see Miller and Williams, 1998) were encouraged to adopt public relations for three obvious reasons: (a) the need to communicate with the British public, (b) the introduction of 'market reforms' and business practices in the running of public institutions, and (c) rising competition for dwindling government resources as the state attempts to decrease its public spending (see Pollard, 1992, Lowe, 1993).

Media campaigns have always been a means by which pressure groups, charities and trade unions raised interest and support. What changed in the last decade was the influx of PR professionals into these sectors. Deacon's (1996) survey of the voluntary sector in fact found that 31 per cent of all organisations had press/publicity officers, 43 per cent used external PR agencies and 56 per cent monitored the media. These figures increased to 57 per cent, 81 per cent and 78 per cent for organisations with annual budgets above £250,000. As chapter seven shows, two-thirds of unions have at least one part-time press officer, 25 per cent use PR consultancies and 57.4 per cent use other agencies to monitor the media and provide other services – significantly more that observed in earlier studies

(Glasgow University Media Group, 1976, 1980, Manning, 1998). That such organ-isations are increasingly using professional PR methods to achieve political and economic objectives is further evidenced in research on pressure groups and trade unions, in work on: environmental issues (Anderson, 1991, 1993, 1997, Cracknell, 1993, Hansen, 1993), the 'criminal justice arena' (Ericson et al. 1989, Schlesinger and Tumber 1994), gay and lesbian pressure groups (Miller and Williams, 1993), industrial disputes (Jones, 1987, Manning, 1998) and paramilitary organisations in Northern Ireland (Miller, 1993, 1994). Amongst charities PR has also become fundamental for raising profiles and gaining funding. The National Children's Home (IPR, 1992), St John's Ambulance (IPR, 1994), the Women's Royal Voluntary Service (IPR, 1995) and the Royal British Legion (IPR, 1997) have all won top IPR 'Sword of Excellence' awards for their campaigns in the 1990s – a signal that PR in the charity sector has become as professional as that employed by businesses.

In 1971 Tunstall wrote (p175) that 'The history of public relations in Whitehall is to a large extent the history of public relations in Britain'. This is obviously no longer the case. What was once the exclusive domain of government in Britain has moved first to business and then into every sector of society which feels a need to compete in the public sphere.

The interaction of journalists, sources and public relations practitioners

This expansion of professional public relations offers up a number of potential research questions. The question addressed in the rest of this chapter concerns the impact of public relations on news production. The PR industry may have expanded considerably, but is there any indication that it is actually affecting the way news is produced and, if so, how?

Two common approaches to answering this question appear to have emerged in studies of sources/PRPs and journalists. The first of these has involved attempts to look at content. It seeks to determine how much news content is primarily PR information and how much is the result of proactive journalism? The second approach puts the emphasis on 'conscious control'. It asks: who is in charge and who is setting the media agenda – journalists or sources and their PRPs? This section looks at both of these approaches and concludes that they deliver rather inconclusive results. This is because the evidence collected tends to be vague and subjective, confused by too many variables, and based on ad hoc collections of anec-dotal evidence.

Public relations content or journalism?

Both journalists and PRPs have made attempts to determine what proportions of news content are PR instigated and what are simply hard journalism. However the polls and estimates produced to date, in addition to being methodologically weak, show very little agreement. A Gallup (1991) survey of 100 heads of in-house PR departments and twenty-six editors of national media found that PRPs believed that 40 per cent of output was based on PR. Editors, in contrast, estimated it to be an average of 25 per cent – with national newspapers the lowest at 10 per cent and the trade press the highest at 53 per cent. Those in radio and television said it was 30 per cent. A Two-Ten Communications survey (1993) of twenty-five national and 100 regional news and features editors found that 10 per cent of national news content and 18 per cent of regional news content was considered to be 'derived from PR'. Additionally, 15 per cent of national and 23 per cent of 'feature content' was 'derived from PR'. A poll produced by the PRCA (1.7.94) estimated that between 10 and 20 per cent of the stories in the national press were PR generated. The *Financial Times* used most PR – estimated at 26 per cent. The *FT* was followed by *The Times* (16 per cent), *Daily Mirror* (14 per cent), *Star* (14 per cent), *Independent* (11 per cent), *Guardian* (10 per cent), *Sun* (9 per cent) and *Mail* (9 per cent). The question continues to be posed periodically within the industry (see, for example, Michie, 1998), and was in fact put to over a third of those interviewed for the research. For both journalists and PRPs, if the question was not dismissed out of hand, estimates continued to vary wildly from between 20 and 80 per cent.[1]

The reason for the variety of responses is that it is almost impossible to break down and determine empirically what is PR and what is journalism. The first problem is caused by the difficulty of distinguishing PRPs from their source ties. There is no compulsory register of professional PRPs – only professional associations with voluntary membership. Many practitioners avoid the PR label, preferring titles like 'communication strategist', 'image consultant, 'information officer' or 'researcher'. Additionally, it is now standard practice that figures such as politicians, chief executives and pressure group leaders are media-trained and used to present material to journalists – in press releases and interviews – regardless of who manufactured the statements. More confusingly still, PR messages are considered most effective when working through third parties. Indeed, the most telling definition of PR is that relayed by Tim Bell (BDO Stoy Hayward Management Consultants, 1994, p7): 'Whereas advertising is the use of paid-for media space to inform and persuade, PR is the use of third-party endorsement to inform and persuade'. Public relations practitioners thus frequently get others outside their organisation to present their material as a means to gain objective support or a sympathetic hearing (see chapters five and eight). Much material is also simply pumped through to news-gatherers and wire services such as Reuters or the Press Association; material which itself is circulated as news gathered rather than PR supplied.[2]

---

1 For example, Quentin Bell, former chairman of the PRCA, estimated that up to 80 per cent of news output is public relations (in Michie, 1998). The current executive director of the PRCA, Chris McDowell, estimated that (interview, 26.7.98) 'In the nationals it's [PR] less than 20 per cent, but in the financial sections an enormous amount is. It's virtually all connected to PR in some way. The *FT* is at least 50 per cent PR ...'

2 As several PRPs explained: Jon Elwes (interview, 31.7.98), 'For getting blanket coverage do syndicated articles. You do a feature wire or a news pack service through someone like Two-Ten. You send an article to them and they send it down the feature wire and it's often printed straight in. It might go to 700 publications – regionals, locals and trade – and be printed, as is, in 70. It's quite an

Second, for every story fed to the media, there is one being carefully kept out. For many organisations, half or more of the work of PRPs involves restricting reporter access and information and/or attempting to quash negative stories. Berkman and Kitch (1986), Tiffen (1989) and Ericson et al. (1989) all noted the prevalence of such activities when looking at corporate news sources. Several of those PRPs interviewed confirmed such tendencies across businesses, pressure groups and government. For example, Tim Blythe, Director of Corporate Affairs at WH Smith explained (interview 15.9.98): 'Over the year it's 50:50. 50 per cent of the job is keeping stuff out of the press. I had ten years in Whitehall, and 70 per cent of press relations there was keeping stuff out of the papers.'[3]

Perhaps the most significant obstacle to defining where public relations ends and journalism begins is the fact that the two have become inextricably linked in a relationship that is largely invisible. Media and PR practices are most successful and appear most legitimate when the process of interaction between the two remains undeclared. Thus, PRPs and journalists alike are not keen to admit publicly their relations for fear of undermining their professional integrity. Even where the relationship is simple to document, many PR ploys for getting organisa- tions and messages into the media have become so commonplace that neither the public nor journalists themselves now seem aware of the differences. Several observers have described the range of ploys commonly used by political party and government PRPs attempting to gain frequent and favourable coverage (e.g., Boorstein, 1962, Nelson, 1989, Tiffen, 1989, Gaber, 1995, Rosenbaum, 1997). As Nelson declares (1989, p50): 'The press release, the press conference, the photo op, the pre-arranged interview, and press tour have all, over the years, become fully integrated into the fabric of what we perceive as "the news".' There are now numerous public relations DIY books which explain the methods for producing potential copy that journalists, if not sidetracked by 'real' news, will faithfully reproduce as a seemingly 'independent and newsworthy' story. 'The survey', 'the

---

effective way of getting wide coverage'; Paul Barber (interview, 20.8.98), 'The new area is the wires – Reuters, Bloomberg, the Press Association, AFX. If you get it on the wires then journalists every- where will take the story from the news wires. As papers reduce their numbers of journalists the news wires become the most cost-effective way of getting stories'; Martin Adeney (interview, 17.12.98), 'Increasingly they just take it off the wire services, which is one of the significant developments in the last three or four years. In my time we never took the wires too seriously and you wouldn't write many stories based on the wires. Now a lot of stories come straight from the wires – the Dow Jones, Bloomberg, Reuter ...'.

3 Paul Barber (interview, 20.8.98), 'Keeping something out of the papers might be the most signifi- cant thing we do all year but it can't be measured ... If you're in an area like banking, half your work might involve keeping stuff out of the media, taking on negative stories and so on'; Jonathan Russell (interview, 14.1.99), 'There is also a lot of work involved in keeping your profile lower. There are as many instances of when you would want to keep your company out of the press as when you would want to put them on the front page'; John Richards (interview, 20.5.97), 'We get a better press but it does depend on how we handle our media relations ... individual members can't talk to the media. Only the General Secretary, Assistant General Secretary, I and the eight regional reps talk to the media now'.

debate', 'the human interest story', 'the demonstration', the 'new research' or 'report', 'the charity action', 'the record breaker' and another story on the 'in-vogue theme', are all PR devices for getting information into the press. 'Yes that's all a survey really is', says Michael Bland and Associates (Michael Bland Communications, 1989, p6), 'the use of statistics to give authority and news appeal to a story you want to promote ... Even the serious press is happy to publish an interesting survey without questioning the quality of the research'.

For several journalists and PRPs interviewed, the methods for feeding PR output to journalists are often recognised as such but they are still considered valid means of news-gathering. Much news is instigated by external sources but is still regarded as 'newsworthy' and in need of being followed up. The real concern is then about how PR information is used. If handled appropriately, it becomes journalism rather than PR. As one financial journalist explained (anonymous, 1999):

> I hope none of it [journalism] is PR. Certainly not here. A lot is initiated by PRs ... there's a constant trickle of results, information on share price movements, acquisition and merger stuff announced by the Stock Exchange and so it goes on. The majority comes to you like that. But then you also get a feel for what we call a sector. You get a feel for what's going on. You can guess, if you follow the industry closely, you can see something is going to happen before it's announced and you follow it up.

In the view of Chris Hopson of Granada (interview, 13.10.98):

> It's about fifty-fifty [PR–journalism]. Most stories are generated by the companies themselves. Almost by definition, little or nothing, in some cases, is discovered by journalists. But the other fifty is that most good journalists don't just take the press release, they ask around a variety of sources. They are not just swallowing hook, line and sinker what the company is telling them what the story is about.

Evidently the ability to determine what is news and what is PR in any single publication is virtually impossible. In which case, determining whether a rise in public relations activity has resulted in more PR-produced news or not becomes a hopeless task.

Who is in charge and who is setting the agenda?

An alternative approach to separating public relations supply and journalist output is to investigate which side is in control and to ask: is the balance of power changing? This debate continues to appear periodically in studies of journalism, media sociology and political communications. In media sociology, the fourth estate line on journalistic autonomy, although not as resolute as before, is still assumed in many liberal studies (Alexander, 1981, Tiffen, 1989, Dayan and Katz, 1992, Schudson, 1996). Such things as 'professionalism', 'newsworthiness' and audience demand, mean that journalists maintain a fierce independence from sources and continue to fend off attempts to influence their output. Other commentators (Sigal, 1973, Gans, 1979, Fishman, 1980, Gandy, 1980, Ericson et al., 1989, Schlesinger and Tumber, 1994) have found a greater degree of complexity in the continuing relations between sources and journalists. However, the common consensus of much media sociology in the 1990s has tended to agree with Gans's earlier assessment; that (Gans, 1979, p117): 'The source-journalist relationship is therefore a tug of war: while sources attempt to "manage" the news ... journalists concurrently "manage" the sources in order to extract the information they want', but that, more often than not, sources 'have the edge'.

The recent expansion of public relations and, in particular, the rise in power of 'spin doctors', has managed to reignite interest in this debate (see Franklin, 1994, Blumler and Gurevitch 1995, Crewe and Gosschalk, 1995, Jones, 1995, 1999, Kavanagh 1995, Scammell, 1995, Crewe et al., 1998, King, 1998, Norris et al., 1999). The general assertion of these works, one that finds many advocates in the media itself, is that PRPs are becoming too powerful and, consequently, journalists are losing their conscious autonomy. Public relations power has manifested itself in several ways. First, with the rise in media outlets, more journalists are likely to be competing to get the attention of prominent sources. As a result, top PRPs are finding themselves in the position of being able to control media access and/or exclude journalists altogether. This power to exclude journalists from, for instance, the briefings of the Prime Minister's press secretary, has been a frequent cause of complaint for journalists operating in the lobby system at Westminster (see Cockerell et al., 1984, Negrine, 1994). It was also apparent in interviews with financial journalists who felt that their access to key business sources was being increasingly restricted by PRPs. As Richard Northedge, deputy editor of Sunday Business declared (interview, 25.5.99):

> They are a very powerful intermediary ... A PR consultant will work for a journalist on behalf of fifty different companies so there are fifty different reasons for the journalist to know the PR consultant ... They have certainly come to hold a much more powerful role in the last ten to fifteen years. Most journalists now complain about them. While PRs help to make contacts with the companies they have also moved to a position where they automatically intervene.[4]

Second, the power of PRPs can be quite significant if their source employers own, advertise in, or have other personal connections with, the publications they deal with (Herman and Chomsky, 1988, Curran and Seaton, 1997). Such factors have become highly influential in smaller, weaker publications, such as trade magazines and local papers where large companies dominate a sector and are an irreplaceable source of advertising revenue. As one 'senior magazine editor' explained (Spillius 1996, p10): 'If a PR wants you to go to an event involving a company that spends thousands of pounds on advertising in the magazine then you go. And you turn up where they want, when they want and wearing whatever cocktail dress they want.'

---

4 Raymond Snoddy (interview, 17.5.99), 'Sometimes they act as a block to keep one away from companies in trouble. I try to go to principals as much as possible. But they have some control in terms of who you get to speak to. It's a certain power over access. Sometimes it can get very heated and shouting matches follow ...'; Alex Brummer (interview, 16.6.99), 'There is also the fear that the PR is a barrier between you and the source that you want to get to. And the CEOs (Chief executive officer) who are happy not to go through the filter of the PRs are becoming less and less. There are very few now and there is a sense of losing something there'.

Few journalist interviewees had experience in these sectors but those that did all mentioned it as a strong influencing factor.[5]

Third, PRPs can harass journalists at all points in the news production process. Such badgering has increased according to many popular accounts – and is now taken to extreme lengths directly before and during elections. In preparation for the 1997 election, Tony Hall, head of news and current affairs at the BBC, was forced to announce that the Corporation was to set up a log to monitor party pressuring of its staff. It was a tactic that had also been adopted by the Independent Television News (ITN) news-rooms (interview with Jon Snow, 22.1.97). Jones (1995, 1999), Gaber (1998) and Rosenbaum (1997) all offer further accounts of media harassment in all its forms. Thus, like 'flak' producing PRPs in the USA (see Berkman and Kitch, 1986, Dreier, 1988, Herman and Chomsky, 1988) British PRPs have increased pressure on journalists. For all these reasons, it is clear to several observers such as Gaber (1995, p1) that 'in the debate as to who – between the politician, the broadcasters and the press – is in control of the national political news agenda, it is the politicians and their advisors who are firmly in the driving seat'. From these descriptions one might thus conclude that PRPs are gaining more than an 'edge'.

However, accounts produced by PRPs and journalists themselves frequently refute claims about the extent of PRP power. The question of control in media-source relations was put to almost all journalists and a third of PRPs interviewees. Once again the responses of both sets of constituents varied considerably, but very few supported the account of powerful 'spin doctors' leaning on or controlling journalists.

First, while the number of media outlets has expanded, so has the number of sources attempting to use the media. There is thus a corresponding growth in competition among PRPs attempting to get media access and favourable coverage. The general impression given by most interviewees was that PRPs, as a rule, had a lower status than journalists and that the powerful 'spin doctors' made up only a tiny minority of practitioners. According to Michie (1998) only 10 per cent of PRPs have any kind of status or power – in that journalists know who they are and/or they are able to control access to key sources. As Stephen Farish, editor of *PR Week*, explained (interview, 25.7.96): 'When you're a journalist and you come into a room you are the most important person there. When you are a PR, you are the least important person there. As journalists, people get to speak to anyone almost instantly. As a PR person it could take you months to speak to the same person.'

---

5 Ellis Kopel (interview, 23.7.96), 'Now there is an enormous amount more pressure by proprietors on editors, and editors on journalists, to try and influence stories, suppress stories, etc. ... especially on the magazine side'; Neville Davis (interview, 29.1.97), 'You have to work within the industry. You can't sit in an ivory tower and say "I am a journalist" and criticise. Because you will be out of a job. You can criticise all sorts of non-advertisers, but you can't have a large proportion of criticism of your own industry'.

Second, even for those in positions of power, the great swell of media outlets makes attempts to monitor and control news a difficult task. Ingham (1991, pp187–8, see also Ingham, 1996): 'Of course I tried to manage the news. I tried – God knows, I tried ... But news management, in the sense of ensuring that nothing is allowed to get in the way of the story the government wants to get over, is impossible in the modern world ... The real news managers today are the media themselves.' Journalists at the end of the day write the stories and have the final say as to what goes into the piece. Even if they cannot access a source, suffer intense PR harassment or are pressured by other considerations, they still determine what is covered. As many prominent sources and PRPs are aware, what goes in can bring down individual leaders as well as governments and large companies. As Wilson (in Crewe and Gosschalk, 1995, p49) declares: 'And let there be no doubt; when it comes to power to really hurt, we cannot touch the media compared with what they can do to us.' Thus for the vast majority of PRPs interviewed it was journalists who tended to be in control.[6]

For almost all journalist interviewees too, although they complained about PRPs, they were adamant that they were still in conscious control on a day-to-day level. In fact, none of the journalists would go so far as to say that they were losing their professional autonomy to PRPs. As Alex Brummer, financial editor of the *Guardian*, declared (interview, 16.1.96): 'The idea that financial journalists can be led one way or another by the communicators, whatsoever the latter may promise to their paymasters, the corporations, is preposterous.'[7]

Ultimately, there exist a colourful range of accounts which may be used to support a case for one side or the other. The evidence to date consists merely of irregular recordings of anecdotal evidence. The variables and vested interests involved make quantitative assessments impossible. Once again one cannot derive

---

6 John Aarons (interview, 5.7.96), 'there are far more PRs with far more media outlets with rapidly changing staff. The modern PR is more proactive and skilful and has to work much harder than 20 years ago ... Now today, definitely the journalists have the power and we have to hassle for attention'; John Elwes (interview, 23.7.96), 'At the end of the day it's the journalist who is in control because he writes the article at the end ... We treat the press like gods and they are ... Journalists know they are in charge and act like it'; Michael Sandler (interview, 19.10.98), 'In most situations the journalist has the upper hand. In fact 90 per cent of the time it's the journalist who is in control and 10 per cent it's PRs'; Martin Adeney (interview, 17.12.98), 'Once the press gets hold of it it's very difficult to keep it out ... It's very rare to get it pulled although occasionally you can. We can only work hard at putting the company's point of view and try to limit any misconceptions. But it's very difficult'.

7 Melanie Essex (interview, 5.2.97), 'There is an element of me that simply sees spin as a self-perpetuating myth ... They begin to believe in their own power. But we [the BBC] are very robust in dealing with it. It's unnatural to expect everyone to get it right 100 per cent of the time, but 99 per cent of the time ...'; financial journalist (interview, 1999), 'A lot of PR people, when they're talking to the companies and trying to get their contracts, will say that they control the press. They like to feel they often use the management to control us. But that's not so – not on the XXX anyway. We try and have an arms-length relationship with them and we do it on our terms, not theirs ... With the pressures we are under there's no opportunity to interfere. There is no window for fine-tuning. The article's done and dusted in no time so there's no time for them to complain or pressure us'.

clear conclusions – only suggest certain patterns. In terms of control one might tentatively argue that power relationships are governed by the law of supply and demand, in part related to evolving hierarchies of PRPs and journalists. In other words, the more in demand a source or journalist, the more power they are likely to have in their relations.

However, the most obvious pattern is that journalists and PRPs work together in a strained relationship – rather similar to Gans's (1980) original 'tug-of-war' description. As Jon Snow of Channel 4 (interview, 22.1.97) typically explained: 'The thing is that people tend to think the spin doctor is just there spinning but he's also a source; so you can't differentiate between a spin doctor and a source. Many of the recipients of spin doctors are very happy to hear from them ... So it isn't a one-way street. It isn't simply nasty spin doctor hassling innocent victim journalist.'[8] Whatever the power balance involved, the process of news production could not take place without a consistent long-term and daily working relationship between PRPs and journalists. News predominantly starts with source supply rather than media investigations, and PR is far more a part of news production than journalists have hitherto admitted.

But still the question posed at the start of this chapter remains. Professional public relations has grown and, as a consequence, sources are more professional in their dealings with the media, but is PR becoming more influential in the news production process? Attempts to gauge changing levels of content and/or journalistic autonomy have proved to be inconclusive.

Resources and the shift to source supply

The decline of British journalism and the rise in information subsidies

This section takes an alternative approach to answering the question by putting a greater emphasis on changing resources and organisational practices. As established above, sources, their PRPs and journalists work closely together in the production of news. Sources and PRPs, whether active or passive, provide most of

---

8 Alex Brummer (interview, 16.6.99), 'I talk to one or two PR men each day ... Basically there are about three or four senior people who have got something useful to say and they work across several firms. I regard them as semi-friends – I have known and worked with them for a long time ... I think it's a relationship of tension. There is a mutual distrust of PRs by most financial journalists. But there is also a recognition that they have to keep in with them and that they work within a very tense relationship'; Roland Gribben (interview, 21.5.99), 'It's like politicians and journalists. It looks adversarial in print but both need each other. PR is a selling business. We are in a consuming business. They are undoubtedly trying to massage the message. It comes down to our judgements of what we consume in the end. You are trying to get behind the layers of PR sugar'; Barrie Clement (interview, 25.5.99), 'It's very good. It can break down if you are doing a story about the internal changes of a union. But generally it's a mature relationship in which journalists realise that the union people are trying to spin things in their direction and they realise that the journalists have their own story to write. And as long as both sides understand that that's a working relationship'.

the raw materials and journalists manufacture the finished products. It therefore stands to reason that if the resources and working conditions of the two sides change it is likely that the production process itself will be altered. What is argued here is that, in the last two decades, national news-gathering resources in Britain have declined, so forcing journalists to economise and rely more on external information supplies. Simultaneously, public relations resources have increased, therefore enabling them to supply a much needed demand for information. Consequently, journalists still decide what goes in an article and have not lost conscious control, but the process of information supply has changed. Without trying to separate and identify the sources of news content, or ask who is setting the agenda, emergent trends suggest that news texts are being composed less by active journalists and more by public relations sources.

An alternative way of looking at PR output is as a source of information supply for journalists who have to fill space. An argument put in different ways by Boorstein (1962), Sigal (1973), Gandy (1980) and Fishman (1980) in the USA, is that PRPs are 'information subsidy' (Gandy, 1980) suppliers to journalists, and that the less resourced a media outlet is, the more it becomes dependent on such 'information subsidies'. As Fishman (1980, pp148–50) explains:

> Thus as story quotas increase while the labour force and the time to fill this quota remain constant, workers turn to reporting pre-formulated and pre-scheduled events in an anticipation of the speed up of their production line ... the overall economic logic of news reporting dictates the minimisation of labour costs by under-staffing the news room.

In theory, if investigative (or 'enterprise') reporting is a resource-intensive activity, then as resources go down, so does independent investigative journalism. At the same time dependence on sources, information subsidies and 'pseudo events' (Boorstein, 1962) goes up.[9]

News production in Britain, along with many other industry sectors, has been subjected to the effects of intense competition during the 1980s and 1990s (see Barnett and Curry, 1994, Tunstall, 1996, Williams, 1996, Curran and Seaton, 1997, Franklin, 1997). The application of new technologies with greater communications capacity, increasing concentration and conglomeration in the industry, media-friendly politicians and media legislation driven by free-market imperatives, have all intensified competition. As 'the market' has taken over from publicly owned and regulated media production, news has become looked upon as a financial millstone rather than a service. With far more readers, viewers, sponsors, advertisers and finance attracted to entertainment, the will to resource costly news programmes and a serious broadsheet press has consequently dwindled. Thus, as Jones concluded (1995, p8):

---

9 Sigal's 1973 study of the *Wall Street Journal* and *New York Times* – between 1949 and 1969 – is one of the few studies that correlated staffing levels with output. Sigal found that as staff numbers and resources on both papers increased in the period, reporters became less reliant on official sources, and, the level of investigative/'enterprise' stories rose.

'During the 1980s they [the Conservative Party] had unleashed and encouraged unparalleled competition between newspapers, television and radio. These commercial pressures had inevitably had an impact on editorial standards.'[10]

An overview of the declining national newspaper industry suggests that, in an effort to remain profitable, it has simultaneously increased output and cut back on staff. National newspapers have consistently struggled as long-term declines have been hastened by rising competition. Sunday papers have lost sales steadily since 1977 and dailies since the mid-1980s (figures in Greenslade 1994, pp4–5). A 1980s tabloid war, instigated by Murdoch's *Sun*, was followed by a 1990s broadsheet war, instigated by Murdoch's *Times*. Since 1993, there has been a sustained press price war which has seen significant losses across the industry. Despite the cuts and a temporary halt to declining sales, the long-term trends looked the same. Between 1994 and 1998 national papers lost a further half a million daily sales (3.6 per cent) and a further 1.16 million Sunday sales (7.3 per cent; figures in *Press Gazette*, 17.7.98, 18.7.94).

To keep pace all newspapers have raised prices well above inflation and attempted a series of sales gimmicks and new layouts. A common ploy has also been to introduce multiple new sections to appeal to alternative readers. This in itself has produced a high rate of page inflation. During the period 1984 to 1994, increases were as follows: the *Sun*, 32 pages to 52; the *Mirror*, 32 to 48; the *Star*, 28 to 36; the *Mail*, 36 to 64; the *Express* 36 to 64; the *Telegraph* 36 to 38; the *Guardian* 28 to 72; *The Times* 32 to 72; the *FT* 48 to 78. (figures in Greenslade, 1994, pp4–5). At the same time, it appears that journalist numbers per publication have been cut or, in the best cases, increased slightly. Almost all papers have reported minor cuts in staffing levels over the last five years. The *Guardian*, *Observer*, *Mirror* and *Sunday Mirror* have implemented small but regular rounds of redundancies in this period. Others, such as the *Independent*, *Daily Express* and *Daily Star*, have gone considerably further, cutting the numbers of editorial staff by between a third and a half.[11] Tunstall (1971) estimated that in 1969 there were approximately 3,550 journalists working on national newspapers. Two more recent estimates, by the NUJ and Delano and Hennington, are 2,666 and 2,462 respectively – indicating a drop of between 25 and 31 per cent over the last thirty years (figures in Franklin, 1997, pp51–3).

Even those papers which have maintained profits and increased journalist numbers have not kept up with page inflation. Table 2.4 records the changes in

---

10 The sea change in the way news is viewed is partly evidenced in the comments of programme controllers. As Paul Jackson, Carlton's director of programmes, declared in May 1992 (in Barnett and Curry, 1994, p249): 'If *World in Action* were in 1993 to uncover three more serious miscarriages of justice while delivering an audience of three, four or five million, I would cut it.' As John Wilson, former controller of editorial policy at BBC, was similarly to comment (in Douglas, 1998, p46) 'news is a way of making money just as selling bread is a way of making money. No-one believes that news and journalism are simply a service to democracy'.

11 Figures reported in the *Press Gazette* (e.g., 3.7.95, 24.7.95, 4.3.96, 9.8.96, 6.9.96, 24.1.97, 6.6.97) and the *Journalist* (e.g., Aug./Sept. 1995, Apr./May 1996, Oct./Nov. 1996, Jul./Aug. 1997).

pagination and staffing levels of the three most profitable national dailies of the late 1990s. It is a clear indication of the growing disparity between resources and output. While technology (new means of information retrieval and transfer, printing costs, etc.) has been responsible for many savings, it is also likely that journalist workloads have increased considerably. Indeed, Tunstall (1996, p136) estimated that 'Between the 1960s and the 1990s the amount of words written and space filled by each national newspaper journalist certainly doubled and perhaps trebled'.[12]

Table 2.4 Increase in page and staff numbers at the *FT*, *Sun* and *The Times*

	FT	Sun	The Times
Page nos, 1984	48	32	32
Page nos, 1994	78	52	72
Percentage increase	62.5	62.5	125
Staff nos, 1986	362	236	253
Staff nos, 1996	417	296	309
Percentage increase	15.2	25.4	22.1

Sources: Greenslade (1994, pp4–5) and newspaper personnel departments

For the majority of remaining staff, conditions have clearly worsened. Since the 1986 Murdoch-led move to Wapping, the power of the NUJ has waned. Currently, amongst national newspapers, only the *FT* and *Guardian* give full union recognition (*Journalist*, Oct./Nov. 1998). Consequently the workforce has been increasingly casualised and new working conditions imposed. Approximately 40 per cent of journalists now work on a freelance basis or are employed on part-time or short-term contracts (NUJ, 1998). Other changes include the introduction of 'multiskilling', 'pooling' of journalists, merging of sister papers, discriminatory practices against union members, attempts to make journalists take legal responsibility for their articles and the loss of journalists' copyright to publishers. A 1996 survey revealed that 62 per cent of journalists claimed to work 59 or more hours in the office each week, and that journalism was now the third most stressful occupation – on a par with airline pilots and prison officers. One-third claimed to have recently suffered from stress-related illnesses and 60 per cent said stress levels had increased in recent years (*Press Gazette*, 12.7.96, p10). A similar survey in 1997 (*Press*

---

12 Broadcasting companies have fared little differently. The BBC has simultaneously expanded its news operations (with twenty-four hour coverage in particular) and been forced to introduce internal market conditions and staffing cuts in an attempt to maintain its charter and licence fee. Franklin (1994, p70) estimated that 7,000 jobs were shed from the BBC between 1986 and 1994. Over 90 journalist job cuts were reported during 1996 and a further 25 per cent cut (to be phased in over five years) was announced in 1997. Regional and foreign news services have been particularly hard hit. Independent Television News has followed similar cost-cutting paths and moved further downmarket – most significantly with the undermining of *News at Ten*. The newest news operations at Sky and Channel Five operate on marginal budgets with skeleton staff. Only Channel 4 remained relatively unscathed during the 1990s, but its future remains far from secure.

Gazette, 2.5.97, p13) reported that 87 per cent now thought stress levels were increasing.

This impression of increased competition, rising stress levels, and a decline in thorough, let alone investigative, journalism is indeed common among journalists and is voiced with some regularity in the media trade press. For example, Bill Hagerty (*Press Gazette*, 29.1.99, p14):

> but the system is now dictating that journalists stay at their desks. They are over-worked – multi-skill mania has taken over – and are not allowed the time to investigate and certainly not the time to go abroad and investigate. That kind of thing is actively discouraged because it costs money ... It's all fast-food journalism these days.[13]

Quite clearly, the less journalists find news the more they become reliant on information coming to them and the less time they have to assess that information critically. The obvious conclusions filtering through point towards an increased dependency on 'information subsidies'. A Gallup survey (1991, p11) found that 60 per cent of editors agreed that 'The growing role of PR practitioners has made journalists more reliant on supplied information'. A 1996 survey (*PR Week*, 11.10.96, p1) of sixty broadcasters found '62 per cent said that, with budget restrictions and increased demand for stories, they expect to use more outside generated material in the coming year'.

The general description offered above was consistently confirmed in interviews with both PRPs and journalists. Although journalists tended to deny the strong influence of PR on their work (conscious or unconscious) they almost unanimously agreed about the above trends and the declining standards of investigative journalism. All but two financial journalists interviewed were quite clear that demands on journalists had gone up and that stress levels had consequently increased. As one financial journalist, who was leaving, said (anonymous, 1999):

> I got totally pissed off at the starving of resources at the XXX ... If you get to the stage, as I did, when you are asked to do too much for too long, you start looking elsewhere ... The XXX is one particular case and we didn't keep up. I left, quite frankly, because I was furious. The paper has been starved of editorial resources ... I was a high-profile journalist, a senior journalist. But with all that, I had no say and I

---

13 Henry Porter (*Media Guardian*, 20.6.94, p4), 'Today the reporter who leaves the new hi-tech facility to collect facts and exhaustively researches a story is a rare bird and certainly the zealous inquiries of investigative reporters are more or less a thing of the past'; Jon Snow (*Press Gazette*, 20.9.96, p5), 'We are under siege, there is no question ... Ratings will be the determinant because the money comes from advertisers ... Within a couple of years there could be no serious analytical news programmes on American TV and that is the way we are heading'; Ian Hargreaves (*Press Gazette*, 18.4.97, p11), 'The biggest threat to the media is the explosion of media firms and new products and the sight of companies investing in these firms trying to milk journalists harder and harder'. See also: Geoffrey Goodman (*Press Gazette*, 18.12.95, p17); Colin Bourne (1995–96, pp18–19); Roy Greenslade (1996, p25); Alan Rusbridger (*Press Gazette*, 22.3.96, p15); Anthony Sampson (1996, pp42–51); Hugh O'Shaughnessy (1998, pp56–9).

had to work under more and more pressure. I'm just extremely angry about the whole thing. I expected to be in financial journalism for the rest of my life and, if I had the choice, I still would be.[14]

Almost all talked about journalists no longer leaving the office, the decline of investigative journalism, and the dependency on outside source materials. As Barrie Clement of the *Independent* explained (interview, 25.5.99):

> Journalists everywhere are expected to produce more copy because there are fewer people to fill papers. And with less reporters the papers think twice about sending people out to get stories. It's much more bums on seats now and people don't get out much. So people are increasingly reliant on the wire services and Internet and other information coming to you. Some people get 80 per cent of their materials from the Internet and wires. So journalists sit in the office much more because that's what management want them to do – it's like a comfort blanket. They like to look around and see lots of bodies at their desks.[15]

The PRP's perceptions of deteriorating conditions in journalism were also unanimous. Public relations practitioners, many of them ex-journalists, were conscious of the fact that they tended to succeed quite simply because of the needs of their journalist consumers. As Nick Miles (17.8.98), CEO of Financial Dynamics, explained: 'What is increasingly the case, and worryingly so, is that journalism is becoming recommodified. Since the newspaper price wars of the mid-90s

---

14 Also: Raymond Snoddy (interview, 17.5.99), 'They [demands] have increased. There is a lot more financial pressure to deliver ... There is a greater pressure on financial budgets and at the same time the amount of supplements, and therefore page numbers, have kept going up. As these pressures have increased, people have to work longer hours to keep up. It's now a very busy and stressful occupation'; Barry Clement (interview, 25.5.99), 'There are fewer people, fewer journalists. There have been mass redundancies in journalism – the same as in other areas. They have got rid of older, more experienced journalists and brought in younger, cheaper ones ... It's no longer annual pay rises – it's much more hit and miss. You can only get rises now if you are prepared to sign inferior contracts'; anonymous financial journalist interview (1999), 'Output has increased at the same time as numbers have gone down. That's across writers and subs. The output of the subs has increased phenomenally with new technologies. Everyone is working a lot harder. Over a period of years, newspaper chapels have become almost defunct. You don't hear about disputes anymore. Threats of action don't halt production anymore. That's all gone now, which means that journalists work harder'.
15 See also: Linda Rogers (interview, 7.1.97), 'I have no evidence for this but it seems that journalists are a lot less assiduous. They have less time to investigate stories. Less time to investigate the story behind the story ... The temptation is to get stuff you can just get across your desk, not to go out so much'; anonymous national editor (interview, 1997), 'We spend more time at our desks rather than going out and spending time getting a feel for this or that. There are more supplements, special projects, and other activities organised by the paper'; Richard Northedge (interview, 25.5.99), 'On a daily paper, unusually compared to other news sectors, financial information has to be issued through the Stock Exchange or the government statistics office and most of the news you read in your daily paper comes from these announcements. It's an easy source of news ... I would say that 10 per cent or even less is news that didn't appear over the wires – which is why the news is almost the same across newspapers'.

journalists have become cannon fodder, except at the top end, such as the city editor. Most of them are being asked to do more and more for less and less.'[16]

Who guards the guards? The transfer of media knowledge

As already documented in this chapter, PR expenditure has expanded at the same time as journalist resources have declined. As such, the PR profession has been ideally placed to supply the rising demand for information subsidies – either directly or through third parties. What has also helped the PR profession to become regular suppliers is a rising level of knowledge about journalists and the media production process itself. Public relations practioners are now not only better resourced than journalists, they know an increasing amount about their customers and can thus produce tailor-made products without arousing suspicion or applying pressure.

Knowledge about journalists and publications has been built up in several ways. First, many PRPs have been journalists before entering the profession. Their experiences give them a strong sense of 'news values', how and when journalists like information subsidies, and many ready-made contacts in the news industry. What percentage of PRPs have come from journalism is unknown and varies across sectors. However, it appeared quite significant in the sectors observed in this study. Amongst unions, 55.6 per cent employed communications staff with experience in journalism (see chapter seven). Over 50 per cent of the 36 PRP interviewees working in corporations and consultancies had media experience. Similarly, a considerable proportion of the top 'spin doctors' in the main political parties have senior press and/or broadcasting experience.

Indications are that the journalist-turned-PRP appears to be a rising phenomenon as journalists lose their jobs and/or seek the better conditions and pay of the public relations industry. Public relation practitioners work fewer hours, earn larger salaries (see figure 2.3), have better working conditions, and are better resourced. Just over 50 per cent of both employment sectors are likely to have some kind of company pension (IPR, 1998b, NUJ, 1998). However, PRPs are more likely to receive additional benefits, such as: an annual bonus (31.9 per cent), private medical insurance (33.7 per cent), or a company car (36.9 per cent). They are also rather less likely to be on part-time or short-term contracts. In fact, not only have PR numbers increased, but the proportion of NUJ members who work in PR have also risen.[17] In 1994 (NUJ, 1994, p8) the 'press/PR' sector made up 7.3 per cent of

---

16 Ellis Kopel (interview, 23.7.96), 'the whole of journalism has suffered from … a slow drift that has made the journalist more dependent on PR … In some ways they [journalists] are more investigative, but only on the scandal side'; Stephen Farish (interview, 25.7.96), 'journalism can't function without PR of some description because modern media operations simply don't have the resources to be driven entirely by investigative reporting'; Stewart Prosser (interview, 22.6.98), 'At the same time newspapers are under increasing financial pressures, with fewer staff, so it's easier to place stories'.

17 In 1984, the IPR had approximately 2,300 members and the NUJ 33,400. By 1998 the IPR had over 5,700 members and the NUJ 27,700 (figures from IPR and NUJ membership departments). Forty per cent of NUJ members were also in irregular or short-term employment (NUJ, 1998).

Figure 2.3 Comparison of earnings of PRPs and journalists, 1998

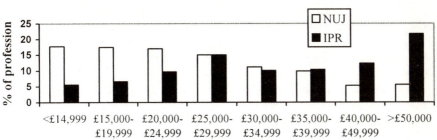

Source: IPR (1998b) and NUJ (1998) membership surveys
(IPR collated slightly differently, in the form 'Up to 15,000', '15001–20,000', etc.)

NUJ membership. In 1998 (NUJ, 1998, p30), 24.4 per cent of members worked part or full-time in 'press/PR'.

Second, for those without media experience, there are many other means of acquiring knowledge about journalists and their personal information subsidy requirements. In fact, more than at any other time, journalists themselves are the subject of investigation. An expanding secondary industry is developing to support the specialist information need of PRPs. Databases and reference books, containing information on individual journalists, particular publications and market trends, are widely available. Any PRP may currently employ specialist companies for 'media monitoring', 'media evaluation', 'media analysis', 'press cutting services', 'media training', 'PR delivery services' and 'video and audio news release services'.

Two of the largest service suppliers, Two–Ten and PiMS offer extensive, and regularly updated, databases on publications and journalists across the UK. Names, addresses, telephone and fax numbers, and e-mail addresses, are all available on-line to PRPs. Although as Colin Taylor, Marketing Manager of PiMS, explains, the available information has become rather more extensive (*PR Week*, 6.11.98, p14):

> We have always collected basic information on journalists but are constantly getting requests from clients on their specific areas of interest … We can also build up more personal background material, such as their career history, so that clients can bring these things up in conversation, helping them to develop a closer relationship … This business is all about establishing relationships so it can also be useful to know about journalists likes and dislikes and even the names of their children.

At the other end of the news production line are the media evaluation companies such as Computer Aided Research and Media Analysis (CARMA) and polling companies such as the Market and Opinion Research Institute (MORI). They offer a range of services that effectively monitor and evaluate media outlets and individual journalists and gain journalists' opinions on PR clients: 'CARMA defines how

your messages are being presented by the media, the favourability of news organisations and individual journalists, who is setting the agenda, and the relationship
between journalists, analysts, lobbyists and others' (CARMA promotional material,
1996). Whether this information is used to blacklist journalists, lobby them, or
shape PR copy, it is another powerful means of news management available to
PRPs.

The suppliers of information subsidies are thus able to research their targets as
effectively as journalists research their stories. Key journalists are now observed at
all stages of news production. As journalists now investigate sources and act as
public guardians, PRPs investigate journalists and act as source guardians. Most
PRP interviewees made use of such tools and devices and were capable of using
their information to clinical effect. As one financial PR director (anonymous, 1998)
explained:

> What we try and do in a campaign is home in on a particular journalist and keep
> them on the case throughout the event. We can't chose who necessarily … We will
> try to go for journalists who we know will have credibility. It's down to the city
> editor. We try and interest other journalists if we can … If we know about a bid in
> advance, we draw up from the database a list of who we want to talk to. So before
> even the analysts or journalists know we know, we contact them ahead and try and
> get our key journalists interested.

Conclusion

As has been demonstrated, arguments about who is in control, who is setting the
agenda, when is news news and when is it PR, are all rather vague and inconclusive.
None of these approaches give a clear indication of whether news production has
been significantly altered by the rise of professional PR. However, by looking at
resources – information, economic and human – trends are rather more
discernible. Study from this perspective suggests that while journalists continue to
act with a high degree of conscious autonomy, that autonomy is subject to resource
constraints.

Clearly, as British journalism is repeatedly cut and squeezed, its fallibilities
increase, its standards and objectivity decrease, and its need to cut corners becomes
crucial. Journalists must do more with less resources and, therefore, are increasingly reactive and less discerning in their activities. Under such a state of affairs,
the weakened media industry remains an easy prey for an increasingly powerful and
predatory PR sector. Journalists are becoming outnumbered and out-resourced by
their PR counterparts. Although PRPs may be in direct competition with each
other, and journalists get to pick and choose, they are in effect making a reactive and
less critical choice – rather than pursuing a proactive investigation. Without any
arm-bending, dominant ideology, loss of editorial control and so on, the influence
of PR has slowly expanded its role in news production. In effect, the liberal gate-
keeper models that have relied on journalistic autonomy have been strongly undermined by the effects of increased competition and the rise of PRPs.

The next question to ask is: which elements of society benefit most from the changes in news production and the dependence on PR-supplied information subsidies? Is public relations simply a means by which particular elite interests can further dominate access and manage media agendas? Or does it enable poorer and more excluded groups to gain a level of coverage in the media that was previously denied to them? So far, the implications indicate that those with greater resources – institutions and businesses – will be more able to supply information subsidies consistently, and will thus gain greater benefits from the new PR-mediated environment. However, as chapter three on corporate PR argues, the production and reception of information subsidies in the media is a rather more complex process.

PART II

CORPORATE PUBLIC RELATIONS

3
CORPORATE PUBLIC RELATIONS
AND CORPORATE SOURCE INFLUENCE ON
THE NATIONAL MEDIA

This chapter looks at the rise of corporate public relations in the UK and asks: how effective has PR been in achieving corporate objectives? As the previous chapter noted, the expansion of professional public relations has been most impressive in the business sector. The occupational survey of IPR members (IPR, 1998b), in conjunction with the client profile of the PRCA (*Year Book*, 1998), indicates that approximately two-thirds of PRPs are currently employed in in-house corporate PR departments or act as consultants to businesses. One might therefore assume that corporate public relations has had the most significant impact on news production and public discourse.

That the public relations profession is so heavily skewed towards the business sector adds weight to radical media sociology assertions about strong corporate influence over the media and public opinion. Common radical explanations for such influence have usually involved a focus on either macro-cultural trends and belief systems or economic explanations of ownership, advertising and news commodification. Although there has been little research on British corporate PR, the available information on the sector, when combined with critical work on PR in North America, produces an account that strongly supports the radical case. Simply put, since 1979: corporate PR has expanded; social and economic policy-making has been dominated by pro-business and free-market thinking; and the majority of national media producers have continued to support political parties which advocate such policies. Thus there appears a strong case for arguing that corporate PR has been instrumental in influencing both the media and public opinion towards an acceptance of business norms and values. In other words, corporate PR has contributed to a corporate 'propaganda model' (Herman and Chomsky, 1988) or, as Habermas earlier argued, a corporate 'refeudalisation' of the 'public sphere' (Habermas, 1989 [1962]).[1]

This chapter evaluates this thesis critically. By looking more closely at (a) media–business source relations, and (b) the corporate PR industry itself, problems with the radical thesis become apparent. Arguably, direct corporate source influence on national news production in the UK has been significantly weaker than most accounts assume. The logics that guide both journalist routines and business communication objectives each suggest that companies are neither able, nor strongly

---

1 Habermas has since acknowledged the deficiencies of his earlier work in Habermas, 1997.

inclined, to concentrate their efforts on influencing the output of mainstream news texts. Rather, they tend to pursue public promotion through advertising, and political objectives through direct contact with policy-makers. Thus, if public relations is benefiting the corporate sector it cannot simply be on account of its ability to influence national journalists and public opinion.

Public relations and corporate control of news production – the radical thesis

Public relations and the legitimisation of capitalist democracy

Looking at the development of public relations historically there appears to be a strong case for arguing that PR is closely connected to the management of public opinion by elites. In North America, the history of public relations in the twentieth century is linked almost exclusively to governments and corporations (see, for example, Dreier, 1982, 1988, Gandy, 1982, Berkman and Kitch, 1986, Herman and Chomsky, 1988, Nelson, 1989, Cutlip *et al.*, 1994, Stauber and Rampton, 1995, Ewen, 1996, Hall-Jamieson, 1996, Marchand, 1998, Tye, 1998). According to many of these accounts the evolution of public relations is indeed tied to the needs of elites in capitalist democracies. The introduction of universal suffrage, the industrialisation of economies, the expansion of mass communications, the emphasis on the consumer society, and the continuing need to legitimise both the state and the process of capitalist accumulation, are all factors requiring increased management of public opinion. Thus the needs of the governments and corporations – to control information flows within the public sphere in the name of the consumer citizen – necessitate the creation of a professional public relations sector. At crisis points, caused by union activity, war or economic depression, public relations has expanded as social psychology has been coupled with sophisticated propaganda methods to influence 'the American masses'.[2]

According to many of these same accounts (see, in particular, Warner and Silk, 1979, Dreier, 1982, 1988, Nelson, 1989, Cutlip *et al.*, 1994, Stauber and Rampton, 1995, Ewen, 1996), the more recent rise in corporate public relations came in direct response to a general crisis of corporate perception in the 1970s. Economic downturn, together with the rise of media-oriented social movements and pressure groups, and a post-Watergate media suspicion of government and big business, combined to produce a wave of negative coverage for 'corporate America'. The response was the investment of billions of dollars in attempts to manage public

---

2 Thus, Cutlip *et al.* (1985, p23) write 'The history of public relations is meaningful only when it is related to these power conflicts and recurring crises of change. For example, it is not mere coincidence that in the past, business interests have taken public relations most seriously when their positions of power were challenged or threatened by the forces of labour, the farmer, the small shopkeeper'; Ewen (1996, p10), who interviewed the elderly Bernays, 'grandfather' of the industry, explains 'Bernays conveyed his hallucination of democracy: A highly educated class of opinion-moulding tacticians is continuously at work, analysing the social terrain and adjusting the mental scenery from which the public mind, with its limited intellect, derives its opinions'.

opinion and the media, including: media training of corporate executives; the rise of government relations and public affairs PR; the establishment of pro-business think tanks; the establishment of corporate-sponsored business journalism courses; pressuring the media with 'flak'; the buying-up of media organisations by corporations; use of libel laws; and, above all, advocacy advertising. An obvious by-product of this corporate communications offensive was the growth in US PRPs. Their numbers rose from 19,000 in 1950 to 162,000 in 1990, with 197,000 predicted by the year 2000 (Cutlip *et al.*, 2000, p31). Like the UK, approximately two-thirds of PR employment was, and continues to be, in business (*ibid.*, p32). Thus, in theory, the corporate sector has developed the capacity to drown out opposition voices by sheer volume of its promotional output alone. Indeed, each of the above studies presents detailed case studies of large corporations using PR to manufacture news and sway public opinion to achieve particular objectives.

These critical descriptions of the development of public relations clearly have some affinity with radical political economy accounts of news production (e.g., Herman and Chomsky, 1988, Schiller, 1989, 1992 Bagdikian, 1997, Herman and McChesney, 1997, McChesney, 1997). All offer detailed accounts of the power of market forces and the ability of corporate interests to influence largely privately owned news media. The 'filters' of business ownership, advertising, and news commodification join with a widespread media workers' view that is positive towards business and the notion of private property, and is conditioned to accept the dominant ideology of capitalist production and/or condemn communism. Such studies, as well as revealing a number of occurrences of media bias, myopia and inconsistency, also identify a steady stream of political legislation which has favoured business interests. This includes legislation which has resulted in: the marginalisation of anti-business organisations such as environmental pressure groups (Gitlin, 1980); the use of advocacy advertising by businesses and the funding of pro-business think tanks and politicians (Dreier, 1988, Schiller, 1989, McChesney, 1997); a reduction of workers rights and union activities; moves towards privatisation, deregulation of industries, international trade, and the promotion of national business interests abroad (Herman and Chomsky, 1988, Nelson, 1989, Schiller, 1989, 1992); a switch from direct to indirect taxation and the reduction in the proportion of tax paid by corporations to government (Schiller, 1989).

Few of the above-mentioned studies have actually looked at the reporting of businesses in the media or media—business source relations. However, if corporate public relations has expanded so significantly and above all other forms of PR, and business interests appear to win the political and media debates far more often than they lose, then clear links appear likely. The obvious conclusion is that corporate PR has helped businesses to further their influence over journalists and the general public and worked to support free-market policy-making agendas.

Corporate public relations in the UK

The radical thesis, although developed in North America, seems quite transposable to Britain. The recent history of public relations and government policy-making in the UK fits the above analysis well. First, as several historical accounts of the period record (see, for example, Middlemas, 1979, 1991, Kavanagh and Seldon, 1989, Young, 1989, Letwin, 1992, Pollard, 1992), the Conservative governments of the 1980s decisively broke with the post-war tripartite consensus and initiated a period of free-market policy-making. These policies resulted in: greater concentrations of economic power in fewer companies; a crippling of union power, a steady casualisation of working practices and increasing insecurity for workers; rising inequality, greater levels of poverty and homelessness; a decline in manufacturing industry while the service and financial sectors expanded; extensive privatisation and deregulation of industries and the financial sector; the shift of the tax burden towards indirect taxation and away from top earners and corporations; and attacks on the Welfare State and public spending (see accounts of such shifts also in, for example, Lowe, 1993, Taylor, 1994, Hills, 1996, Hutton, 1996, Mitchell, 1997). In effect, the power of international capital (the interests of the City and multinational corporations) has been strengthened at the expense of national wage labour (trade unions, manufacturing industry and the welfare state) and elected government.

Conditions consequently required the rapid expansion of corporate public relations, in order to maintain the support of a majority of consumer-citizens – many of whom stood to lose out by such changes. The corporate PR industry did indeed expand impressively during the 1980s (see chapter two). Much of it also appeared to be directly linked to the Thatcher policy agenda as a three-way alliance seemed to develop between the Conservative government, the corporate sector and the public relations industry.

Several of the top public relations companies that grew to dominate the industry in the UK simultaneously worked closely with the Conservative Party, gained many Conservative government contracts, and were employed by many of the UK's top companies. For example, Shandwick, Lowe-Bell (now Bell-Pottinger) and Dewe-Rogerson (now Dewe-Rogerson-Citigate) all grew at tremendous rates during the period of Conservative government – each becoming top-three companies in the PR consultancy sector. The chief executive of Shandwick is Peter Gummer, brother of the former cabinet minister, John Selwyn Gummer. Shandwick also headed a consortium of four consultancies that freely advised the Conservative Party throughout its term of office. Its directors/advisers (including its subsidiaries) during the period included: Lord Chalfont, Lord Strabolgi, Sir Michael McNair-Williams MP, Sir Fergus Montgomery MP, Alan Haselhurst MP and David Mellor MP. In 1996 the company listed eighteen of the FTSE 100 companies as clients. Lowe-Bell was run by Tim Bell, personal adviser to Margaret Thatcher and the Conservative Party. Its directors/advisers (on subsidiaries also) during the period included: Anthony Grant MP, Michael Mates MP and Peter Archer MP. In 1996 the company listed nineteen of the FTSE 100 companies as clients. Dewe-Rogerson(-Citigate) made donations to the Conservative Party, was employed to promote a total of fourteen privatisation projects in the UK, and has gone on to repeat the process in many other countries. In 1996 the company listed fourteen of the FTSE top 100 companies as clients.

Burson-Marsteller, Hill and Knowlton, the Rowland Company (owned by Saatchi and Saatchi), Valin Pollen (now Gavin Anderson) and Charles Barker have all also dominated *PR Week*'s 'top 10' list for long periods. The directors/advisers listed for these companies have included: Sir Bernard Ingham, David Crouch MP, Ted Garrett MP, Lord Orr-Ewing, Peter Fry MP, Dudley Smith MP and Tim Rathbone MP. Between them they listed another thirty-four of the FTSE top 100 companies as clients in 1996 (sources for all figures and connections, PRCA *Year Books*, 1989–97 and FT 500, 1997). Even *PR Week*, the industry trade journal, is owned by Michael Heseltine's Haymarket group and has Bernard Ingham as its star columnist.

Each of these PR consultancies benefited by being awarded communications contracts for government departments, privatisations, and former nationalised industries. A look at the budgets for some of the Conservative privatisation campaigns of the 1980s (most of which were awarded to PR consultancies) gives some indication of the extent of finances being filtered towards these companies. The promotional budget for the privatisation of British Telecom (BT) in 1984 was £25 million, for British Gas in 1986 £40 million, for British Petroleum (BP) in 1987 £23 million, for the water utilities in 1989 £40 million and for the electricity companies in 1989 £76 million (Franklin, 1994 p103). In fact, over 100 contracts for government departments, state institutions, privatisations or recently privatised companies were awarded to the above consultancies during the Conservative period of government (see also Miller and Dinan, 2000).[3] As Kavanagh (1995) has also

---

3 These included: Amersham International, Anglian Water, the Atomic Energy Authority, British Airports Authority (BAA), the Bank of England, British Aerospace, British Airways, the British Army, British Coal, British Coal Pension Fund, the British Council, British Energy, the British Film Institute (BFI), British Gas, British Leyland, the British Library, British Nuclear Fuels, British Oil, BP, British Rail, British Railfreight, the British Railways Board, British Steel, BT, Cable and Wireless, the Central Electricity Generating Board, the Central Office of Information, the Departments of Energy, the Environment, Health, Social Security, Trade and Industry, and Transport, the Driver and Vehicle Licensing Authority (DVLA), East Midlands Electricity, East of Scotland Water Authority, Eastern Electricity Board, the Equal Opportunities Commission, Eurotunnel, the Falkland Islands Government, the Health Education Authority, the Health Education Council, Her Majesty's Customs and Excise, Her Majesty's Stationery Office (HMSO), the Home Office, the Industrial Development Board of Northern Ireland, the Information Technology Parliamentary Committee, the Inland Revenue, the Independent Television Commission (ITC), the Office of Fair Trading, Leyland, the London Electricity Board, London Buses, the London Stock Exchange, London Transport, Manpower Services Commission, Manweb, Marconi, the Meat and Livestock Commission, the Ministry of Defence, the Monopolies and Mergers Commission (MMC), the Motor Industry Parliamentary Committee, North Atlantic Treaty Organisation (NATO), the National Audit Office, the National Council for Vocational Training, National Grid, National Power, Northern Ireland Electricity, North Western Electricity Board (NORWEB), North West Water Group, Northumbrian Water, Nuclear Electric, the Office of Fair Trading (OFT), Office of Telecommunications (OFTEL), the Post Office, Powergen, Railtrack, Rolls Royce, Royal Mail, the Royal Mint, the Rural Development Commission, Scottish Nuclear, the Scottish Office, Scotrail, South Wales Electricity, Southern Electricity Board, Southern Electric, the Territorial Army, Thames Water, the TSB Group, Vickers, the Water Authorities Association, the Water Services Association, Southern Water, the Welsh Development Agency, Welsh Water (PRCA *Year Books* 1980–98).

pointed out, these same companies also benefited by gaining numerous corporate contracts because of their government connections. Saatchi and Saatchi, for example, five years after it took on the Conservative Party account, had increased pre-tax profits by 600 per cent (Kavanagh, 1995, p18) and had become the largest advertising agency in Britain.

Throughout, the media in Britain appear to have played a part in this neo-liberal drive. For most of the period in question, the majority of national media organisations supported the Conservatives – only becoming more ambivalent as New Labour adopted many of those same free-market policies (see, for example, Curran *et al.*, 1986, Hollingsworth, 1986, Williams, 1996, Curran and Seaton, 1997, Franklin, 1997). That the media were pro-business was given further support in the few studies of business sources in Britain that were to emerge at the time. Work by the Glasgow University Media Group (1976, 1980, 1982), more recently supported by Tumber (1993) and Mitchell (1997), all suggest that management and government sources have managed to dominate reporting of industrial relations and the economy (see also the discussion in chapter six). Mitchell's 1988 (1997, p47) survey of trade union and business relations with the media found that only 3 per cent of unions said the media were 'sympathetic' and 66 per cent said 'unsympathetic'. This was opposed to employment groups – 42 per cent sympathetic and 21 per cent unsympathetic – and individual firms – 30 per cent sympathetic and 17 per cent unsympathetic.

Radical miscalculations and the failure of business sources

Undoubtedly, the public relations industry has been widely employed by corporations and government and has also been significantly involved in the promotion of free-market policy-making. The question is: how successful has it been in its promotional goals? As the next two sections in this chapter argue, if it has been successful, it is unlikely to have been entirely through attempts to influence mainstream journalists and the general public.

The principal problem with the mass influence model outlined above is its lack of empirical evidence on business source activities, corporate source–media relations or corporate public relations in Britain. In effect, the power of business sources and corporate PR to influence day-to-day reporting has been assumed rather than demonstrated. Arguably, the few radical studies that have managed to observe business sources and mainstream business reporting fail to convince with their evidence (see critiques by Harrison, 1985, Tiffen, 1989, Schudson, 1996). More importantly, these studies do not explain several empirical inconsistencies in their work – each of which tend to suggest that business–media relations require substantial reconsideration. In fact, there is a rather significant body of evidence which suggests that (a) business sources are not particularly effective at gaining access to mainstream news, and (b) influencing mainstream news with public relations is not necessarily a major objective of business elites at all.

Reviewing elite source dominance – the economics of news-gathering

It is often assumed that because elites generally dominate news, business sources do also. However, although journalists tend to pursue institutional and government elites the same can not be said of corporate elites. In fact, the findings of most empirical studies of news-gathering and production (Tunstall, 1971, Sigal, 1973, Tuchman, 1978, Gans, 1979, Fishman, 1980, Gitlin, 1980, Tiffen, 1989, Ericson *et al.*, 1989, 1991) suggest that mainstream journalists are rarely likely to cover business sources for clear economic and organisational reasons.

First, all of these studies note that journalists attempt to cover beats, build up regular sources and follow routines for news-gathering. In other words, news organisations must employ journalists efficiently by gaining regular and accessible sources of news supply in order to produce a consistent and continuous flow of news stories. It is for these organisational reasons, as much as the need to find authoritative and powerful sources, that institutional sources dominate most forms of news. However, businesses do not conform to these journalist requirements. As Ericson *et al.* (1989, 1991) discovered, they are not part of regular news-beats, do not have physical spaces for journalists to occupy and generally do not offer a regular supply of 'newsworthy' stories.

Further barriers, which hinder active business source–journalist relations, have been recognised in both corporate and media circles for some time. Unless there is an emergency, business executives rarely make or have the time to give interviews to meet urgent journalist deadlines. Another problem is that economic and business issues can be very technical and complex and thus demand levels of specialist knowledge and time that journalists do not have. Finn's (1981) survey, of 187 business executives, 204 PR directors and 198 journalists, found that both sides agreed that journalists were too ignorant of business and did not adequately research their business stories. Each of these points have been repeatedly stressed by both journalists and corporate elites (see Warner and Silk, 1979, CBI and Abbey Life Assurance Co. Ltd, 1981, Finn, 1981, Hoge, 1988, Smith, 1988, Rees-Mogg, 1992). Thus, in the increasingly fast-paced news-gathering environment it is simply not efficient for businesses and business leaders to become regular sources for mainstream reporters.

From the point of view of audiences, and therefore sales and advertising revenues, journalists are also less likely to cover businesses. Mainstream journalists are aware the general public is not interested in good business news, which is technical, not personality based, and seemingly irrelevant to most people. As Silk explains (in Warner and Silk, 1979, p44), news media, with large audiences, often shy away from business reporting because of: 'the fear of dial-switching, as listeners tune out an explanation of the economics of gas pricing or energy development for a rock singer, a baseball game, a quiz show, a soap opera, or some other piece of entertainment that will raise its ratings and hence its advertising dollars and profits.' Thus, as news outlets try to expand their audiences in order to draw wider audiences and more advertising (see Curran, 1978, Dreier, 1982, Garnham, 1990, Franklin, 1997), so businesses are less likely to be sources in mainstream news. This is particularly the case in tabloid newspapers, which depend more on sales than advertising (see Curran, 1978). As Kahle (in Rubin, 1977, p171) concludes, 'The irony, then, is that as the media become bigger businesses, they become more problematical for big business'.

In fact the few quantitative studies that exist, in which business and other sources are compared, all tend to agree that business sources are amongst the least cited. Several studies of industrial relations reporting (Glasgow University Media Group, 1976, 1980, 1982, Annan Report, 1977, McQuail, 1977, Harrison, 1985) all produced content analysis data demonstrating that both union and government sources gained significantly more coverage than business ones. Finn's survey (1981, p37) similarly found that three-quarters of 'Journalists and public relations directors are both aware that business executives have few outlets in which to express their views'.

Reviewing journalist–business relations – antagonism and scandal

What several studies have also noted is that the majority of British journalists are union members and more sympathetic to the political left than they are to the pro-corporate right (e.g. Annan Report, 1977, McQuail, 1977, Philo *et al.*, 1977, Jones, 1986, Harrison, 1986, Seaton, 1991). Lichter and Rothman's (1988) study in the USA produced similar results. A survey of 240 journalists and 216 business executives found that, in all elections since 1964, over 80 per cent of journalists had voted Democrat. Asking their opinions on a series of issues, the study found that the majority of journalists could be classified as 'welfare state liberals' who supported policies and followed voting patterns that were in marked contrast to those of business leaders. Such observations suggested that business elites and journalists were unlikely to communicate on a positive, like-minded basis.

Research by Lichter and Rothman (1988) and Finn (1981), in fact, recorded high levels of antagonism between the two groups. Lichter and Rothman's survey found that individuals from both business and the media regarded the other as constituting 'the most powerful group' in society (from a choice of seven excluding the state) and believed that its influence should be severely reduced. The American Management Association's (AMA's) study (Finn, 1981, p10) 'of public relations executives found that 73% believe reporters don't accurately research their topics, 62% believe reporters play on public emotions, and 72% see anti-business feelings and public sentiment being on the side of the media'. For their part, 61 per cent of journalists thought 'business people are not honest'. Several US and UK publications, produced by the business sector since the late 1970s, record a high level of concern amongst business leaders about reporting patterns and 'the social evolution of "consumerism, environmentalism and employeeism"' (Rubin, 1977, p170). For example, the CBI's media guide for businessmen, under the heading 'Media people – are they human?' (CBI and Abbey Life Assurance Co. Ltd, 1981, pp14, 16), warned that: 'In general, those entering journalism are not "business-oriented" – nor are they much helped in training to appreciate business … Worse, from the businessman's viewpoint, he may well have picked up the fashionable anti-business attitudes common to some higher educational courses.' A decade later,

Rees-Mogg was to observe that (1992, p9) 'there is still a good deal of misunderstanding about how business and the press can best relate ... Businessmen in general have an uneasy feeling the press is liable to go off like a bomb'.[4]

Relations are not helped by the tendency for most journalists to report businesses only when there is a negative story. Since consumers are drawn to stories about personalities, drama, crime and the environment, businesses are most likely to be reported when they are involved in wrong doing or crises such as environmental catastrophes. As Hoge explains (1988, p422): 'The media write about the bad and ignore the good; they are fascinated by corruption, unsafe products, lawsuits and bribery, and sensationalism and conflict.' Such findings are clear to those studies that look at business sources (Dreier, 1982, Tiffen, 1989, Ericson *et al.*, 1991) and painfully obvious to businesses (Warner in Warner and Silk, 1979, CBI and Abbey Life Assurance Co. Ltd, 1981, Hoge, 1988, Smith, 1988, Rees-Mogg, 1992).[5] Thus for businesses, appearances in mainstream news are unlikely to be advantageous.

Returning to the work of Tumber (1993) and Mitchell (1997), their data in fact suggests that businesses get little actual positive coverage. Tumber's (1993, p354) figures show that less than a third of national newspapers have more positive than negative coverage, with the *Financial Times* being most pro-business by only producing 48.2 per cent negative coverage. Mitchell's figures (1997, p47), while showing that businesses have more positive coverage than trade unions, also show that business coverage is not particularly positive. Looking at his figures in more detail, only three papers have 50 per cent or more 'sympathetic' news coverage of business, while all the tabloids are more 'unsympathetic' than 'sympathetic'.[6]

Fracture and conflict in pro-business ideology

Another significant problem with the notion of business ideology influencing news is that businesses are far from united in their thinking. Studies of business elites

---

4 See also: Annan (1977, p273), 'On the other side, management equally believes that its case rarely gets a fair hearing'; Warner (in Warner and Silk, 1979), 'The truth is that by speaking out, business is only beginning to redress an obvious imbalance ... If anything, it is the anti-business forces who manipulate the media'; Berkman and Kitch (1986, p275), 'Business had long believed that journalists give a bad name to profits and exaggerate workplace and environmental hazards'.

5 CBI and Abbey Life Assurance Co. Ltd (1981, p6), 'Bad news will be with us as always. Media people want a good story, which disasters always are'; Norman Manners (in Englefield, 1992, p10), 'There is little doubt that the avarice of the 1980s caused the public perception of business to change quite radically. The public has come to mistrust the dominance of big business'; Tumber (1993, p358), 'Stories appearing on the front and main pages are exceptional and dramatic with an emphasis on crime, sex and scandal. The news values involved have not deviated from the old definitions of what is, or makes, news'; PRP (in Ericson *et al.*, 1989, p270), '[news coverage] can kill you more quickly than it can make you. Ten times as fast as it can make you. The news is by definition more interested in crisis, agony problems ...'

6 It should also be taken into account that in 1988, at the time of the survey, the economy was very strong and unions were in the depths of economic and political crisis. In the late 1990s, figures are rather different (see chapters six and seven on trade unions).

and pressure groups (e.g., Ball and Millard, 1986, Richardson, 1993, Grant, 1993, 1995, Boswell and Peters, 1997, Mitchell, 1997), while noting the advantages of businesses in the policy-making process, also stress the great divisions within the business community. The needs of the financial, service and manufacturing sectors are often quite different. In addition to being part of industry associations, businesses may also belong to a number of associations with conflicting aims, including the Confederation of British Industry (CBI), the Institute of Directors (IoD), the Federation of Small Businesses and the Association of Independent Businesses. The effects of taxation and interest rates policies, European integration, financial regulation, industrial and trade policy, energy and environmental policies, health and consumer policies, each impact the various businesses and business sectors in different ways. Thus, as Grant is led to conclude (1993, p18):

> Britain has a business sector in which there is an increasing concentration of economic power, but that business remains politically weak ... It is not easy to define its interests or to select the best political strategy for pursuing them, in part because there are important divisions of interest between different sectors of business (and not just between financiers and industrialists), in part because the optimal strategy to secure a desired end is not always readily apparent or, at any rate, is the subject of dispute.

In effect the fact that business sources are often in competition does much to dilute their corporate messages.

That business elites have been unable to consistently promote their views, through the mass media, to the general public is further supported by studies of 'dominant ideology' and audiences. Abercrombie *et al.* (1984, 1990) concluded that, historically and sociologically, there has never been a coherent dominant ideology that has persuaded the masses to accept many of the tenets of the prevailing system of production. Elites have remained too divided and fractured for that. Subordinates, in turn, have never been particularly persuaded by ideas as much as by social and economic pragmatism (see Held, 1989, Hill, 1990 and Turner, 1990b). Work on audiences (Morley, 1980, Ang, 1985 Fiske, 1989) has similarly argued that dominant ideas are disrupted by the fact that audiences actively consume, have very different habits of consumption, take pleasure in consumption, and respond quite differently to products according to their social and cultural backgrounds. As Abercrombie concludes (1990, p221): 'The net effect of these features is a great deal of diversity, pluralism and indeterminacy.'

However corporate sources are reported, public antagonism towards businesses and business ideals seems to have increased rather than diminished. Fidler's study of business elites (1981, p254) found that: 'Even within the middle classes, businessmen feel they have no particularly high status, for they remark on the traditional dislike of the British for industry.' Page *et al.*'s (1987) research found that viewing publics distrusted information from business sources, as they did with special-interest groups generally. A MORI poll in 1993 (Poll Data, Dec. 1993) placed business leaders eleventh out of fifteen in a list of who the public trusted to 'tell the truth' (with only 32 per cent support). A similar poll two years later (MORI Poll Data, Dec. 1995) found that company directors had dropped to twelfth out of fifteen.

Similarly, while there is considerable tacit support for the capitalist system, many specific corporate elite ideals have failed to gain general public support. According to Jowell *et al.* (1992, p135), when people were asked who benefited from increased profits, 54 per cent answered shareholders and managers, 28 per cent said investment in machinery, research and training, and 8 per cent said the workforce. When asked where increased profits should go, only 3 per cent said shareholders and managers, 42 per cent said investment and 39 per cent said the workforce. Throughout the period 1975 to 1995, MORI poll data found that: between 71 per cent and 82 per cent of respondents agreed that 'Trade unions are essential to protect workers' interests'; and that between 51 per cent and 71 per cent thought that 'Generally speaking ... trade unions are a good thing' (between 18 per cent and 34 per cent disagreed). According to Jowell *et al.* (1993) 85 per cent of the British think the rich should be taxed more and 85 per cent are in favour of a 'progressive taxation' policy of direct rather than indirect taxation. More recently, *PR Week* (2.10.98, pp10–11) reported on the Institute of Directors 'Hub Initiative' – a £300,000 PR campaign deemed necessary to improve the public perception of business. It reported that a 1998 MORI survey found that 67 per cent believed profits were too high – up from 55 per cent in a 1990 survey, and only 28 per cent believed company profits helped everyone – down from 46 per cent in 1990.

In effect, either corporate public relations investment has given poor returns to the corporate sector or it has been used more effectively for other purposes. Aggregating the findings of all these studies, the clear conclusion is that, on the whole, reporting patterns are not consistently favourable to the needs of business. In general news coverage, corporations have no advantages of access and are unlikely to gain it according to factors governing routine reporting and audience demand. Clearly, despite the tremendous investment in corporate public relations during the last two decades, the ability of businesses to promote themselves in the news media has not really improved.

Alternative business communication objectives

Looking at corporate communications activity the indications are that businesses actually avoid mainstream news coverage altogether. Indeed, according to several studies of business sources (Berkman and Kitch, 1986, Ericson *et al.*, 1989, Tiffen, 1989), corporate public relations appears to have best served businesses by restricting reporter access and information – not by promoting company views. As Ericson *et al.* (1989 p390) conclude: 'For the private corporation, power over the news is power to stay out of the news. Their news proactivity goes no further than reminding the news outlets that benefit from their advertising that the corporation would appreciate the odd 'free' news or feature item on the wonders of its products.'

Indeed, business elites seem to have realised the limits of proactive public relations when it comes to influencing news production and, as a result, have decided
that it is not an effective means of achieving many business ends.[7] Companies
advertise if they want to promote particular products or opinions and go direct to
politicians if they want to influence policy. Thus, total business advertising expenditure is still several times higher than that on public relations. In 1994, UK advertising rose to £10.136 billion (Advertising Association, 15.6.98). In that same year
DTI estimates for PR, acquired from the PRCA, IPR and WPP, varied between
£400 million and £1.4 billion. Even taking this top estimate, advertising expenditure is still more than seven times that of public relations. A report by Mintel
Marketing Intelligence in 1995 estimated that advertising accounted for 50 per cent
of UK expenditure on marketing services while PR accounted for 5-6 per cent –
roughly a tenth. In the USA in particular, corporations spend a large part of their
advertising budgets on 'advocacy advertising' (Warner and Silk, 1979, Vogel, 1983,
Berkman and Kitch, 1986, Dreier, 1988, Schiller, 1989, Bagdikian, 1992) in order to
express their views on politics and the economy. Businesses, in effect, find advertising a more useful and controlled means by which to communicate with the public.

In terms of political influence, studies also suggest that business elites already
have considerable access to policy-makers, or the means to gain access through
lobbyists – and so have less need to use the media. Studies of pressure groups and
politics in the UK (Ball and Millard, 1986, Kavanagh, 1990, Richardson, 1993,
Grant, 1993, 1995) generally agree that businesses have an 'insider status' not
equalled by other organised interests. Apart from contact through business associations (e.g. the CBI, IoD, Association of British Chambers of Commerce [ABCC],
amongst many others), individual businesses are represented on a wide range of
economic, legal, technical and financial committees. Business access to civil
servants and ministers (and even prime ministers) is both regular and institutionalised. That access has been further improved by the employment of expensive
lobbying firms – the recent expansion of which in the UK has been noted in several
studies (Crouch and Dore, 1990, Jordan, 1990, Grant, 1993, 1995, Mitchell, 1997)
and drawn considerable media attention.

All of this suggests that businesses have realised that political objectives are not
necessarily best achieved by marshalling public opinion. Businesses are more
successful going direct than using a potentially hostile, unpredictable and inaccu-
rate news media. Ball and Millard (1986), Berkman and Kitch (1986), Ericson *et al.*
(1991) and Mitchell (1997) have all reached the same conclusions. Mitchell's survey
of trade unions and business associations demonstrates this most clearly (see table
3.1). Business associations, engaged in political activity, are far more likely to meet

---

  7 See also: chapter two; Cutlip *et al.* (1985, p478), 'It was obvious to many sophisticated heads of
     large businesses that the credibility and confidence they had lost could not be regained through
     traditional public relations "techniques" openly bidding for public support'; Berkman and Kitch
     (1986, p293), 'Business interests rarely promote initiatives in their own interest, and, when they do,
     these initiatives are not especially successful.'

Table 3.1 Types of political activity – percentage frequency of use
and effectiveness for business associations and unions

	Most often used		Most effective	
	Business Associations	Unions	Business Associations	Unions
Committees	7	6	0	0
Meeting Ministers	47	6	27	17
Meeting Civil Servants	86	21	58	10
Written Submissions	78	43	6	3
Lobbying	57	29	10	24
PR Campaigns	21	38	3	38
Protests/Strikes	0	14	0	13

Source: Mitchell, 1997, p158

with civil servants and ministers, and to lobby, than they are to use PR campaigns or committees. Meeting ministers and civil servants is also regarded as the 'most effective' form of political activity. In contrast, the most effective means of political activity for unions is lobbying and public relations.

The obvious conclusion is that, if public relations is effectively achieving corporate political objectives, it must be doing so in other ways and in other forum. Two ways suggested in this part are: (a) by restricting information and journalist access, and (b) by increasing direct access to politicians through lobbying. However, this account does not really explain the continuing corporate investment in public relations – the vast majority of which is still directed towards media relations. The questions remain: how does corporate public relations influence media texts – if it does at all – and how does it benefit business?

Corporate public relations for corporate audiences

The answers lies in the fact that a significant proportion of corporate PR in Britain is not particularly focused on 'the masses' or mainstream news at all. This is initially demonstrated with a closer look at the PR consultancy industry itself. A breakdown of the major occupations of PRPs in rank order (see table 3.2), during the period 1989–96 are financial, consumer, corporate, trade and industry, government relations, international, employee relations, high tech and other. Consumer relations is the only one of these aimed at a wider public audience. Financial, corporate and trade/industry, three of the four major categories, are actually directed at the corporate sector itself.

As table 3.2 reveals, the dominant PR employment sector for most of the last two decades has been financial public relations.[8] For many commentators, the impressive expansion of the whole PR industry in the 1980s was in fact led by the rising demand for financial PR (Kopel, 1982, Nicholson and Trundle, 1986, Olasky, 1987, Bowman, 1989, Smith, 1989, Mintel Marketing Intelligence, 1995, White and Mazur, 1995, Hanrahan, 1997). The 'City and Financial' section of the IPR, initiated in 1972, has remained the largest specialist group within the IPR and

Table 3.2 Employment sectors for PR consultants (percentages)

	1989	1990	1991	1992	1993	1996
Financial	28	25	16	20	22	19
Consumer	22	24	20	21	18	19
Corporate	16	17	16	12	16	12
Trade/industry	14	15	8	9	10	14
Government relations	7	6	8	7	7	3
Employee	3	3	3	3	3	3
High Tech	2	3	5	7	9	4
Health	1	4	6	7	10	4
Other	9	3	18	14	5	22

Sources: PRCA, *Year Books*, 1990, 1991, 1992, 1993, 1994, 1997

currently has 440 members. The Investor Relations Society (IRS), in existence since 1980, has expanded to over 350 members since individual membership was introduced in 1993. City and investor relations is also considered to be the most prestigious and financially rewarding employment sector in public relations. An IRS (1998) survey of its members revealed that the average salary in investor relations was £78,000 (plus generous benefits) – more than double the average of the industry (see 'PR Week Salary Survey'). According to the same survey, companies with a market capitalisation of over £5 billion spend £546,000, on average, just on investor relations. Companies with a market cap of between £500 million and £5 billion spend £447,000 on average. Thus it is clear that considerable resources have been invested in City and financial public relations with rather more specialist target audiences.

The rise of financial news

Parallel to the recent expansion of public relations has come an equally impressive increase in the production of business and financial news. A number of media scholars have noted the rise of financial news media (Curran, 1978, Dreier, 1982, 1988, Berkman and Kitch, 1986, Jones, 1987, Parsons, 1989, Tumber, 1993, Williams, 1996), both in the USA and Britain. Jones (1987, p12) observed in the 1980s that industrial relations reporting was seriously declining and that the main growth area was in financial reporting – a sector that had come to occupy a third of the editorial space in *The Times*, the *Independent* and the *Daily Telegraph*. For Tunstall (1996, p354–5), within the last two decades 'financial news has tended to

---

8 These figures are also likely to underrepresent public affairs and financial PR work. This is because, in order to retain anonymity for themselves and their clients, the majority of top City consultancies have not joined the PRCA. For example, at the time of writing, eleven of the largest eighteen financial consultancies (as listed in *Crawfords Directory*, 1998 and *The Hambro Company Guide*, 1998), are not PRCA members and remain virtually unknown outside City circles.

take over from political news and foreign news as the premier serious news field'. As part of this transition the *Financial Times* has taken the place of *The Times* as the most respected broadsheet newspaper, acting 'as the semi-official voice of the City of London'. As well as the promotion of the *Financial Times*, Tunstall also argues that *The Economist*, Reuters and the London Stock Exchange have combined to form the basis of an expanding international centre for financial news. Tunstall estimated that by 1994 there were 200 financial journalists amongst the national press and a further 200 on the *Financial Times*. Tumber (1993, p350), from a different vantage point, observed a similar expansion of financial news in television and radio news as well as in the development of 'many new investment magazines, newsletters and tip-sheets offering share recommendations to subscribers'.

Of these works, only Tunstall (1996) made the connection between the rise of the financial media and that of corporate PR. However, for the PR industry, the two are obviously inseparable. For several authors (Bowman, 1989, Williams in Bowman, 1989, Michael Bland Communications Consultancy, 1989, Andrew, 1990, Andrew, 1995, White and Mazur, 1995), corporate public relations has directed an expansion of financial news in response to financial activity – and has often acted as a direct subsidy for news outlets not prepared for this expansion. In Bland's assessment (Michael Bland Communications Consultancy, 1989, p4), the space for financial PR opened up because 'The financial coverage of newspapers has increased, but the supply of financial journalists has not kept up. Good financial journalists are in short supply.' Regardless of what came first, the financial news text 'chicken' or corporate press release 'egg', the two have followed very similar patterns of development. Financial PR and financial journalism are both now considered the premier employment sectors of their respective industries. Both led the expansion of their industries in the 1980s; both halted expansion during the recession of the early 1990s, and both have begun expanding again since the mid-1990s.

Clearly the two are closely connected. One might therefore conclude that if public relations is benefiting the corporate sector it is likely to be doing so in specialist magazines and news sections that offer business, financial and economic news. Thus, further research in these areas would be the next logical step. How effective financial PR has been in the area of business and financial news, and its influence on financial decision-making processes, are the subjects of the next chapter.

4
CITY AND FINANCIAL PUBLIC RELATIONS
AND BUSINESS NEWS

Following on from the conclusions of the previous chapter, chapter four explores the development of financial public relations and its relationship with financial and business news in the national press.

The chapter begins with what appears to be a classic liberal pluralist account of the expansion of financial and business news and corporate public relations. This account argues that financial and business news expanded because of (a) rising public interest, and (b) the greater information requirements of an expanding and volatile market. Increased post-war prosperity amongst the expanding middle classes led to greater personal investment in financial products which, in turn, led to greater interest in financial news and thus generated more corporate advertising. Privatisation programmes, as well as the promotion of wider home and share ownership in the 1980s, intensified such trends. At the same time government and stock market regulations required that companies become more open and account-able by supplying more information about themselves and their products. Business news therefore expanded – its funding provided by financial product advertising, and its fourth estate role established by the needs of the public and the require-ments of a fair and perfect market. Thus financial PR grew reactively to service the information demands of a growing public audience.

This account, however, is particularly narrow because it does not take account of the information needs of businesses themselves. As the greater part of this chap-ter argues, it is corporate communication imperatives that have been more instru-mental in shaping business news in the last two decades. City corporations, aided by the employment of proactive financial PR, have managed to 'capture' financial news production. In this news sector, businesses pay for all advertising, dominate as sources, have a monopoly in the supply of information subsidies and are the main consumers of business and financial news. It therefore stands to reason that, even if companies are in conflict, business agendas and business norms and values will shape financial and business news. Ironically, as corporate competition has intensi-fied in the last two decades, so business and financial news has become less pluralis-tic and autonomous.

This has resulted in business and financial coverage being confined to reporting the concerns of 'financial elite discourse networks', thus excluding both the general public and rival elites. One might argue that such tendencies have contributed to the following trends: there is a greater level of unchallenged consensus in the beliefs of the financial elites that govern the City; financial elites have increasingly become the de facto experts on the economy, an expertise which continues to influence policy-makers and regulators in successive British governments; and the interests and requirements of non-financial elites are excluded. As such, corporate public relations has benefited parts of the corporate sector, most specifically the City, not so much by controlling public opinion as by excluding the general public altogether.

Most of the supporting evidence for this chapter comes from a series of thirty-eight semi-structured interviews.[1] This material was combined with quantitative data from professional bodies in the PR industry, the Stock Exchange, City Business and Guildhall libraries, *PR Week* and the Advertising Association.

Financial news and the transition from public interest to corporate need

Studies of corporate journalism and PR (e.g., Kopel, 1982, Newman, 1984, Parsons, 1989, Bowman, 1989, Andrew, 1990, Tumber, 1993, Andrew, 1995, Tunstall, 1996) provide a range of explanations for the rise of financial and business news – many of which were repeated by interviewees. These included increased financial activity in the City, the rise in financial products and personal finance advice, investor and regu-latory demands for greater flows of financial information, the expansion of private share ownership and greater competition and volatility in the City. Within these accounts two broad counter theses are discernible. The first, popular amongst finan-cial journalists and the City, is that financial and business news expanded to serve the needs of an interested public and to impose a necessary transparency and equality on the London Stock Exchange. The second is that corporations, operating in an increasingly competitive environment, have sought to actively use financial PR to make business news serve corporate information needs. Arguably it is corporate influences which have increasingly come to shape business and financial news.

Public demand for financial news

For the majority of financial journalists and ex-journalist PRPs, business news expanded because newspapers and advertisers perceived a rise in public interest in the subject. This developed as a result of post-war economic affluence. According to social and economic historians (e.g., Cairncross, 1992, Pollard, 1992, Rubinstein, 1993) the standard of living for the general population rose considerably in this period. Consumer spending has grown as a proportion of gross domestic product (GDP) in every decade since 1950 (Cairncross, 1992, pp274–5). Home ownership

---

1 These include: ten with in-house directors of corporate affairs of FTSE top 150 companies (as listed in the FT 500, 1998); fifteen with financial and City PR consultants at chief executive or director level – all from the top twenty financial PR consultancies (as listed in *Crawfords Directory of City Connections*, 1998, and *The Hambro Company Guide*, 1998); nine with financial journalists and editors of the national press; and four with individuals with a direct interest in financial PR – including the director general of the Takeover Panel, the executive director of the PRCA, and the director of external affairs of the Investor Relations Society.

increased from 29 per cent in 1951 to 56 per cent in 1981 (Rubinstein, 1993, p42).
As an increasing proportion of the population began to possess surplus capital, so
the financial sector developed a range of financial products for them to invest in –
from basic savings accounts and pensions to unit trusts and share investment
schemes.

Personal finance generated high rates of advertising which, in turn, increased
financial sections and paid for more coverage of companies, financial products and
economic and business news. According to Curran (1978), by far the largest increase
in advertising and advertising-related features, in the period 1946 to 1976, took place
in the business and financial sections of newspapers. Newman's figures also show a
strong rise in financial advertising from the 1950s onwards. In Newman's assessment
(1984, p193): 'The space occupied by consumer-targeted, financial editorial was
directly related to the amount of financial product advertising. As the advertising
grew, so did the columns and the number of financial journalists.'

Advertising for these products was matched by the perception of editors that
the general public wanted more information on these products. Journalists operating at the time saw it as their duty to open up the closed world of the City and to
advise and speak for the small investor, be it on personal finance schemes or share
dealing. As one recounted:

> If you go back historically, the financial media were very restricted. The number of
> people holding stocks and shares was low, and financial public relations was little
> more than a delivery service … Suddenly the newspapers woke up to the fact that
> there was a whole new generation of shareholders, and it was no longer the privi-
> leged few. This was a potential readership for financial news and it spawned the City
> pages … On the back of these, very quickly, came the personal finance pages, as a
> number of new financial products were launched. So came the growth of financial
> journalism, which attracted readerships and their advertising.[2]

---

2 See also: Graham Williams (interview, 26.10.98), 'When I was a young man, the amount of coverage
   given to finance was tiny. Apart from the FT it was relatively small. Now it is huge … The welfare state
   expanded and taxation changed and became more complicated. Suddenly people had savings and
   wanted pensions and mortgages to buy houses and life insurance to cover the mortgages. People began
   having bank accounts and to buy things on higher purchase, and then came credit cards. None of these
   things really existed in great numbers before the war … It was a revolution involving money management … So we are developing as a society which is financially literate – involved with savings and
   investments – a society which sees savings, for whatever purposes, as routine from the moment they
   leave school, if not before'; anonymous financial PR and former journalist (interview, 1999), 'At the
   time [post–Second World War period] it was Beaverbrook's *Express* that was the pioneer of modern
   financial journalism. The *FT* and *Telegraph* were not the sort of papers that would rock the boat and
   question the establishment. But Beaverbrook was a Canadian and not part of the City club. The *Daily
   Mirror* was another innovator. *The Times* also began offering investment advice in response to readers'
   letters. It was a chance to increase circulation. Derek Dale of the *Mirror* also decided to have a City
   column and the *Evening Standard* produced its own City page. So the City pages came in response to
   readership and advertising demand. At the start they were all very simple. The *Mirror* even had a strip
   cartoon which was used to give investment advice. As a result, letters poured in and the City editors
   could identify what was wanted'.

These trends were boosted by the policies of the Thatcher administration in the 1980s. Government legislation promoted home ownership, the privatisation of nationalised industries, the widening of private share ownership, and incentives to invest in various savings schemes. Home ownership increased from 57 per cent to 69 per cent from 1979 to 1989 (Pollard, 1992, p379). Between 1979 and 1996 there were fifty-nine major public sales of government-owned businesses, worth £65 billion, and eighty-eight private sales, worth a further £6.7 billion (Gibbon, 1997). In 1980 there were 3 million shareholders. The privatisations of the 1980s increased this number to 11 million by 1991. Following a number of demutualisations by leading building societies and insurance companies the total reached 17 million in 1997 (London Stock Exchange, *Fact File*, 1998). Consumer interest again increased, as did financial advertising, which tripled in the period 1975–83 (Newman, 1984, p221). Journalists were consequently given yet more space with which to cover business and financial news and to offer personal investment advice.

Thus, the majority of interviewees tended to agree with Richard Northedge's (interview, 25.5.99) account:

> The greater space devoted to business matters is partly an expression of reader interest. People have more money to dispose of. There are PEPs, ISAs, they invest directly in shares. It was all part of the business environment that was there during the Thatcher years ... The other pressure comes from the corporate sector in the form of advertising. To be clear, if there wasn't the increase in corporate advertising there wouldn't be such expansion in the business sections. It goes hand in hand with advertising.[3]

The regulation of financial information and the needs of the perfect market

Another reason for the expansion of financial news, according to studies of financial PR (Kopel, 1982, Newman, 1984, Bowman, 1989, Andrew, 1990, White and Mazur, 1995) and several interviewees, is the increased demand for publicly available information for investors. According to Andrew (1995, pp11–12) 'perfect communication' flows are essential for the functioning of the 'perfect market' – and

---

3 See also: Alex Brummer (interview, 16.6.99), 'In the main it [business coverage] has played an increasingly important part in people's lives. The concept of a cradle to grave welfare state has changed and it has become necessary for people to provide for themselves. We have had the opening up of the stock market, the Big Bang, privatisations, demutualisations – all the while with a sense of events connected to the Reagan-Thatcher era'; anonymous financial journalist (interview, 1999), 'The growth of financial news in the *Telegraph*, *The Times* and others has come because of financial advertising. They have seen that it's a lucrative area to get into because of the financial advertising revenues that can be gained. The second reason is things like pensions and life assurance which have produced all the personal finance sections'; anonymous financial journalist (interview, 1999), 'It's expanded to a certain extent because of privatisations and the growth in the number of "Sids" (small shareholders) – which has increased the shareholding proportion of the general public. So the issue has been forced on the public and they want to know a lot more about what is going on in the Square Mile ... You have also got a more affluent public with more spare income and they are more prepared to put that spare income at risk in investments. Low unemployment also encourages more risk with savings'.

work to ensure the inclusion of multiple, informed buyers and sellers and multiple transactions. As Alistair Defriez, director general of the Takeover Panel, explained (interview, 11.11.98):

> It is important in any public market where investors are dealing and investing in shares that they have access to sufficient information in quantity, and also complete and accurate information in terms of quality. Anything that assists in achieving those objectives – information quality and quantity – is a good thing. The rise of all these things has meant that we have more transparency and better information.

Directed by such principles, successive companies acts, in conjunction with increased stock market regulation, have demanded the publication of greater and more regular quantities of information by listed companies (see account in Newman, 1984, ch. 1). During the 1980s, such factors as the introduction of the Unlisted Securities Market (USM), a rise in flotations, an extensive privatisation programme, and wider share ownership, led to greater calls for public accountability and the need for yet more financial information to be published (see Pratten, 1993). A number of acts and codes followed or were enlarged (including the 1985 Companies Act, 1986 Financial Services Act, 1993 Criminal Justice Act, Stock Exchange Listings Rules, the Takeover Code, and the Price Sensitivity Guide).

Public relations practitioners interviewed were all very aware of the regulations and the financial watchdogs which had developed to oversee their activities. Infringement of these could result in investigation, censure and prosecution by a number of bodies, including the Stock Exchange, the Financial Services Authority, the Takeover Panel, the Monopolies and Mergers Commission, the Office of Fair Trading and the Department of Trade and Industry. Indeed, for many PRPs, all these restrictions made much of financial PR a fairly routine activity and ensured that financial or media manipulation would be limited. Several held quite firmly to their beliefs in the mechanisms of the market and denied that PR could have more than a temporary influence on market values. Michael Sandler's (interview, 19.10.98) remarks were fairly typical: 'At the end of the day the market always gets it right. Public relations can only delay things – it can speed them up or slow them down. Any public relations person who thinks they can influence it any more than that is ahead of themselves.' This belief in 'the market' also appears to be common amongst financial journalists who continually refer to such things as 'market sentiment', 'City opinion' and 'shareholder sentiment' as if they were objective universal laws.[4]

Thus a popular liberal thesis seems clearly in evidence amongst those who work in the City and are involved in the production of financial and business news. According to the views of journalists in particular, the rise of financial and business

---

4 For example: Bob Gregory (interview, 21.8.98), 'Most of these things are standard and you have to show them according to Stock Exchange regulations and law – things like profit and loss accounts, balance sheets, cash flow … There are standards for all these things and they are regulated as such … This stops people generally from putting out inflated or false information'; anonymous financial journalist (interview, 1999), 'Coverage is something and you really can affect the market … Prices

news was driven by increased public interest, financial product advertising and the information demands of investors and regulators. The corporate sector responded by seeking to employ professional communicators and the financial public relations industry expanded accordingly.

The rise of corporate conflict and alternative corporate communication needs

The counter-thesis begins not with journalists, consumers and regulators, but with businesses themselves. From this perspective, financial public relations was initially driven by the corporate need to fulfil regulatory demands and to minimise the financial risks associated with increased coverage. But, in the last fifteen years, it has become more proactive – developing into another means by which companies seek to gain a competitive edge in the marketplace. Under such circumstances, PR has advanced from its basic function of 'neutral' public information supplier, towards a role that is occupied with fulfilling corporate economic objectives through the generation and supply of partial information. Consequently, because corporate interests dominate news production in this sector, financial and business journalism has become reshaped accordingly.

As several authors have noted (e.g., Parsons, 1989, Grant, 1993, Hutton, 1996, and Boswell and Peters, 1997), the rise of Thatcherism, while being broadly supportive of the business community, also did much to exacerbate competition and conflict within the UK markets. Legislation in 1979 and 1980 brought the release of exchange and credit controls and thus initiated a new credit boom. Financial deregulation continued, most notably with the 1986 Financial Services Act, leading to the frenzied activity of the 'Big Bang'. Privatisation programmes, the demutualisation of building societies, the application of General Agreement on Trades and Tariffs (GATT) directives, a rising level of merger and acquisition activity, expanding international trade, and the developing sophistication of communications technology, have all kept financial growth and competition at a pitch not experienced before the 1980s (see Cairncross, 1992 and Pollard, 1992, for an overview).

In fact, for much of the financial PR sector, it is increased competition in the financial markets that has spurred the need for greater control of information by businesses and institutions operating in the City (see Olasky, 1987, Bowman, 1989, L'Etang, 1996, Meech, 1996, Hanrahan, 1997, Maloney, 1997). Financial public relations thus became another tool, like information technology (IT) or advertising, with which corporations attempted to gain 'an edge'. As a DTI report (BDO Stoy Hayward Management Consultants, 1994, p10) on the expansion of corporate PR observed: 'The boom period of the mid 1980s, with an aggressive, free-market, US

---

will change with announcements. But in the end the market is always right because things will settle back down – just like water'; anonymous financial journalist (1999), 'You can't buck the market but that's different from the market always being right … It's very difficult to go against the market which is why you very rarely see the foreign markets getting involved'; Nigel Whittaker (interview, 14.10.98), 'Some guys will say yes they can double your share price. But the things that make a difference are performance, management and prospects … Where a share price is hyped by PR it's only transitory and that share price is going to go down again'.

inclined attitude towards business, a swathe of mergers and acquisitions and significant privatisation, saw increasing commercial interest in image and reputation,
with a consequent boost to the level and variety of PR activities.' This view of PR as
a competitive tool was one sketched out in several PRP interviewees.[5]

As interviews with corporate affairs directors revealed, financial public relations is currently used to compete in a number of areas. First, on a day-to-day level,
it involves the constant promotion of company products, services and brands over
those of rivals. Second, it can involve the winning of government contracts and the
influence of decision-makers involved in the creation of new legislation and regulation.[6] As Chris Hopson of Granada explained (interview, 13.10.98):

> We frequently try to persuade the regulatory bodies – the ITC, OFT, the MMC, as
> well as influence the development of EU [European Union] directives. The balance
> and priority order entirely depends on what today's project is. … A while ago we
> wanted to change the ownership rules to enable us to take over LWT [London
> Weekend Television] and Yorkshire Tyne Tees. Were it not for our and other PR
> departments' activities, changes would not have happened and we would not have
> been able to take those companies over. That change and those takeovers have
> helped to increase our profits ten times since 1991. We have saved the company
> around £40 million on recent regulatory questions and probably saved the ITV
> [Independent Television] companies £100 million in total.

Almost all of the in-house corporate affairs directors interviewed had participated
in similar communications work to affect company-relevant bits of regulation/
legislation.[7]

Third, for City and financial PR consultants the most frequent communications
objective was to sustain and/or raise shareholder interest and support. As Kopel

---

5 Similar remarks were made by: Angus Maitland (interview, 17.9.98), 'It's not at all about Stock
   Exchange regulations. It's all about getting a competitive edge. It's 100 per cent about competitive
   edge. It's about proving that if people invest in you they will get proper value for their company in
   terms of investment'; Chris Hopson (interview, 13.10.98), 'There is a group of thirty-somethings,
   brought up in the business world – not just ex-journalists or politicians – who know that the aim of
   the business world is to make profit. They, as individuals, are motivated by that task and they are
   mentally attuned to doing it. We add real value in PR. We now have people who understand how the
   whole business works. The aim is to improve profits and not just have lunch with journalists';
   Alistair Defriez (interview, 22.12.98), 'I have been in companies where we did not deal with the
   press as well as we should have done … By the time we came to the critical bit, the institutions said
   they didn't know anything about us. We had lost the press battle and we were ignoring the press. We
   had taken the high-handed City attitude that who cares what the press says. You will not find
   anyone in the Square Mile with that kind of attitude now … It's a necessary evil – necessary to
   make sure that you are still on the playing field by the time it gets to the closing stages'.
6 Two documented examples include: (a) Devonport Dockyards used the Rowland Company to gain
   a lucrative government shipbuilding contract by defeating rivals Rosyth Dockyards and their PR
   company GJW (IPR 'Sword of Excellence Awards', 1994); (b) Charles Barker PR carried out a
   successful public affairs campaign on behalf of Virgin and British Midland to gain a greater share
   of European business trade from British Airways (IPR 'Sword of Excellence Awards', 1992).

explained in an early financial PR guide (1982, p4): 'The price of the share is directly related to supply and demand and therefore the amount of information known about the company ... This concern for the share price, and the means by which it can achieve and maintain its peak, is a thread running through everything that is done in financial public relations.'[8] Related to the promotion of company share prices is the use of financial PR to engineer mergers and fight takeover battles. According to Sudarsanam (1995, pp2-4) merger, acquisition and divestment activity reached a new pitch in the mid to late 1980s. The years 1986 to 1989 inclusive saw record highs in all these areas. At the 1989 peak, 1337 companies were acquired, worth a total of £27.25 billion. Between 1979 and 1997, despite a steady flow of company flotations, a significant increase in the total value of the stock market, and the introduction of the USM, the number of listed companies declined from 3,249 to 2,683 (figures in London Stock Exchange, 1994). In fact, for PR consultants, takeover work is both the most strenuous and the most financially rewarding, with consultancies earning millions of pounds for short-term contracts.[9]

Financial elite spinning and market rhetoric

While the majority of PRP interviewees had a certain faith in 'market principles' they also acknowledged that: (a) the markets left much room for short-term promotional manoeuvres, and (b) skilled financial PR work was about rather more than presenting tightly regulated information. As Nick Miles of Financial Dynamics admitted (interview, 17.8.98):

> The market isn't all that efficient. If it were then there would be no reason for us to exist. In the long term you can outperform the market by looking at your audiences, seeing what they believe and giving them what they want. It's a matter of bringing the mountain to Mohammed because Mohammed won't come to you. There are many things you can do which amounts to telling them the truth about your

7 These included: financial regulation (Stuart Prosser, interview, 22.6.98), pensions (Jan Shawe, interview, 7.10.98), the regulation of commercial airlines and changes to the health system (Peter Jones, interview, 9.9.98), newspaper distribution (Tim Blythe, interview, 15.9.98), and environmental legislation and regulation of the privatised water companies by the Office of Water Services (OFWAT) (Jonathan Russell, interview, 14.1.99).

8 Three award-winning examples of increasing share prices are: (a) College Hill PR helped raise the value of Surrey Free Inns in 1997 from 75p to 443p – a rise of 477 per cent ('PR Week Public Relations Awards', 1997); (b) Standard Chartered Bank, in the course of its 1996 campaign, increased its profit by 30 per cent and rose from 84 to 32 in the FTSE 100 index ('PR Week Public Relations Awards', 1996); (c) Ludgate PR's work for FKI in 1993 trebled the share price in the space of a year after generating widespread interest amongst institutions and analysts ('PR Week Public Relations Awards', 1994).

9 Two documented examples include: (a) Ludgate's work for Lloyds Chemists during its takeover of Macarthy in 1991, which also involved fending off competition from Grampian Holdings and UniChem, as well as pushing the bid through a MMC investigation (Mintel, 1995); (b) Dewe-Rogerson helped defend William Cook against a hostile take-over bid in 1997 and, in the process, raised William Cook's share price from 312.9p to 425p – a rise of 36 per cent ('PR Week Public Relations Awards', 1997). See also the example of the Granada takeover of Forte in chapter five.

company in a structured and interesting way which plays to their prejudices and
interests.[10]

In effect, subjective judgements are inextricably linked with seemingly objective
decision-making by investors, and PRPs can supply information which is
constructed with the intention of affecting those judgements.

Impartial information is transformed into partial rhetoric at all levels and
begins with the presentation of figures. Accounting dates, financial measures and
forecasts can all be selected according to what corporations want to demonstrate.
The 'reputation' of the chief executive and the management team are also highly
influential factors for investors. A study by Burson-Marsteller, of 2,500 people
across 360 *Fortune 500* companies in the USA, found that (*PR Week*, 3.4.98, p2):
'Chief Executive reputation accounts for 40% of a company's reputation ... [and
that] 75% of respondents believe the CEO's reputation will enhance the company's
ability to attract investment capital and earn the company the benefit of the doubt
in times of crisis.' In a MORI opinion poll (Poll Data, Nov. 1998) of 'Captains of
Industry', 51 per cent of business leaders said that the 'quality of management' was
one of 'the most important factors' to take into account when making
'judgement[s] about companies'. Particular market sectors, in themselves, are yet
another pull to investors (see Andrew, 1995). In the view of another experienced
financial PRP (interview, 1999):

> investment is a fashion business. There is no doubt. It's just like clothes, houses,
> universities – they are all fashion businesses ... what you don't know over a long
> time is whether a company is just riding the fashion or genuinely doing well because
> of the management. That's very difficult to calculate and I don't know anyone who
> has been consistently good at calling that.

At the same time PRPs are also aware that regulation of their activities will always
be limited. Currently there exists no legislation and no form of regulation that
specifically deals with their occupation. Although Stock Exchange regulations have
been made tighter in recent years many practices – such as the 'Friday night drop',
the leaking of information via third parties and 'conditioning the market' with

---

10 Other remarks include: Nick Boakes (interview, 18.8.98), 'Share price is really what people are
    prepared to pay and of course that varies. If something suddenly is in demand than the share price
    goes up and vice versa – it's all supply and demand. The answer is you probably can [buck the
    market]. A strong share price is very important for organisations ... If they feel they are misunder-
    stood by the market, if they are not getting their share of voice and there's a lot of competition out
    there for a share of voice ... and normally these things can be corrected'; Tim Jackaman (interview,
    8.10.98), 'You can't defy reality in the long term. But in the short term the market is often drasti-
    cally wrong. You can do a lot in the short term but it all evens out over time'; Alistair Defriez (inter-
    view, 11.11.98), 'There are times when, for various reasons, the market forms the wrong perception
    of a company – too harsh or too favourable. It's one of the great conceits of economic theory – the
    idea of a perfect market. But of course if that was the case there wouldn't be a market at all. if we all
    had the same information and the same views then nothing would be bought or sold'. See also the
    work of Klamer *et al.* (1988) on the use of 'economic rhetoric' in markets.

partial information – are common and almost impossible to monitor. Much PRP communication with audiences takes place on telephones or face to face, thus leaving no incriminating evidence. Although, in principle, financial PR consultants could be disciplined or ultimately prosecuted for breaching Stock Exchange rules, in practice PR companies have been no more than publicly reprimanded in a handful of cases. The professional associations, the IPR and PRCA, have their own codes of conduct. However, the majority of financial PR consultants are not members of either association. Those that are, are rarely monitored, let alone disciplined. The problems associated with regulating financial information flows are actually acknowledged by the industry itself with some frequency (Nicholson and Trundle, 1986, BDO Stoy Hayward Management Consultants, 1994, and in regular pieces in *PR Week* and the PRCA annuals).

The rise of public relations subsidies in financial news

That corporations have become more proactive in their attempts to influence financial news is indicated by the growth of financial PR relative to that of financial advertising. Reading Newman's (1984) detailed history of financial marketing in the UK, it becomes clear that much of the financial PR consultancy industry was actually born out of the decline of City advertising agencies. During the post-war era, Newman identified a steady switch from City-based company advertising to financial product advertising dealt with by West End advertising agencies. Additionally, financial institutions objected to excessive corporate advertising bills, especially during takeover battles. In order to survive, the traditional City advertising agencies began to branch out and use their communications expertise in other ways. Several were already responsible for providing press cuttings, as well as presenting company results, dealing with new issues, and mergers and acquisitions, in the form of advertisements, to the financial press. A number of these hybrid agencies – for example, Dewe-Rogerson, Charles Barker, Good Relations, Broad Street and Valin Pollen – eventually formed the foundations of the modern financial PR consultancy sector. Corporations accordingly turned to financial PR as a means of fulfilling their communication needs and there was a consequent shift from paid-for advertising space in the financial pages to PR-fed journalism.

According to reports by the DTI (BDO Stoy Hayward Management Consultants, 1994) and Mintel Marketing Intelligence (1995), during the 1980s and 1990s, financial PR spend in fact increased at a much greater rate than financial advertising. Looking at table 4.1, between 1984 and 1994, financial advertising rose by 144.4 per cent. Next to this, PRCA consultancy fee income increased by 400 per cent (inflation not accounted for in figures), and financial PR has been the largest PR employment sector. Thus, although advertising continued to increase, it never equalled the growth rates experienced in the previous three decades. According to Mintel Marketing Intelligence (1995), whereas general PR expenditure in the UK is roughly 10 per cent of that spent on advertising, in the financial sector the disparity has become much smaller. Between 1984 and 1994, financial PR expenditure was between 30 and 40 per cent of that spent on financial advertising.

All of the above tentatively suggests that proactive financial PR has played a significant part in the recent expansion of business and financial news. But have corporate communication needs influenced the shape of business news more than factors such as wider consumer demand and the imperatives of fourth estate journalism?

Closed discourse networks and the corporate capture of financial news

As this section argues, the evidence suggests that corporate communication needs have indeed come to dominate the production of business and financial news. This is because, in contrast to mainstream news, journalists are not torn between the competing demands of their suppliers and consumers. Corporate elites are simultaneously the main sources, advertisers and consumers of business and financial news. Thus, corporate PRPs are likely to find themselves in a strong position, vis-à-vis news producers, and the communication needs of corporations are likely to override the information requirements of regulators and the general public.

In fact, the most significant consequence of increased corporate source/PR influence on business news production is the exclusion of the general public altogether. The principle that financial PRPs have managed to impress upon their City clients, is that their 'key audiences' are not the general public but rather those who count most – other corporate elites. This combination of corporate source advantages and corporate elite focus has resulted in the 'capture' of business news within 'closed discourse networks'. In these networks, corporate elite debate and conflict are reflected in the business media but only within limited parameters. Journalists can report on a range of matters but have severely restricted remits. As a result, news paid for by advertising financial products to the general public has instead become a means of financial elite communication and debate.

Corporate source advantages in business news

For several reasons, corporate sources are likely to have considerable success in their attempts to influence business news producers. First, business journalism, despite its apparent buoyancy, is highly dependent on information and advertising subsidies. Because of the complexities and speed of financial news, journalists are less able to investigate stories properly or generate independent data. As many business sources have complained, and journalists admitted (see especially Finn, 1981, but also Warner and Silk, 1979, CBI and Abbey Life Assurance Co. Ltd, 1981, Hoge, 1988, Rees-Mogg, 1992), reporters cannot keep up – something confirmed in interviews with several PRPs.[11] This not only leads journalists to rely on PR information subsidies and 'expert' business sources, it also entails a reliance on the specialist financial news press, and wire services. Both of these, like most sectors of the trade press, are even more reliant on PR and a few key business advertisers (see chapter two).[12]

Second, just as corporate sources are severely hindered by the constraints of journalist routines and consumer demand in mainstream news (see chapter three),

Table 4.1 Increases in financial advertising, *FT* journalist numbers
and PRCA members' fee income

	Financial advertising (1997 prices) (£million)	FT journalist numbers	PRCA members fee income (£million)
1984	176.7	379	33
1986	258.2	362	58
1988	367.5	403	101
1990	367.7	441	146
1992	284.7	391	156
1994	431.8	410	165
% increase	+144.4	+8.2	+400

Sources: *Advertising Statistics Yearbook*, 1998,
Financial Times personnel department, PRCA *Year Book*, 1998

so they are advantaged by these factors in business news. Unlike many other forms of news, the needs of sources, advertisers and consumers are much closer. In effect, the main consumers of business news want the 'expert' comments and influential opinions of leading figures in the business world – including chief executives, finance directors, and analysts. The main advertisers in business and financial news want those same comments and opinions. There is thus no longer a conflict of interest which determines that journalists must neglect one side or the other in the production of business news.

In fact, indications are that public relations and advertising have a greater influence on financial news production than on any other news section of the national press. In the post-war period, advertising increased most in the area of business news (Curran, 1978, Newman, 1984). As table 4.1 shows, both advertising and public relations expenditure continues to outstrip the increase in financial journalist numbers. For example, between 1984 and 1994, *FT* journalist numbers increased by 8.2 per cent while pagination for the paper increased by 62.5 per cent – from forty eight to seventy eight pages (figures supplied by *FT*). In the same period, financial advertising

---

11 Paul Barber (interview, 20.8.98), 'There are a large number of people with interests a mile wide and with knowledge an inch deep. Newspapers just don't have the specialists. Standards per se have not got worse. If a single journalist has to cover banking, aviation, etc., then your level of knowledge gets worse because there is just too much'; Richard Oldworth (interview, 26.8.98), 'But there is a large element of young people who know very little and it can be a frightening thing ... There are some basic bits of information that any financial journalist should be able to read – but increasingly the new ones get it wrong, not because they are malicious, they just don't know'; Nick Chaloner (interview, 16.9.98), 'Even experienced journalists who have been covering the financial services sector for years are not experts and some have admitted to me that they don't really understand the field'.

12 That the trade and local press are the most vulnerable to PR and advertisers is also borne out in: a Gallup survey (1991), a Two-Ten report (Two-Ten Communications, 1993), Franklin (1997), Seymour-Ure (1996), several public relations handbooks and much of the rest of this book.

rose by 144.4 per cent and PRCA consultancy fee income increased by 400 per cent. Surveys by the public relations industry provide further evidence. A poll produced by the PRCA (*PR Week*, 1.7.94, p2) found that the *FT* used considerably more public relations material than any other national paper, with 26 per cent of its output being PR-generated – 62 per cent in the companies and markets section. The majority of PR practitioners interviewed, also picked out the financial press as the largest consumer of PR information.[13] Thus, Parsons's earlier predictions now appear fairly accurate (1989, p213): 'The danger is that, as in the past, the financial press may become more participants and "puffers" than observers and more extensions of PR companies than independent commentators and reporters.'

The financial elite focus

The most significant thing about increased corporate PR activity is that is has been increasingly directed at a narrow group of established corporate elites. A survey by Fleishman Hillard (White and Mazur, 1995) of eighty US and 113 EU companies, demonstrates the lack of corporate interest in the mainstream media and general public (table 4.2). For each it is shareholders and analysts that count most.

The focus on elite target audiences has a fairly clear logic. Although share ownership has increased since 1980, the actual proportion of shares held by private individuals has decreased. In 1964, private shareholders owned 59 per cent of shares and City institutions 41 per cent. By 1980 private ownership had dropped to 30 per cent and institutional holdings had risen to 70 per cent. By 1997, despite

Table 4.2 Fleishman–Hillard 1993 survey of US and EU companies and their communications priorities

	US (%)	EU (%)
Shareholders	53	48
Securities analysts	51	29
Employees	49	35
Government officials/agencies	23	19
Business media	18	21
General media	6	7
General public	6	6
Activist groups	3	0

Source: White and Mazur, 1995, p7

---

13   Tim Jackaman (interview, 8.10.98), 'More than 50 per cent [of financial news is PR]. Sometimes you look through some Sunday papers and it seems to be almost 100 per cent '; Roland Rudd (interview, 15.10.98), 'Undoubtedly there is more PR in financial news than other sections'; Martin Adeney (interview, 17.12.98), 'I would say it [financial news] was 85 or even 90 per cent driven by formal announcements or events … The majority of journalists wouldn't even go down to Companies House to look up the annual reports and accounts'.

the fact that the number of individuals owning shares had increased more than fivefold, total individual holdings amounted to only 15 per cent of all UK shares (figures in Newman, 1984, p83, and London Stock Exchange, *Fact File*, 1998). According to Newman (1984) and several PRP interviewees, the 1980s was a period of transition when corporations realised they had to reorganise their communication efforts. Instead of an 'unsophisticated courtship' of the media, the focus became the smaller number of institutions which held effective control of the company and those that influenced them – analysts, fund managers, financial journalists, and other City elites. In Graham Williams's words (interview, 26.10.98):

> By around 1980 the term 'investor relations' began to appear, almost imperceptibly, within corporate affairs departments ... Companies also realised that instead of the majority of shares being held privately they were held by say 50 institutions ... It was no longer the 25,000 shareholders in Bournemouth and Bristol and Edinburgh that mattered any more. Rather, it was these fund managers ... The takeover battles of the 1980s and 1990s made this abundantly clear to the company – that a few institutions owned the company and could make the decisions that affected its future ... The companies now wanted to make sure that the institutions were happy and the institutions wanted to make sure their investments were safe.

The communications focus on other financial elite audiences was rather obvious to all the PRPs interviewed. In fact, each one had a very accurate idea of who their targets were in the City. In every case, PRPs explained that the publicly quoted company they worked for had an audience of no more than a few hundred individuals – with a maximum of 100 being considered to be significant. As Angus Maitland of the Maitland Consultancy explained (interview, 17.9.98):

> You have three significant audiences – the press, the sell-side brokers and the buy-side institutions. Any company has three sets of groups interested ... Out of these there are roughly two dozen journalists who are really influential. On the relevant sell-side you have the top-rated analysts and the most mentioned analysts – out of which about twenty are really key. On top of that you have about twenty top fund managers with about twenty to fifty people. So you could say that the perceptions of a company are dependent on fifty to a hundred individuals.[14]

---

14 Other examples include: Bob Gregory (interview, 21.8.98), 'In John Menzies, for example, there are a dozen big shareholders, the business press with maybe twenty key editors and journalists, and ten analysts ... fifty maximum'; Tim Jackaman (interview, 8.10.98), 'The private investor, most of the time, is regarded as an irrelevance. Ninety per cent of shares are now held by institutions, so private investors are generally ignored. So we concentrate our efforts on institutions. Fifty per cent of shares for any reasonably sized company can be held by between six and twelve institutions, depending on the size of the company. If you look at the market as a whole probably the top ten to twenty fund managers control 70 per cent of the market'; Jan Shawe (interview, 7.10.98), 'There are about 200 or 300 [key individuals] at most – of which ninety or a hundred are critical, seventy analysts of which eight are critical, 100 journalists of which ten are critical. Twenty institutional shareholders with three or four decision-makers in each – sixty or seventy people. Then there are the personal finance journalists of which ten are critical'.

The City and the formation of financial elite discourse networks

The group of elite decision-makers in the financial sector has always been small and exclusive. The City itself has remained a highly restricted sphere with limited entry and limited interests (see, for example, Parsons, 1989, Grant, 1993, Hutton, 1996, London Stock Exchange, *Fact File*, 1998). Many of the financial associations and institutions which now make up the City began originally as 'gentlemen's clubs'. The Bank of England itself was traditionally a privately run bank, managed by City merchants and bankers (until it was nationalised in 1946). The Stock Exchange has continued to operate under its own authority, avoiding direct government regulation. All its regulatory bodies tend to be made up exclusively of City insiders (the Monopolies and Mergers Commission being the only obvious exception). Its board of directors is drawn entirely from the City and any company seeking a listing must appoint an 'approved sponsor' – of which there were 119 by the end of 1997. It also operates with its own police force and in an enclosed geographical space within London.

The few sociological studies of the City and financial elites that exist (Fidler, 1981, Scott and Griff, 1984, Useem, 1984, Hill, 1990, Hutton, 1996) have each observed that the City is bound together by extensive financial and personal networks. Top managers, owners and fund managers all benefit through similar wage structures, share options and other performance-related perks and, as such, pursue similar objectives. As Hill explains (1990, p11):

> This primary network of capital relations is supplemented by another form of inter-corporate linkage, namely networks of interlocking directorships which are mainly centred on the major banks. Their personal relations link different company boards, provide channels of information across the corporate world and link firms to the major capital brokers.

The financial PR consultancy sector has developed, and continues to develop, as an integral part of the City elite establishment.[15] Its activities have resulted in an increase in intercorporate elite communications. As a result closed discourse networks have been formed around top company managers, PRPs, fund managers, analysts, merchant bankers and financial journalists. In Martin Adeney's experience (interview, 17.12.98), one repeated in several PRP interviews:

> It is quite obvious that investor relations is becoming much more important than it was. Our current chairman and chief executive are spending more time in the City

---

15 Many of the established financial PR agencies can be traced back to advertising agencies (see Newman, 1984) established in the City for most of the century. The Investor Relations Society holds all its initial meetings in the Stock Exchange itself and its president has always been the chairman of the Stock Exchange. As all financial PRP consultants confirmed, the vast majority of clients are obtained through word of mouth rather than through any advertising or marketing. Most of the top financial PR companies avoid publicity, even in the industry's own forums – the PRCA and *PR Week*. At the time of writing, eleven of the largest eighteen financial consultancies (as listed in *Crawfords Directory*, 1998 and *The Hambro Company Guide*, 1998) are not PRCA members and remain virtually unknown outside City circles.

than the previous ones and those spent more time than their predecessors ... Now I have noticed during my nine and a half years here that the interaction with the City has steadily increased.

According to the IRS (1998, pp33, 43), 77 per cent of analysts have at least weekly contact with their investor relations counterparts, 78 per cent of chief executives have more than eleven one-to-one meetings with fund managers per year, and 10 per cent of chief executives spent 30 per cent or more of their time on investor relations.[16]

On a day-to-day level, financial PRPs, analysts and senior corporate staff maintain the parameters of financial discourse networks with constant two-way exchanges. Several studies of PR (e.g., Kopel, 1982, Michael Bland Communications Consultancy, 1989, Andrew, 1990, Cutlip *et al.*, 1994, Andrew, 1995) and business news (Dreier, 1982, Ericson *et al.*, 1989, Parsons, 1989, Andrew, 1995) have observed the development of such closed communication channels. Within these networks PRPs both bestow access and information on analysts and journalists, and gain access and information from them. Those same analysts and journalists also communicate with fund managers and other corporate elites in order to get their views and keep abreast of their activities. In effect, communication is frequent, multidirectional and exclusive.

PRP interviewees all tended to confirm this picture of intense communications taking place within exclusive networks and saw it as an accepted part of the job.[17] The responses of financial journalists and editors suggested similar patterns in their news-gathering activities. When asked who they liked to quote in their pieces, the answer was invariably chief executives, followed by other senior company figures and analysts.[18] Asked where they got their information from, the answer

16 Thirty-five per cent spent between 11 and 20 per cent of their time on it; 47 per cent spent between 6 and 10 per cent of their time on it. Seventy-two per cent said they spent more time on investor relations than two years ago and 47 per cent predicted it would increase still further in the next two years. Of the fifty fund managers interviewed, 91 per cent wanted greater contact with the finance director and 82 per cent wanted greater contact with the chief executive.

17 For example: Tim Jackaman (interview, 8.10.98), 'There was a long tradition at the *Sunday Telegraph* of putting on a Christmas party. It was the establishment paper read by City-type people. And to that party would come, and still come, very eminent industrialists, businessmen and PRs. They would all stop by, even if it was just for half an hour ...'; Martin Adeney (interview, 17.12.98), 'We are very conscious of where we are with the analysts. That is generally seen as primarily the role of investor relations, but what is quite apparent is that journalists and analysts swim in the same waters. Journalists increasingly write stories based on analysts' reports and comments'; Graham Williams (interview, 26.10.98), 'At the same time brokers, institutions, and the press all wanted and needed more current information. A constant dialogue was created, a daily exchange of views. Some analysts used to speak to me daily, or at least two or three times a week in the 1980s. And so IR has grown'.

18 For example, anonymous financial journalist (interview, 1999), 'Chief executives are the ones you want. If you can't get the chief executive you want the finance director and then the chairman'; Roland Gribben (interview, 21.5.99), 'First of all the chief executive or someone from the company itself – rather than the PR or analyst. Analysts don't want to be quoted directly although they are useful in terms of judgements that are reflected in the market'; anonymous financial journalist (interview, 1999) 'First of all you like to quote the chief executive or the chairman or a top analyst – and you like to quote them on the record if you can'.

invariably was established contacts in the City, including analysts, fund managers, the companies themselves and PRPs. As Alex Brummer, financial editor of the *Guardian*, explained (interview, 16.6.99): 'But we are also working all the time with chief executives and chairmen. I see CEOs four times a week. I also see Treasury officials, Bank of England officials and others on a regular basis ... I talk to one or two PR men each day. The people I talk to are usually the more senior people who ring up with stories.' As another senior City editor (interview, 1999) replied: 'you still have lunches. My diary is still full of lunches with chairmen and chief executives – that hasn't changed ... But in the end it's a village. They need you as much as you need them. Usually they need you more, so there's always a negotiation to be done'.

Financial journalists also said little to dispel the notion that financial news was written increasingly for City elite consumption. When asked who they wrote for, in order of importance, only two of the nine placed small private investors at the top. The others all put business managers, fund managers and professional investors at the top of their lists. Analysts and City institutions, even other financial journalists, were often mentioned over private investors. As one financial journalist typically confirmed (interview, 1999): 'We have the highest percentage of businessmen and managers – the highest proportion after the *FT*. So it's businessmen, managers of big and small businesses and professional investors. Then there are also the private investors, financiers, corporate accountants and lawyers'.[19]

Conclusion

As one financial PRP (anonymous, 1998), confidently asserted: 'The national financial press are written for the City by the City. So we know that when we are getting coverage we are getting through. What you use the press for is to provoke a thought or confirm a thought. So if an investor is interested and if it's in the press then it gets discussed.' In effect, business news has been 'captured' by financial elites. Even though it is a space for business conflict and competition, and journalists operate with a degree of conscious independence, coverage remains fairly restricted. Journalists are significantly limited by the fact that they are highly dependent on the goodwill of City elites in their roles as sources, advertisers and consumers. They must therefore abide by the unsaid 'rules' of financial reporting in order to

---

19 See also: anonymous financial journalist (interview, 1999), 'For us it's the people who are running companies and investing in them – the company managers and the fund managers [we write for] ... There aren't any private investors. I don't know what percentage of the Stock Exchange is invested in by private investors – between 10 and 20 per cent'; Alex Brummer (interview, 16.6.99), 'Traditionally we wrote for Guardian readers rather than City ones. Now the view is that we are a much more mainstream paper, which means we spend more time on traditional City and business coverage'; Richard Northedge (interview, 25.5.99), 'On Sunday Business we write for people who are in business. Certainly we write for the captains of industry but there is a limited number of them. So a lot of our readership are middle managers and personal investors, many of whom have a day job in business. But there are different sections for different people. The bread-and-butter stuff, though, is about business for business – take-overs, new directors and other changes'.

maintain their access to the City's 'elite discourse networks'. As Michael Walters of the *Daily Mail* explained (interview, 19.10.98):

> In a way the vacuum is filled much more easily by PR. They offer you an interview or some other source – and you have to be very stubborn-minded to pursue an investigative story on your own. The companies don't like it, the PRs don't like it, the brokers are against it and the City doesn't want a knocking story. There's a million and one reasons why you can't do it. But if you want to do a positive investigative piece then everyone will help you.

The ideological and material consequences

The corporate capture of business and financial news suggests a number of long-term consequences. First of these is the exclusion of non-financial elites from the production and consumption of business news texts. Second, business, financial and economic news coverage has been shaped to the needs of corporate elites; thus bringing more technical and pro-business news rather than debate and critical analysis. Third, an unchallenged business consensus has developed that promotes policy-making and regulation which naturally support City institutions, large multinationals and City elites. As a result, important questions of economic and industrial policy that affect the larger population, from entry into the Exchange Rate Mechanism (ERM) to levels of corporate taxation, are covered less and/or are covered from the point of view of business elites. Consequently, non-financial elites, from ministers to voters, when seeking 'expert opinion' on a variety of economic and industrial issues in the business pages, are unlikely to come away with a balanced overview.

Public exclusion

The expansion of business and financial news has never been matched by a corresponding increase of public interest in corporate activities. Curran (1978, p238), noted that the rise of business features in the post-war period, being advertising-driven, did not tally with readers' interests. A 1993–94 survey, reproduced by Tunstall (1996, p217) makes the point more explicitly. A list of twenty-three items which readers of the *Sun*, *Mail* and *The Times*, 'specially chose to read', placed 'personal finance' sections at number 22, with only 6 per cent of readers wanting to read them. At number 23 was business and company news with 4 per cent of readers interested. In the *The Times*, with the highest proportion of AB readers and shareholders, personal finance came thirteenth with 14 per cent of readers interested, and business news came seventeenth with 12 per cent interested.

The information exclusion of the general public through more subtle means is also evidenced in share dealing. Although, in principle, the rules of the Stock Exchange are designed to treat all investors equally, in practice, private investors are continually disadvantaged. As well as being excluded from financial elite networks, they are hindered by the slow speed of their information delivery, a lack of specialist knowledge and little research time. Professional dealers now get up-to-the-minute information through wire services such as Reuters, Extel and Bloomberg. These services are too expensive for private investors and, once again, are largely sourced by financial PRPs (although the opening of markets to Internet trading may overcome this to a degree). Even where time is not a consideration, City documents and financial news texts are really directed at professional investors. They are therefore full of specialist jargon and accounting procedures that are unintelligible to non-specialists (see comments in CBI, 1990, London Stock Exchange, 1996). Even for those who do understand, the rising Stock Exchange demands for more financial information mean that private investors have impossibly large amounts of data to consume – a job that employs several full-time analysts in each investing institution. As such, the production of more financial information and business news has only worked to disadvantage private investors. The gap between the information 'haves' and the 'have-nots' means that institutional shareholders will continue to benefit at the expense of private ones.

The end result, despite repeated government attempts to encourage wider share ownership, is minimal private shareholder interest and no power in corporate decision-making. As Sir Peter Thompson of the CBI Wider Share Ownership Taskforce was to admit (CBI, 1990, p7):

> Like many others, I suspect, I thought the 1980s was the decade when popular capitalism really took root in the UK ... The reality is very different. Millions of the new investors have never traded a share, nor do they know how. They only own one or two shares bought in the generously priced and heavily marketed privatisation issues.

According to a 1996 report (London Stock Exchange, 1996), when private share ownership hovered around 10 million, only 4 per cent of private shareholders had substantial holdings, owning 74 per cent of all privately owned shares, only 3 per cent were active traders, trading at least once per month, only 5 per cent had obtained any advice from brokers and only 6 per cent had ever attended an annual general meeting (AGM). In effect, although individual share ownership had, at that time, increased to 10 million, only about 400,000 people had any significant shareholding and/or took an active interest in share dealing – roughly the readership of the *Financial Times*.

Pro-business news and City elite consensus

According to Parsons, critical discussion of industrial and economic policy in the financial and business pages ended with the debates over monetarism in the late 1970s and early 1980s. Instead, the information needs of the financial community have come to dominate business news. As he concluded (Parsons, 1989, p8): 'nowadays you are more likely to read a piece by an economist from a firm of stockbrokers on the latest set of figures or predictions than a professor from a university offering some explanations or solutions'. Not only is business news catering to business needs, it is also likely to be 'pro-business' and unquestioning of business norms in its outlook. Indeed, this is the picture drawn by several observers (Dreier, 1982, 1988, Newman,

1984, Berkman and Kitch, 1986, Parsons, 1989, Tumber, 1993). Thus, whereas companies are often reported as negative, scandalous and self-interested in mainstream news, they appear positive, respectable and objective in business news.

Such conclusions are also implied in the quantitative data collected in other studies (e.g., Rubin, 1977, p172, Finn, 1981, p10, Hackett, 1992, Tumber, 1993, p354, and Mitchell, 1997, p47). Looking at Tumber's figures, for example, it should be noted that negativity ratings do not, as would be expected, correlate with the party political leanings of newspapers. Instead they appear to correlate rather more with the size of financial sections in newspapers. In other words, the more financial news there is, the less negative a newspaper is towards business. Thus the *Financial Times* is the least negative, followed by *The Times* and *Daily Telegraph*. All the tabloids – the *Sun, News of the World, Daily Mirror* and *Sunday Mirror* – are the most negative. A return to Mitchell's 1988 figures shows the same pattern. Only the *Financial Times, The Times* and *Daily Telegraph* are more 'sympathetic' to business than 'unsympathetic'. All the tabloids, including the *Sun*, are far more unsympathetic.

Although financial elites may be in constant competition, that competition is constrained by a great deal of cultural consensus. Several studies (see Fidler, 1981, Pool *et al.*, 1981, Useem, 1984, and Hill, 1990) noted that senior business elites frequently shared a number of social and cultural similarities and/or that moved in the same social circles. Fidler (1981) went further, arguing that, in general, they had little contact with those outside their circles, knew little about their company employees and generally assumed that employee interests and expectations simply concurred with their own. As one might assume, if City elites had similar social and cultural backgrounds and pursued similar objectives, albeit it in competition, they ought to share a number of norms and values. Indeed, these and other studies (see also Abercrombie *et al.*, 1984, 1990, Hutton, 1996, Boswell and Peters, 1997) have suggested just that.

For Hill (1990), Hutton (1996) and Boswell and Peters (1997) these common corporate elite ideals found a large degree of coherence in 'Thatcherism', or what Boswell and Peters (1997) refer to as, 'liberationism'. This outlook broadly believes and argues that business is the creator of wealth, should be free to develop as it wants without state control and interference, and if business benefits so does the country. As long as business flourishes, government income, employment levels, consumer spending, etc., all rise. In terms of specific policy directions this involves such measures as: the end of collectivism and continued privatisation; the weakening of trade unions; the endorsement of material inequality and the end of the commitment to full employment; an end to high levels of public expenditure; and a reduction in taxes, 'red tape' (regulation) and other barriers to the 'enterprise culture'. Poole *et al.* (1981, pp74, 80, 85), for example, found that 81 per cent of business elites wanted cuts in public expenditure, 89 per cent wanted controls on secondary picketing, 79 per cent wanted legislation to deal with strikes, 91 per cent were against the establishment of state monopolies and 87 per cent thought unions were not acting in the country's economic interests. Attitudes towards the Labour

Party, the traditional opponent of all these measures, is even more striking. In the 1987 General Election, 91 per cent of business leaders voted Conservative. In 1992, 94 per cent voted Conservative and 2 per cent voted Labour. In the 1997 General Election, in the face of Labour's landslide victory, 69 per cent voted Conservative and only 7 per cent voted Labour (MORI Poll Data, 1987, 1992, 1997). Such attitudes are clearly in marked contrast to the beliefs of the majority of the population (see chapters three, seven and eight).

According to Hutton, these belief systems are clearly identifiable in the City, the Treasury and Bank of England; which all work to enforce London's position as an international financial centre with (Hutton, 1996, p144) 'its basic credo that the promotion of the City of London's financial markets is synonymous with the public interest'. Within the City, these beliefs are most obviously translated into the need to make profits and demonstrate shareholder value. Hill's (1990, p13) study of forty-eight directors in top companies echoed the findings of Fidler (1981) and Pool *et al.* (1981) almost a decade earlier:

> These main board directors were unanimous in their belief that the role of the board is above all to serve the interests of shareholders … A board serves the owners by maximising the sustainable return on assets and providing a good flow of dividends, and, in so far as this can be influenced by what the company does, by maintaining or increasing the price of shares.[20]

A 1998 MORI poll of 'Captains of Industry' (MORI Poll Data, 1998) makes the same point. Asked 'What, in general, are the most important factors you take into account when making your judgement about companies?', the top two answers were financial performance (45 per cent) and quality of management (51 per cent). In contrast, 'social responsibility' was noted by only 6 per cent, treatment of customers by 7 per cent and treatment of employees by 6 per cent.

Business news influencing political policy-makers?

There is some suggestion that the pro-business and free-market consensus, that has come to dominate in business and financial news in the last two decades, has acted as a form of influence on government policy-makers. Corporate elite views are already privileged over others because they have much greater direct access to ministers and civil servants (see, for example, Ball and Millard, 1986, Crouch and Dore, 1990, Jordan, 1990, Grant, 1993, 1995, Richardson, 1993, Mitchell, 1997). Arguably, these 'insider' advantages have become regularly reinforced with the very public output of business and financial news – news that privileges business elite views on the economy. As such, one might surmise that policy-makers, in their

---

20 Pool *et al.* (1981, p144) concluded that for managers, even for those without shares, 'equally it was clear that owners and shareholders were placed highest in the overall priorities of our respondents'. Similarly, Fidler found that (1981, p253): 'Although I distinguished carefully between capitalists and managers in the sample, a distinction recognised by the interviewees themselves, I found no deviation from the traditional goals of capitalism. Profit remains the aim and measure of success.'

search for guidance on economic and industrial policy, would find it hard to go against the considerable 'expert' consensus that has accumulated.

Although it is impossible to determine conclusively how much influence such news texts have had on government policy-making, several authors have indicated that it has been quite significant. For Herman (1982), Parsons (1989) and Hutton (1996), debates in the financial press have always been a crucial part of the adoption of new economic theory and policy, from the late nineteenth century onwards (see also Klamer *et al.*, 1988), and such influence was clearly in evidence in the 1980s. Herman (1982) argued that economists, businessmen and analysts were becoming regular 'co-opted experts' for the presentation of neo-liberal economic policies in the Thatcher–Reagan era. According to Parsons, the adoption of monetarism took place more as a result of (1989, p7) 'its impact on influential sectors of press and political opinion than its ability to make converts in economic departments in British universities through the weight of its scientific arguments'. For Hutton (1996, p23): 'The powerful voice of the international financial community has helped to sanctify the New Right's calls for budgetary austerity, free trade, and price stability. Economic analysts from the great City investment houses regularly broadcast the capital's incantations on TV and radio.'

Whatever the level of business media influence, with the arrival of the Thatcher administration, Keynesianism was rejected and corporate – or more specifically City – influence once again came to the fore. Many of the policies listed above came to be regarded as part of the new economic consensus. The material consequences have been two decades of policy-making that have benefited those who dominated City 'elite discourse networks'. The interests of 'big business' have predominated at the expense of many other parts of society. For example, government attempts to intervene in the regulation of the financial sector have repeatedly collapsed or been made ineffective (Hutton, 1996, Farrelly, 7.11.1999). Manufacturing industry has steadily declined (Cairncross, 1992, Pollard, 1992, Hutton, 1996) as corporate profits and shareholder dividends continue to outstrip manufacturing investment. Public expenditure as a proportion of GDP has decreased and remains the second lowest in the EU (Cairncross, 1992, Pollard, 1992, Lowe, 1993). Union power has been severely pruned (Taylor, 1994, McIlroy, 1995), employment made increasingly insecure, and the disparity between rich and poor has grown (Hills, 1996, Goodman *et al.*, 1997). Taxation policy has clearly contributed to this. Between 1979/80 and 1996/97, income tax was reduced from 33 per cent to 24 per cent, the top rate of tax from 83 per cent to 40 per cent and corporation tax from 52 per cent to 33 per cent (Hutton, 1996, pp7, 13). Perhaps the most significant indication that corporate elites have benefited lies in a comparison of the finances of the UK government and the London stock market. In the first year of Conservative power, in 1979/80, the equity value of the stock market (£30.8 billion) was roughly 40 per cent of government income (£76.6 billion). By 1996/97, its value (£1,012.5 billion) had risen to more than three and a half times government income (£284.8 billion, figures in HMSO 1980/81 and 1997/98, and in London Stock Exchange, *Fact File*, 1998).

Added together these social and economic changes appear significant. That there has not been an outcry in the national media suggests collusion or approval on their part. However, it is more likely that opposition has been diluted simply because many of these macro-scale outcomes have resulted from an accumulation of less visible micro-scale events and activities. Most legislation, regulation, budgetary directives, takeovers and other financially relevant changes, on their own, do not appear particularly significant. They are either not given space in the news or, more often, confined to the financial and business pages – to be discussed in terms amenable to corporate 'elite discourse networks'. Understandably most observers, including very knowledgeable journalists, cannot perceive what the long-term social effects will be of a takeover and dismemberment of an established company, or the privatisation of a minor national utility, or a small shift in taxation policy towards indirect taxes, or the demutualisation of an established building society.

Conclusion

The strongest conclusion to be derived from chapters three and four is that corporate public relations has benefited the corporate sector as a whole, less by manufacturing 'mass consent' than by excluding both the general public and non-corporate elites. In terms of mainstream news, corporate sources and their PRPs have failed to inculcate the mass of the population with pro-business thinking. While the majority do support 'capitalist democracy' per se, they are not persuaded by many free-market policy ideals and have a negative view of the business community overall. Instead, corporate PR has been used to (a) minimise profiles and negative coverage in mainstream news, and (b) slowly gain more control of news more favourable and relevant to the corporate sector – financial and business news.

Arguably it has been extremely successful in this latter task. The impression given by other studies and journalist interviewees was that, in the post-war period, financial product advertising aimed at the expanding middle classes was the main impetus for the expansion of financial and business news. To a large extent the economic policies of the 1980s perpetuated these trends, and both public interest levels and financial advertising increased again. Such trends forced companies to invest in largely reactive PR operations. However, as competition increased during the decade, reactive public relations measures became proactive operations. Because corporate PR is far more advantaged in the area of business and financial news, corporate communications came to play a much larger part in this news production process.

All of which indicates that, whereas financial news expanded to feed a perceived consumer interest, and as a challenge to the City's closed world, financial PR has been used to reshape financial news to corporate needs. The public interest remits that guided such news production are likely to have been steadily altered to fit corporate information needs in an era of increased competition. The consequences of this corporate battle over financial news has been the virtual exclusion of all non-financial elites and the 'capture' of financial journalism. In other words, financial PR has worked to close off the City once again. As Parsons explains (1989, p217): 'in the beginning the press and political economy evolved in the context of a debate in which the educated classes were participatory observers. However, by the 1870s economics began to develop in an altogether more closed environment. This tendency towards the privatisation of its discourse has continued apace in our own times'.

Within the resulting 'closed discourse networks' of the City, the financial elite consensus on certain macro belief systems frequently guides the ongoing processes of media reporting and micro-level decision-making. Such processes not only affect activities in the City but, arguably, also have some influence on wider economic, political and legal decision-making circles. Non-financial elites are not aware of most of these decisions and their implications – each of which alters conditions in a barely perceptible way. However, if added up during the period of Conservative government the changes are quite stark. As opinion polls show, the average voter does not support such a system. If presented with something clear, as in the case of the 'poll tax' in the 1980s, subordinate and media responses are, accordingly, rather more critical (see Deacon and Golding, 1994). Unfortunately, most of the time, the decision-making process remains invisible to most and, even if made more visible, no single decision appears to be of real consequence.

5

THE GRANADA TAKEOVER OF FORTE

The following case study illustrates the findings of chapter four. The study looks at the professional communication campaigns involved in the Granada Group takeover of Forte Plc in 1995/96.

On 22 November 1995, the Granada Group unexpectedly announced its intention to take over Forte Plc with a bid of £3.28 billion. Forte immediately decided to oppose the bid and both groups gathered together large teams of top City advisers. The bid was vigorously contested by both sides throughout the 60 days allotted by City takeover rules. A large part of this contest involved the communications campaigns managed by two of the largest financial PR consultants in the City – Brunswick for Forte and Citigate for Granada. Both Granada and Forte were considered to be leading companies in high-profile consumer markets[1] and the campaigns accordingly producing several thousand articles across the national, regional and trade press. Both campaigns were ultimately successful. Forte succeeded in forcing Granada to raise its already generous bid to £3.8 billion. The value of Forte's shares rose 54 per cent over a sixty-four day period (from two days before to two days after the bid period) – almost putting the company out of Granada's reach. Granada's campaign eventually helped in winning the bid; a process that involved persuading both Forte and Granada shareholders to back Granada in spite of the rising costs and risks involved. By the deadline, 1 p.m. on 23 January 1996, Granada had received 67.58 per cent of acceptances from Forte shareholders.

However, the success of the two campaigns can also be looked at rather more critically. City elite sources almost entirely dominated the reporting of events in the media. In this closed 'elite discourse network', the future interests of employees and customers, and the long-term development of the businesses themselves, were considered unimportant next to the will of the market and promises of 'shareholder value'. By the end of the bid, the high stakes involved meant that, whichever company won, Forte was going to have to be dismantled and approximately half of it sold off. Thousands of jobs would be at risk, costs cut and high levels of debt incurred – all in order to fulfil promises to shareholders. Ultimately,

---

1 In 1995 Forte (formerly Trust House Forte) came ninety-second in the FTSE index and thirty-fifth in *The Times 1000*. Its market capitalisation was £2.236 billion, its turnover was £1.789 billion and it had 36,000 employees. Granada was one hundred and eighteen in the FTSE and one hundred and twenty-seventh in *The Times 1000*. It had a market cap of £3.278 billion, a turnover of £2.098 billion and 43,000 employees.

the only real beneficiaries were those who dominated the media debates – City advisers, large institutional shareholders and the senior management teams of both sides. Thus a PR conflict between elites, involving elite winners and losers, also ensured that certain financial elites could only win and many non-financial elites could only lose.

The research for this study involved accumulating information on the activities of sources and their PR practitioners, through documents and interviews with participants.[2] The findings were compared with a detailed content analysis of the national press during the sixty-day takeover period and accounts of business jour-nalists who reported on the takeover.[3]

Corporate conflict and communications conflict – the spinning of elites

City conflict

The bid itself must also be looked at as part of a general war of position and manoeuvre that continues to take place in the City. In this case both businesses had grown through a mixture of expansion and aggressive acquisition. Granada, with Gerry Robinson as chief executive since 1991, had acquired several smaller compa-nies, and had proved victorious in a hotly contested takeover of LWT in 1994. Forte's history included a merger then takeover of Trust Houses, a successful defence against an attempted takeover by Allied Breweries, and a protracted battle for control of the Savoy. The Granada-Forte takeover undoubtedly became a full-scale conflict between City elites. Both companies began by assembling impressive teams of stockbrokers, financial advisers, accountants and PR consultants.[4]

Many other parties had an interest in the outcome of the bid and were quickly drawn into the conflict. Seven of the ten largest institutional fund managers in the

---

2 The principal source of documentation, records and news cuttings was the archives of Granada's PR firm Citigate Communications. Available texts included all public documents produced by both sides, most of Granada's and some of Forte's press releases, Citigate/Granada's internal communi-cations documents, analyst/fund manager briefings and presentation materials. Nine interviews were conducted: three with Citigate directors, two with Granada management staff, two with ex-Forte management staff, and two with other Forte advisors.

3 The newspaper content analysis recorded a total of 582 articles appearing in nine national daily newspapers and three Sunday papers. Articles selected had to be specifically focused on the takeover and had to be 6 cm or more for broadsheet publications and 3 cm or more for tabloids. Preliminary analysis was applied to all articles appearing in these newspapers between the 23 November 1995 and the 23 January 1996. Seven of the twelve publications, carrying 425 articles, were selected for closer analysis: the *FT* – 107, *The Times* – 105, the *Telegraph* – 83, the *Sunday Times* – 28, the *Sunday Telegraph* – 19, the *Guardian* – 70 and the *Observer* – 13. For each of these articles a number of elements were coded and recorded. A further six interviews were then conducted with journalists who had covered the takeover.

4 These included Lazard Brothers, JP Morgan, SBC Warburg, UBS, Cazenove and Morgan Stanley (merchant bankers/financial advisers), Hoare Govett and BZW (stock broking firms), Touche Ross and Price Waterhouse (accountants), Linklaters and Paines (solicitors), Citigate, Brunswick and Makinson Cowell (financial PR consultants). All these advisers were rated in the City as being in the top six operating in their sectors (see *The Hambro Company Guide*, 1995).

City had significant share holdings in Forte. Eighty-seven institutions had stakes in both Granada and Forte, including Mercury Asset Management (MAM) which had the largest single holding (13-14 per cent) in both companies. The Savoy (part-owned by Forte), the Council of Forte (which owned 0.1 per cent of Forte shares but 50 per cent of its voting rights), Whitbread (which also bid to buy part of Forte) and other rival hotel and leisure companies all joined the conflict. Many of these organisations stood to gain or lose, and saw movements in their own share prices, as the bid shifted in one direction or another. Additionally, a number of external insti-tutions, including the Takeover Panel, the Inland Revenue, the DTI and the Monopolies and Mergers Commission, were all temporarily pulled into the takeover by one or both sides.

Communications conflict

As part of the conflict the two sides expended significant resources in trying to control communications channels and influence media coverage. Citigate added a team of nine to Granada's in-house team. Forte, in addition to its own award-winning in-house team, brought in six people from Brunswick plus advisers from Makinson Cowell. Both sides ran election-style campaigns, which included investi-gating the other using teams of accountants and analysts, preparing themselves for attack by running their own fake opposition teams, and constantly monitoring the media and operating with a 'rapid rebuttal' system. Between them they generated eight public documents (sent to 75,000 shareholders, all media, analysts, fund managers and others) and over 200 press releases in the sixty-day period. But the public documents were only a small part of what was involved. Most of the communications work involved numerous telephone conversations and private meetings with journalists, analysts and fund managers. Since the written output of respected commentators helped to influence shareholders, every major journalist, editor and analyst also became a target.[5] The communications battle also extended itself towards private investors in the last few weeks when the two groups began advertising campaigns, telephone canvassing and embarked on a series of nation-wide presentations.

Both sides also made extensive use of third parties to put their case for them. The most significant group in this case were analysts; those considered to be the 'experts' in the field. Analysts, like journalists, had to process information and offer advice to shareholders and therefore maintained close contact with the participants. If persuaded to one side or the other their assessments were taken up and used in

---

5 As Granada documents (Granada, 1996) explain, they 'Provided regular and early comment to the wire services to set the tone, ensuring early contact for the Granada team with the most influential City editors, commentators and journalists following the bid; and being accessible to them at all times … Recognised importance of *FT* to investment community, meeting at all stages and gave the *FT* team Granada's institutional presentation'. In Richard Power's (interview, 30.11.98) words: 'We did have a bad start but I do think we won the media campaign …We never convincingly won over the Lex column of the *FT* – except when there was a temporary change of editor – but we won almost all the rest of the columns (*Questor, Telegraph, Tempus, Times*).'

public documents and press releases. Other third parties were also encouraged to get their views on the takeover directly into the business columns. These included William Shawcross, William Rees-Mogg, Melvyn Bragg, Pannell Kerr Forster Associates (PKFA) hotel analysts, several business academics (at Henley Management College, the London Business School, and London School of Economics [LSE] – in Citigate, 9.1.96, 10.1.96) and a number of respected chief executives. A Citigate memo (16.1.96) explains the extent of this activity in the last week:

> Bernard Talyor's piece is still with *The Times* ... The *FT* have agreed in principle to a piece to be submitted by Melvyn Bragg for Friday's paper. XXX and I are liaising with Melvyn and XXX has also agreed to speak to Melvyn to give him some reassurance ... David Blackwell at the *FT* has written an article on Sutcliffe for Wednesday's paper which I think will be OK. He has talked with Don Davenport at Sutcliffe and we have tried to provide him with everything he needed ...

The campaigns focused on a complex mixture of issues, all of which were calculated to have an impact on the deliberations of financial decision-makers. Tables 5.1 and 5.2 record the most common points and arguments that appeared in the content analysis of the broadsheet press. These tables reveal that there were a number of subjective issues that appeared to be linked with the presentation of seemingly objective figures. Thus, commentary on personalities and managements, and general speculation about management styles, future markets and performances, were merged with past and current financial measures. All these factors made up the promotional campaigns in which City decision-makers were the targets to be 'spun'. In response, financial elite opinion and press support for the two sides swung significantly over the sixty-day period (see figure 5.1).

Table 5.1 Most common points/arguments, favouring Granada, appearing in selected newspapers

Most repeated arguments	% of articles
Rocco Forte out shooting/nepotistic family-run business	13.4
Forte management is distracted by 'trophy' assets	8.7
Forte management is generally poor/poor results and 'track record'	9.6
Forte's poor returns to shareholders	7.8
Granada management's 'track record' is better than Forte's	7.5
Granada management's results and 'track record' are very good	8.0
Gerry Robinson has a great 'track record'/profile and philosophy	10.4
Granada can make £100 million savings after takeover in year 1	9.4
Granada's plans to sell assets and 'exploit synergies'	12.7
Forte's new plans unworkable: hotels unstable, dividends high, etc.	15.5
Analysts/the City favour Granada	14.6

Note: Sample, 425 articles

Table 5.2 Most common points/arguments, favouring Forte,
appearing in selected newspapers

Most repeated arguments	% of articles
Granada is a '1980s style conglomerate'/conglomerates are bad	9.9
Granada is an 'asset stripper'/bid has no 'industrial logic'	12.5
Gerry Robinson and Granada know nothing about hotels	8.7
Forte's new management changes, new directors, etc.	10.4
Forte's previous disposals, rebranding and new focus	11.3
Forte disposals during bid	16.5
Forte's sale of the roadside business to Whitbread	9.9
Hotel market has been through a poor cycle/start of upswing	9.2
Forte profit forecasts up	5.9
Forte hotels revalued upwards	5.4
Forte's special dividend payments	11.3
Forte says it is worth more	8.5
Analysts say Granada must raise bid/Forte will escape	11.3

Note: Sample, 425 articles

Figure 5.1 Cumulative favourability of coverage for Granada and Forte
in the broadsheet press

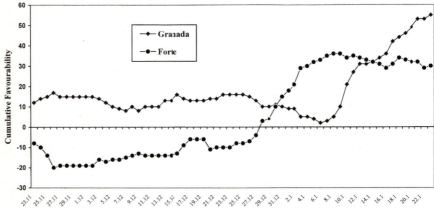

23rd November 1995 to 23rd January 1996

Notes: Sample 425 articles. Favourability ratings: the main participants were each given a favourability
rating of minus two to plus two for each article. Zero denoted either no mention or a neutral presentation. Minus one represented a negative impression of a group and/or policies associated with it; plus
one, a positive impression. Minus two represented an outright attack on that group; plus two, an
outright endorsement. Each daily rating for the participants was the average score gained in the publications analysed. This score was then added to the previous day. This form of analysis is used by many
evaluation companies in the PR industry and is also to be found in some academic studies (e.g., Hansen,
1993, Norris *et al.*, 1999).

Lies, damn lies and statistics

'Spin-doctoring' began with the presentation of very different sets of financial performance figures. At every opportunity Granada unfavourably compared Forte's poor results to their own impressive ones. According to Granada's documents (24.11.95a, 14.12.95, 9.1.96, 16.1.96), Forte's five-year history read: operating profits down 11 per cent, earnings per share down 41 per cent, dividends per share down 24 per cent, net assets down £590 million, share price relative to the Financial Times Actuaries (FTA) All-share Index – down 40 per cent. Granada's own five-year history (*ibid.*) read: operating profits up by 341 per cent, dividends per share up by 68 per cent, cash flow up by £775 million, etc. The two graphs that were widely reproduced at the time (see figure 5.2), of operating profit and earnings per share, illustrated the differences clearly. As a Granada press release (15.1.96) was to proclaim: 'Small wonder that, for total returns for shareholders over the five years prior to our offer, Forte ranked 86th out of the FTSE 100; Granada ranked 5th.' Looking at table 5.1, 7.8 per cent of articles mentioned Forte's poor return to shareholders and 8 per cent mentioned Granada's strong results and track record; 7.5 per cent directly compared the two companies, showing Forte in a poor light next to Granada. Granada also maintained the focus on Forte's financial record by comparing them unfavourably with other hotel groups. Documents were produced by Citigate (20.12.95, 21.12.95) and Touche Ross (19.12.95) which, due to careful selection of examples and figures, made Forte's performance seem below average in the hotels sector as a whole.

Figure 5.2 Granada charts of operating profit (left) and earnings per share (right)

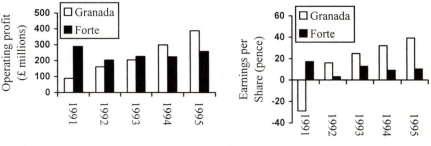

Source: Granada, 24.11.95a, pp10, p11

Forte's first line of defence was to present its figures in ways that made the fluctuating performance of one five-year period into a dramatically improving performance over three years. Using a shorter time-span, alternative accounting periods, and forecasts for a year that had not yet been completed (see figure 5.3), Rocco Forte was able to declare (Forte, 2.1.96a, p1): 'We are forecasting profits before tax and exceptional items for the year ending 31st January, 1996, of not less than £190 million, which represents an increase of 50 per cent over the previous year. We have more than trebled profits and increased earnings per share by five

Figure 5.3 Forte charts of increased profit before tax (left) and earnings per share (right)

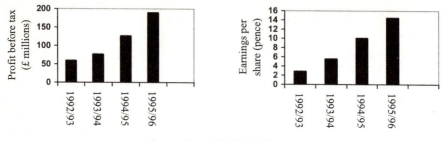

Source: Forte, 15.1.96, inside cover

times over the last three years ...'. Forte also hit back on the issue of its performance relative to the hotel sector as a whole. It commissioned and published research from PKFA which showed that a number of Forte hotels had operating profits of between 9 per cent and 47 per cent above average, and room yields up to 22 per cent above average (Forte, 2.1.96a).

For the first month of the bid, the force of Granada's arguments about its superior track record, and Forte's poor financial record, were the ones that dominated reporting and City elite debates. Analysts and commentators all thought it would be a 'tough battle' but generally predicted a comfortable Granada victory (see figure 5.1). It was clear that Forte would have to do something more radical.

New improved Forte

The company responded by attempting to transform itself completely over the sixty-day period. As Richard Power explained (interview, 30.11.98):

> Our aim was very much to present the company as a new one ... the presentation of a new company for the new millennium. Although Rocco is a strong Conservative supporter and Gerry Robinson a New Labour man, we presented New Forte as the forward-looking business – as opposed to the tired old bureaucratic conglomerate. And it persuaded people, it worked.

The transformation was enacted in three different ways. The first of these was in management. It began with bringing in new, externally recruited senior managers (see Forte, 8.12.95, pp1, 4), continued with changes to the board of directors (Forte, 2.1.96, p2), and was completed with Rocco Forte relinquishing his joint roles as chief executive and chairman (with the CEO role going to Sir Anthony Tennant). By the end of the bid, Forte was able to declare that (Forte, 15.1.96, inside cover): 'Over two-thirds of Forte's management team have joined during the last three years. Forte's new management team is committed to achieving continuing growth for shareholders and is delivering growing profits and earnings.' Looking at table 5.2, 10.4 per cent of articles mentioned Forte's changes of management or announced new board appointments.

The second part of the transformation involved a massive disposals programme – aimed at turning the company into a 'new focused hotels group'. Forte declared in its first defence document that it had sold off £950 million of assets in the preceding three years. As the bid progressed, it announced a series of deals and disposals, the most significant of which was the £1.05 billion sale of its roadside business to Whitbread. Forte's recent disposals and rebranding were discussed in 11.3 per cent of articles, and 16.5 per cent of articles featured one of Forte's many disposal deals during the sixty-day period. The Whitbread sale alone featured in forty-two articles (9.9 per cent). As Forte made clear, not only would the disposals transform Forte into a 'new focused hotels group', it would release enough capital to enable the company to pay off its mounting debts and/or increase dividend payments to its shareholders.

The third part of the campaign involved talking up the financial future of 'new Forte'. In its first defence documents, poor results were blamed on the ailing hotels market which was, in turn, blamed on a combination of the Gulf War and recession. Research, commissioned from PFKA, linked changes in GDP to profits in the hotels market and, on the basis of GDP currently rising, predicted that (Forte, 2.1.96a, p9) 'the UK hotel industry has entered a period of strong growth in profits which should continue for three or four years'. That the hotels market had been through a poor cycle and was now at the start of an upswing was reported in 9.2 per cent of articles. Forte also began to get new valuations of its properties and made much of the higher estimates that were produced. 5.4 per cent of articles mentioned the rise in value of Forte's properties.

The other side of this strategy was to cast doubt on Granada's future profitability. Granada was criticised (Forte, 8.12.95) for its lack of focus, lack of hotel sector experience (33 hotels compared with Forte's 398), and lack of 'commercial logic' in trying to link its existing businesses with Forte's. On top of that, Granada had high levels of debt (£3.6 billion) and several businesses that had stopped growing and/or were in decline. In other words, Granada was becoming 'a 1980s style, acquisition driven conglomerate' at a time when 'the City' had decreed 'focus' was in fashion and conglomerates 'under-performed the market' all too often. As Rocco Forte was to declare (Forte, 15.1.96, p2): 'This highly leveraged break-up bid follows the now discredited pattern of 1980s-style conglomerates – whose shares have consistently under performed in the 1990s. how long will it be before its shares suffer a similar derating? Do not trust the highly questionable value of Granada's shares.' Looking back at table 5.2, 12.5 per cent of articles reported the Forte argument that Granada was an 'asset stripper' and the bid had 'no industrial logic'. Granada was referred to as a 'conglomerate' and the value of conglomerates to shareholders questioned by 9.9 per cent. The charges that Gerry Robinson and Granada knew little about hotels were repeated by 8.7 per cent of articles.

Clearly, six weeks into the bid, Forte's campaign had turned financial elite opinion in its favour. It had persuaded 'the City' that: its figures were respectable compared to others in the struggling hotels sector; it was becoming a dynamic new company with new management associated with an upturn in fortunes; it had focused on hotels at a time when hotels were going to be very profitable; and Granada's bid was an attempt to make short-term profits at the expense of long-term ones and a highly risky venture. Citigate's own research (Citigate, 4.1.96c) found that analyst support had now switched to Forte:

> The robustness of Forte's defence and the perceived inaction of Granada to date means that Granada will have to increase its offer by 15% ... Granada has never shown any understanding of trophy assets ... The basic numbers do not stack up for Granada to take on the bid and they never did ... A number of people think Granada should walk away from it ... Granada will have to raise its offer by at least 10%.

Analysts came out by a ratio of six to one in favour of Granada either withdrawing or substantially increasing the bid (*ibid.*). A swathe of forty-eight articles in the period subsequently reported that 'analysts' and/or institutions thought Forte would escape. The content analysis (see figure 5.1) accordingly shows that Forte had overtaken Granada in the level of favourable coverage it was attracting. Consequently, Forte's share price began to creep up while Granada's own share price edged down – thus indicating that investors would not support the bid.

From focused hotel group to balanced modern leisure company

In response, Granada developed its own version of what the future held. The 'new Granada', rather than becoming an 'unwieldy conglomerate', would be a 'balanced modern leisure company' with 'potential synergies' and protection against 'cyclical markets'. Its plans were most solidly illustrated by repeated claims that it could save an extra £100 million in profits from Forte's operations in the first year of management (Granada, 14.12.95). As Gerry Robinson explained (9.1.96, pp7–8): 'This is the shape of the new Granada and as you can see it is extraordinarily well balanced with 29 per cent in Leisure and Services, 25 per cent in Television, 22 per cent in Rental and 24 per cent in the most profitable and predictable end of the hotel market ... This mix of businesses will leave us with a very well balanced group ...'.

Forte, on the other hand, had suffered by being too reliant on the highly cyclical hotels industry – a matter made worse by its focus on the top end of the market. Doubts were also cast on the viability of Forte's future financial plans. These included a generous share buy-back scheme and a promise to increase dividends by 20 per cent each year for three years. Such promises, according to Gerry Robinson (Granada press release, 12.1.96), would require profits to double in three years. Consequently, new Forte was going to be a very risky venture to invest in (Granada, 16.1.96, pp8–9): 'Forte's defence is flawed ... creating an unbalanced risk ... A buy back scheme that may never happen coupled with an imprudent dividend commitment ... A management change that isn't a change ... retaining up-market hotels which are highly capital intensive, are vulnerable to an economic downturn and provide low returns, even in buoyant times ...'.

Looking again at table 5.1, 9.4 per cent of articles reported Granada's £100 million savings plan, 12.7 per cent repeated Granada's arguments about potential synergies and cash generated from the disposal of 'trophy assets' and 15.5 per cent printed Granada's concerns over Forte's plans. Granada was therefore able to

create a very different interpretation of future markets and appropriate management styles. In the last three weeks of the bid it managed to turn City opinion once
again. Focused companies were now unbalanced, hotels were a risky investment,
Forte's commitments were too difficult to support and Granada offered a balanced
future with a proven management team.

For investors, with the stakes as high as they were, both ventures now appeared
fairly speculative. Since both sides offered very similar financial packages to shareholders,[6] the question of management competence became increasingly important.
The *Investors Chronicle* (1996) summed up 'City opinion' at the time:

> In which case, two other factors loom large:
> * the shareholder's view of risk
> * which management is likely to shape up better
> … Conventional wisdom says that Granada's management is far better. Quite likely.
> We do wonder, however, how much of Granada's recent growth came from improv-
> ing the businesses its management inherited and how much from acquisitions …
> Forte's record is dismal. The question, however, is to what extent the current top
> management is responsible for that and to what extent it has tried to correct the
> mess?

A question of management

The greatest weapon for Granada was the perceived strength of it management
team and chief executive when compared to Forte. Granada thus finished its
campaign as it had begun it – by focusing on management teams and personalities
and, more particularly, on the Forte family. The Fortes, although well connected in
certain political and business circles, were poorly perceived in 'the City' and had
developed a reputation for being 'nepotistic', overly 'extravagant' and outdated in
their working practices. All these elements were played upon and exploited to the
full by Granada. It began on day 1 of the bid when Granada informed the press that
Rocco Forte had been out shooting on the day the bid was launched. As Chris
Hopson of Granada explained (interview, 25.1.99): 'The shooting thing was, in
fact, a perfect analogy for our views and claims about how Forte was running the
business. It summed up a company that was being run as a series of trophy hotels,
that was an archaic family business, that wasted time on pomp and ceremony. So it
was a perfect analogy and it fell into our hands – too good to resist.' Granada
continually referred to Forte's interest in 'trophy assets', the shooting incident and
other wasteful extravagances – all images distasteful to professional fund managers
and analysts. Looking again at table 5.1, 13.4 per cent of articles mentioned either
Rocco's 'shooting fiasco' or made reference to Forte being a family business run on

---

6 The mathematics were somewhat disputed but, according to many assessments, the end offers were
   roughly equal. The *Investors Chronicle* (1996), for example, concluded that the figures were rather
   similar with Forte offering slightly more. It calculated that keeping Forte would be worth £416
   for every 100 Forte shares, as opposed to accepting Granada's offer of £402 for every 100 Forte
   shares.

nepotistic lines. Granada's claims that Forte had been 'distracted by trophy assets' were repeated by 8.7 per cent of articles.

These images were in direct contrast to those associated with Gerry Robinson and the Granada management team – all of whose reputations had been firmly established in 'the City' in recent years. In contrast to Rocco Forte, Gerry Robinson had come from a poor family background in Ireland and had worked his way up through a number of UK corporations. At each he had built up a reputation for improving businesses and profits. In fact, 10.4 per cent of articles in the period talked about Gerry Robinson's track record and management philosophy, or relayed information about his upbringing and past business record. This was how the two chief executives came to be presented throughout the contest. As one former Forte adviser explained:

> Bids become very personal, particularly if you are Gerry Robinson, a highly successful businessman, the smartest man to come out of Ireland in the last twenty years, and especially if your opponent is Rocco Forte, seen as a bit thick, there because it's the family business. If we had been on Granada's side, we would have advised them to focus on management and personalities. Working for Forte the obvious thing was to play that down. And yes, that kind of thing does influence people. If you went and asked all the brokers 'Who would you back, Gerry Robinson or Rocco Forte?', they would say 'Gerry Robinson' every time. It's all part of the calculation.[7]

In the last two weeks Citigate and Granada proved particularly adept at pushing their case. They also pulled off a series of daring manoeuvres, including a last-minute deal to purchase the Council of Forte's shares, and a 'dawn raid' in which they stepped in ahead of Whitbread to buy up 10 per cent of Forte. Crucially, they also increased their offer by a further 15 per cent to £3.8 billion – achieved not by greater borrowing, but by offering to sell off more of Forte and pay back shareholders with a special dividend (Granada, 9.1.96). Once again, analyst and media opinion turned and increasingly began to favour Granada (see figure 5.1) – something the company was quick to publicise. They compiled lists of pro-Granada analysts and analysts' comments (Granada, 18.1.96), presenting them in a letter to journalists (Nolder, 15.1.96): 'Listed below are analysts following the Granada/Forte bid. The majority back Granada either outright on the record, or if pushed, off the record … I thought you might find the list of assistance especially if you wanted to carry out your own survey of opinion.' During the final two weeks, when Granada

---

7 See also: David Nolder (interview, 22.12.98), 'So you had the great debate – drive, enthusiasm, earnings per share, professional management and not a lot of sentiment, versus the old man, autocratically driven, lacking drive, lacking the hard edge, into trophy assets, letting profitability go a bit flabby'; Alistair Defriez (interview, 22.12.98), 'But the previous six or seven weeks were an outstanding example of a full-blown, almost gladiatorial public relations battle – right from the start, as I saw it … Rocco, in some people's minds, was a dilettante playboy inheriting the business from his father and pursuing aristocratic country sports. As opposed to Gerry Robinson, who was a self-made man, one of thirteen children, risen through the ranks on merit, an advocate of meritocracy, a man who through his own skills and abilities had risen to the top of Granada'.

was regaining the initiative, sixty-two articles (see table 5.1) reported that 'analysts' and/or institutions backed Granada to win. Many of these mentioned a straw poll of analysts that had been carried out. By the final offer date (23 January) most of the major shareholders had been convinced and Granada received acceptances for two-thirds of Forte's shares.

Questioning the effectiveness of the PR campaigns

It is very difficult to reach firm conclusions about the importance of the respective public relations campaigns. In many ways they were indivisible from the general campaigns in which financial PRPs contributed to meetings on financial strategy, and accountants, financial advisers and solicitors jointly produced documents and press releases. Everyone involved spent large amounts of time promoting the key messages to analysts, journalists and institutions. All, in effect, became involved in one large communications operation.

Interviewees gave mixed responses when asked about how much the public relations operations contributed to the eventual outcome. Several, including all of the PRP interviewees, played down their role, believing that decision-making came down to simple financial calculations. They argued that advisers, analysts and, above all, institutional fund managers, were, and continue to be, driven purely and simply by figures and profits. Ultimately, Granada won because it made an offer that couldn't be refused. In Simon Rigby's words (interview, 20.11.98): 'For institutional share-holders it all comes down to the finances. Because fund managers all deal with large amounts of other people's money, they don't make decisions on a whim or on who they like or dislike, etc. They make decisions clearly on who offers them the best deal.'[8] Thus, many would argue that the success or failure of the bid rested on the financial manoeuvres of various participants and, above all else, on the sums involved.

However, as this part has attempted to demonstrate, the presentation of accounts varied considerably and financial decision-making was influenced by a number of highly speculative factors. Thus, future profit forecasts, predictions for the market, and the present and past performances of comparable businesses and management systems, were all speculative factors dressed up as objective facts. All too frequently, such factors were dragged into the debate by one or other of the protagonists them-selves. Decision-making was also smothered in personal prejudices and associations – from Rocco Forte's interest in shooting to arguments about what constituted a con-glomerate and whether conglomerates were profitable.

---

8 Richard Power (30.11.99), 'We lost basically on price. I suppose we have all asked ourselves if there was something we could have done differently … But at £4.00 a share, no, I can't think of anything we could have done beyond pushing it to that'; David Nolder (interview, 23.12.98), 'If Gerry is delivering and Carol's all about earnings per share … In the end Gerry was deemed more successful than the old man and that he would have done more with those assets in the long term … Gerry was always clear about the earnings potential and what to sell. He was less sentimental about the deal'; Keith Hamill (interview, 17.2.99), 'A number of our friends said to us we would have to accept simply because of the size of the bid in the end. We had done very well and in the end this is more important than the PR. They [Granada] did it with money. They certainly didn't do it with PR'.

Considering the fact that the final offers were rather similar in financial terms, one would thus assume that decisions were based on more than financial calculations. If not, why were two public relations firms paid £3 million between them for sixty days' work? How could opinions and values swing so dramatically in such a short space of time if it was only a matter of presenting figures? All bids are expected to be raised, but the overall increase in the value of Forte appeared quite dramatic. A share price that had been steadily dropping for some years was suddenly raised by 54 per cent in a sixty-four day period.

Indeed, several interviewees, including journalists and those working on the financial side, admitted that highly speculative, non-financial factors were very important.[9] In fact, for all the journalists interviewed, it was the issues of management and personalities that dominated the story. As Richard Northedge (interview, 25.5.99) recalled:

> Granada had a very good long-term image. Gerry Robinson had managed to build up a specific image of the company and himself over a period of time ... It was one reason why the City was prepared to accept Granada's bid. Citigate's work was important and in Granada's case it was generally true. But on the other hand Brunswick changed the perception of Forte. Before the bid Forte had a terrible reputation in the hotel sector. They were like British Rail in that they were generally thought to be bad. But during the bid it suddenly became an institution we should have been preserving. The bid battle was all the sort of stuff of Jeffrey Archer novels. Both sides had personalities and offered a story with appeal. Granada turned Gerry Robinson into a personality and one could argue that it was the personalities that decided the issue.[10]

---

9 Tim Weller, group financial controller for Granada (interview, 19.1.99), 'Ultimately you would like to believe that institutional shareholders make decisions based on the financial merits. But undoubtedly they were affected. They read the newspapers and they would have been at least a little affected, just as you or I would be. At the time there were multiple issues that could have affected an individual's judgement and all these issues were plastered right across the financial press throughout the bid period. Undoubtedly they would have'; Alistair Defriez, financial adviser for Forte at the time (interview, 22.12.98), 'It's a necessary evil ... you can't afford to ignore your public relations. You do so at your peril. If the other side steals a march on you in PR terms it's very hard to come back. In a closely contested takeover things like PR can tip the balance at the margins. It's not the most important thing but it can tip the balance'.

10 Anonymous financial journalist (1999), 'One really drummed-in thing was that Rocco Forte was out on the grass moors when Gerry Robinson phoned him to make the offer. That was used extensively to show how patrician Rocco was ... Gerry Robinson on the other hand was seen as much more a man of the people'; anonymous financial journalist (1999), 'All I can really remember is that poor old Rocco Forte was out on the grass moors when Gerry Robinson made his lightening strike ... Gerry Robinson was very much the flavour of the time whereas poor old Rocco was seen as the not too successful son of a successful father ... So ultimately Gerry Robinson was highly thought of in the City and Rocco was not'; Raymond Snoddy (interview, 17.5.99), 'I think the decision in the end was taken by a small number of City investors who believed in Gerry Robinson. It was mostly down to financial decisions. There were a few emotional things flying about though that were used as symbols, for example the shooting event. That symbolised in Gerry Robinson's mind what it was all about – the grass moors, old money, lazy money – it was a powerful symbol'.

From spinning corporate elites to corporate elite capture of the media

Although the media actively reflected and relayed the conflict between elites involved in the takeover, it was also highly constrained in its reporting. What is demonstrable is that coverage of the takeover battle was appropriated by the business media and the business media was largely 'captured' by the communications campaigns of Granada and Forte. The results of this capture were that all source input and all debates came from the City. Other voices and other concerns were ignored. As a result, regardless of the outcome, the winners in the whole takeover process were guaranteed to be City elites of one kind or another. The losers were going to be those whose concerns and interests were barely heard. This is not to say that the media was acting in league with their sources, or that they simply reproduced PR material uncritically. Certainly, journalists were critical of the two sides and attempted to get a variety of opinions from those involved and those whom they considered to be independent experts – analysts, fund managers and other CEOs. However, their agendas, and the materials they worked with, came almost exclusively from a small City community which was severely limited in its objectives, priorities and general norms and values.

Corporate capture of the business media

Despite the takeover drawing extensive media coverage, it was a rather select group that participated in the debates. The two companies, their advisers, rival CEOs, institutional shareholders, and analysts, all formed a closed network of communications in which journalists had to be accepted or risk being left out altogether. For the two sides involved the communications emphasis was primarily directed at some twenty-five to thirty key institutions and those that influenced them. This was because this select few owned the majority of shares in Forte.[11] The 75,000 private shareholders that existed together owned no more than 15 per cent of Forte – the same amount as the largest institutional shareholder MAM. The two chief executives accordingly spent a large proportion of their time in one-to-one meetings with top fund managers in City institutions. Rocco Forte visited each major institutional shareholder twice during the sixty-day period (in Forte, 1997); Gerry Robinson visited each of them approximately four times (interview with Chris Hopson, 25.1.99).

Around the CEOs and fund managers, analysts, advisers and PRPs maintained the communication channels and defined the terms of the debate. Those journalists accepted[12] automatically joined the two-way communication channels that stretched

---

11 At the time, the top ten institutional shareholders together owned 34.22 per cent of Forte (Horseman and Shepherd, 4.1.96).

12 Interviews suggested that there was strong competition between journalists to gain access. David Nolder (interview, 23.12.98), 'At the time it was a major issue and they were queuing up to meet Gerry and the Pacemakers. So we talked and set up meetings with all the ones that we thought were important'; Alistair Defriez (interview, 23.12.98), 'With such a big deal every journalist in town wanted to hear about it every day. There was a voracious appetite for stories – some of which had been generated by our earlier actions.'

Table 5.3 Article positioning in national newspapers

Newspaper	Business pages	Home pages	Other	Total
FT	107	N/A	N/A	107
The Times	95	6	4	105
Daily Telegraph	80	2	1	83
Independent	65	8	1	74
Guardian	65	3	2	70
Daily Mail	37	–	2	39
Daily Express	23	–	1	24
Mirror	11	–	–	11
Sun	7	2	–	9
Sunday Times	26	2	–	28
Sunday Telegraph	18	1	–	19
Observer	12	–	1	13
Total	546 (93.8%)	24 (4.1%)	12 (2.1%)	582

Note: Sample, 582 articles

between the companies and the top institutional shareholders. As Alistair Defriez (interview, 23.12.98), explained:

> There was enormous communication with the brokers. You are talking to them all the time. They get feedback from the institutions and we find out what arguments are weak and which are strong and we go back and work on our messages accordingly … At the same time the press are also talking to the analysts. The press is going to the market and asking what they think about all this.

Because journalists covering the story were 'captured' in such a way, the news production process was also. Looking at table 5.3, of twelve national newspaper titles, 93.8 per cent of all articles appeared in the financial and business news sections. Of the 4.1 per cent that appeared in the home pages, nearly all were smaller extracts of larger articles written by financial journalists for the business sections. The 2.1 per cent of other features were generally larger, often written by other journalists, and expressed other concerns – but were, however, always placed in the middle of the paper.

The two sides were themselves the most common contributors to news articles and produced a steady supply of information subsidies – all of which found willing takers amongst the financial press. Three hundred and eighty-three out of 425 (90.1 per cent) articles, of the seven publications selected for further analysis, included contributions from Granada, Forte, or both sides. That is, they included figures, quotations or arguments supplied by those companies, or, they discussed such contributions in comment pieces. Where figures were used, they came almost entirely from the public documents and press releases of the companies or from standard Stock Exchange information on share prices and trades. Even when journalists appeared sceptical of the figures or arguments they were reporting, they rarely found alternative ones.

Table 5.4 Contributors cited

Forte total	*(27.2%)*		
		Rocco Forte	(13.4%)
		Forte named	(6.8%)
		Forte anon.	(7.0%)
Granada total	*(26.3%)*		
		Gerry Robinson	(14.2%)
		Granada named	(6.6%)
		Granada anon.	(5.6%)
Fund manager/broker analyst/consultant	*(34.9%)*		
		Named	(13.4%)
		Anon.	(21.6%)
Other business	*(8.8%)*		
Other non-business	*(2.8%)*		
Total	*(100%)*		

Note: Sample, 501 citations recorded in 425 articles

Looking at table 5.4, it is clear that virtually all other contributions to news texts came from City and business sources. Anonymous analysts and fund managers were the main alternative providers of comment. Granada and Forte between them provided 53.4 per cent. Other business sources – mostly company CEOs and directors in related businesses – accounted for 8.8 per cent. All non-financial elite sources provided just 2.8 per cent of citations.

The target audience for most articles was shareholders – more specifically institutional shareholders. The simple message that both sides wanted to communicate was that they would offer 'more value to shareholders'. Forte attempted to argue that Granada had undervalued the company and therefore shareholders should not sell. Granada attempted to communicate the impression that Forte had not given shareholders value in the past and, if the bid was successful, Granada would offer more value to them in the future. Many of the thirty-six press releases and all eight public documents featured the topic of 'shareholder value'.[13] This focus, in all its guises, was similarly reflected in a majority of news items. For example, looking back at table 5.1, 7.8 per cent reported that Forte 'offered poor returns to share-holders' and 9.6 per cent stated that its general financial results and track record

---

13 For example: Granada (24.11.95a p6), 'Granada believes that in recent years, Forte has failed to deliver adequate value to shareholders …'; Rocco Forte (in Forte, 8.12.95, p4), 'Well structured and carefully timed disposals of businesses have achieved excellent value for shareholders …'; Gerry Robinson (Granada press release, 27.12.95), 'Forte is failing to achieve a decent return on its assets and is not delivering real value for its shareholders'; Forte (2.1.96b, p19), 'On the basis of Granada's latest full-year dividend, any such shareholder accepting the bidder's all-share terms would have suffered a shortfall of income … '.

Table 5.5 Those referred to or addressed

Those referred to/addressed	% of articles
Shareholders/investors (generally refers to institutions)	63.5
'The market'/'the City' (as in 'the City backs Granada')	39.8
'Analysts' (as in 'analysts think the bid should be raised')	21.4
Takeover Panel/takeover rules	12.2
Employees	7.1
Private investors	4.2
Customers	4.2
Total number mentioning one or more of these three	13.4

Note: Sample, 425 articles

were 'poor'. In table 5.2, 8.5 per cent of stories repeated Forte's claims to be 'worth more' and 11.3 per cent stated that analysts actually thought that Forte was 'worth more'. Looking at table 5.5, it also becomes clear that the principal audience for news stories was considered to be institutional shareholders. 63.5 per cent of articles either address shareholders or refer to them.

Articles similarly acted to reinforce a number of other City norms and values. The first of these was that 'the City'/'the market', this objective yet anonymous body of opinion, knew best. News items frequently used such phrases as 'City opinion believes ...', 'Market sentiment dictates ...', 'Analysts have determined that ...' Looking again at table 5.5, 39.8 per cent of articles referred to 'the City' or 'the market' in such phrases, 21.4 per cent referred to 'analysts' in similar ways, 12.2 per cent referred to the Takeover Panel and takeover regulations. Second, those most cited had their status as 'experts' and authoritative sources on corporate/City matters reinforced. As table 5.4 confirms chief executives, analysts and fund managers provided 43.7 per cent of these 'non-aligned' comments.

Non-City elite exclusion

Financial elite capture of the news production process also resulted in the automatic exclusion of other participants. Looking back at table 5.4, fourteen citations, or 2.8 per cent of the total, were taken from non-City elites. These appeared in seven different articles, or 1.65 per cent of the total.[14] Table 5.5 also shows that employees, private investors and customers are only referred to in 13.4 per cent of all articles. Not only were non-corporate elites excluded, so were potential rival elites from the worlds of academia, politics, law and industry. The Fortes actually had extensive links with the Conservative Party, both Houses of Parliament, and business communities around the world.[15] Such connections, although far superior to Granada's own, proved to have little influence on financial news coverage.

---

14 The fourteen quotes were from three customers, eight private shareholders, Egon Ronay (for Forte), Melvyn Bragg (for Granada), one DTI spokesperson, and Alistair Darling – Labour City affairs spokesperson.

Looking at table 5.6, it is clear that few articles questioned the takeover or showed concern about how it would affect those outside the 'Square Mile'. Some sort of cynicism about the takeover – its short-termism and destructive nature – was expressed by 4.7 per cent of articles. Mostly emanating from Forte in the early stages of the campaign, 3.5 per cent articles suggested that jobs might be lost. City adviser fees, tax loopholes and the exclusion of private shareholders voices, were each mentioned in just over 1 per cent of articles. Only twelve (2.8 per cent of the total) articles actually chose to make objection to the process a main theme. The other 97.2 per cent did not significantly challenge the takeover on anything other than grounds of shareholder value.

Table 5.6 Critical points/arguments appearing in selected newspapers

Critical arguments	% of articles
Cynicism about the takeover/takeovers, their short-termism and value	4.7
Jobs will be lost as a result of the takeover	3.5
Cynicism that the main winners will be the advisers involved	1.2
Concern at the tax loopholes being exploited by either side	1.2
Concern at inequality of private and institutional shareholders	1.2

Note: Sample, 425 articles

In effect, the capture of the story, by corporate PRPs and the City more generally, resulted in a closed financial 'elite discourse network'. The parameters of the debate were narrowly defined by the fact that both news sources and news audiences were predominantly from the financial sector. Despite there being a high level of both conflict and critical debate, many City norms were perpetuated and remained unchallenged. All others with a stake, including employees, customers and legislators, could not participate in the debate and, most of the time, were not even aware of it. Thus, the effects of the takeover on 80,000 employees and millions of customers, and the voting intentions of 75,000 private shareholders (many of them loyal Forte customers), were virtually ignored.

The material consequences

The material consequences of the whole takeover process very much reflected the inherent balance of power suggested by this closed 'elite discourse network'. The biggest beneficiaries were in fact the large trading institutions. For the whole sixty-day period Forte and Granada shares were heavily bought and sold. Two days before the bid Granada were trading at 680p per share. They ended, two days after the bid was accepted, at 714p per share – a modest, but respectable increase of 5 per cent. Forte moved from 260p two days before the bid to 402p two days after – a rise

---

15 The Forte family made regular donations to the Conservative Party and Thatcherite think tanks. Olga Polizzi had even redecorated 10 Downing Street for Mrs Thatcher. Charles Forte was made a lord and Rocco Forte knighted during the Thatcher administration. The Fortes regularly dined with politicians, nobility and business leaders across the UK and abroad.

of 54 per cent. The total increased value of the two stocks over a 64-day period thus amounted to £1.534 billion – the vast majority of which was gained by institutional shareholders. Although private shareholders stood to gain too, the great majority of them actually backed Forte.

The other clear winners were the advisers. Estimates of total advisers' fees for both sides were £155 million.[16] Similar fees, of between £1 million and £3 million, were given to each firm of accountants, lawyers and PR consultants – much more to financial advisers and underwriters. Estimates for Brunswick are between £1.75 million and £2 million, and for Citigate, between £800,000 and £1 million. More fees were to be expected when Granada began its disposals programme of large parts of Forte. The final beneficiaries were the senior managements of both companies. Most of the directors on both sides had share holdings in their companies and, likewise, would have seen substantial rises in their personal income. Gerry Robinson, voted the thirteenth most powerful man in Britain (Hutton 1998), added to his growing reputation in the City with yet another successful takeover. The Forte family, although they had lost their business, came away with over £300 million from the sale of their shares. Rocco Forte has since gone on to found a new, international, upmarket hotel chain called RF (Rocco Forte) Hotels. At the time of the research the chain had, in a period of eighteen months, expanded to a total of eight luxury five-star hotels.

The most obvious victim in the battle was the sixty-year-old Forte company along with its 38,000 employees. By the time the conflict was over, the stakes had become so high that, whatever the outcome, either company would be forced to carve up Forte and sell off large parts of it. During the bid, in an effort to stay afloat, Forte began disposing of what would have amounted to 40 per cent of its assets. It also offered to give away its Savoy shares to loyal Forte shareholders and committed itself to raise dividend payments by 20 per cent a year for three years. Granada, on the other hand, had to take on significant debts in order to buy Forte and also pledged a special dividend to shareholders as part of its raised offer. It eventually became apparent that, to pay for this, Granada expected to dismantle and dispose of between 45 per cent and 60 per cent of its new acquisition. In fact, over the next two years it made sales of £1.75 billion – or 46 per cent of the Forte empire. Neil Bennett, in the *Sunday Telegraph* (14.1.96, p2), was thus led to comment: 'On the one side Granada is taking on debts of £3 billion just so it can sell more than half of what it is buying: on the other Forte is naturally disembowelling itself with a fire sale of businesses, a massive share buy back and reckless commitment to increase dividends by 20 per cent a year. Whatever the outcome neither side will win.'

Additionally, Granada claimed it would make savings in the first year, from what remained of the company, of £100 million. Since Forte's profits at the time were £258 million for the whole of the company, it intended to increase profitability

---

16 £105 million was specified in Granada's documents. There were also a number of unconfirmed estimates of £50 million for Forte (Joyce, 1996, p1, *FT*, 1996, p8, Fildes, 1996, p23).

through quite considerable cuts. There were many ways and means by which the large debts incurred were paid off and the extra savings extracted. One obvious way was through job losses and by generally economising on staffing costs. According to Richard Power (interview, 30.11.98), as he described daily events at Forte during the sixty days:

> Every day a piece of news went down the line to employees – telling them both the good and the bad news … We knew that if we won the bid it was going to be a complete blood bath to make the profit increases we had promised. There were going to be lots of cuts and we would have to hack off bits of the business on all sides. But then we knew the same was going to happen if we lost and we thought it was better to do it from our side.

Thus, employees already working in two of the poorest paid and least secure industries (hotels and catering), were about to have job cuts and 'greater flexibility' imposed on them.[17]

The last to lose out were taxpayers. The plans of both companies involved making use of tax loopholes. These meant that one side or the other could claim to be paying shareholders more because the construction of their deals meant that certain fund-holders would not have to pay tax on the deals. According to Graham Searjeant of *The Times* (1996, p1), if Granada won the bid the takeover would have cost taxpayers up to £450 million. Unfortunately, such results were rarely looked at by the financial journalists involved. Most either ignored the implications or were prone to giving such advice as that expressed by the *FT*'s authoritative LEX column (10.1.96): 'No public interest is served by a loophole that involves taxpayers subsidising corporate raiders. But until the rules are changed, bidders would be mad not to exploit them to the full.'

Whether the takeover of Forte was in the best long term interests of Granada has been the subject of much comment and a few academic studies. Interview responses on this matter were divided according to company loyalties.[18] However, as this book goes to press, the long-term profitability of the merger for Granada looks in some doubt. In 1999 they participated in a £17.5 billion merger with the

17 As Richard Thomas (10.1.96), in one of only two articles to focus on employees during the period, reported: 'These are the pawns in the game being played by Forte and Granada – the people from whom "more value" is to be squeezed to boost profits. Those at the bottom of the pile already work long hours for lowly wages … the 312,000 people working in British hotels are at the cutting edge of the Conservative drive for a "flexible" labour market. Big leisure firms spearheaded the campaign for the abolition of the wages councils – which guaranteed minimum rates in industries like hotels and catering – and most vehemently oppose Labour's plans for a minimum wage and adoption of the social chapter.'

18 The Forte side generally believed that Granada paid too much and that, in the long run, its share price had underperformed the FTSE 100 average. Opinion at Granada was different. Within the year the company had managed to increase profits through savings by £124 million, made all its disposals at a 'full price' and had paid back £2.5 billion of its loans. Granada interviewees in 1998 argued that they had therefore made a prudent move that had ultimately produced a 'profitable and balanced business'.

catering group Compass to form Granada Compass. They have since been put under pressure to demerge and/or sell off parts of the group. Despite the subsequent demerger of part of Granada Media (with a proposal to demerge the rest in 2001) the share price of the new company has lost almost a third of its value in 2000 and new pressure has been put on the company to sell off the majority of what remains of the former Forte hotels business. In other words, current 'City opinion' and activity suggests that the original takeover has not been profitable for Granada in the long run. 'City opinion' backed the original takeover and 'City opinion' is now supporting quite different actions – but all in the name of City profits.

Conclusion

Although this takeover gained more media coverage than most in was not atypical in terms of its size or in terms of those who gained or lost most by it. 1995 was in fact a record year for merger and acquisition activity with deals worth £69 billion, or 10 per cent of the value of the stock market (three times that of the previous year) taking place – a figure that now appears small next to current levels of activity. Over £1 billion was paid out in City advisers fees alone. Seven of the principal institutions with shares in Forte were, in fact, amongst the ten largest fund managers in the UK and controlled £313 billion worth of funds – equivalent to 48 per cent of the value of the UK stock market at the time.[19] As stated, they, along with the armies of City advisers involved, made considerable profits from the takeover. Most studies of mergers and acquisitions similarly conclude (see Sudarsanam, 1995, Hutton, 1996) that the main beneficiaries in mergers and acquisitions are the managers of the acquiring business and the shareholders of the target company. The acquiring company rarely benefits in terms of innovation, output or growth. A recent study by KPMG (Buckingham and Atkinson, 30.11.99) typically found that, while 82 per cent of executives thought their acquisitions successful, only 17 per cent actually 'added value' in the long term.

Neither was there anything unique about the low level of mainstream coverage. In fact, this was one of the most high-profile takeovers of the decade, involving well-known consumer companies, employing 80,000 people and serving millions of customers. Even so, it still drew relatively little non-financial media attention. As Will Hutton was to exclaim amidst all the takeover activity at the time (Hutton 1995, p17):

> Hundreds of thousands of workers in a myriad of businesses have been subject to the uncertainty, dislocation and asset-sweating that take-over brings ... But this is not deemed mainstream news: nor has it forced itself into the wider political and intellectual culture ... neither the prevalence of take-overs nor the individual consequences of the companies concerned are reckoned to rank alongside, say, an

---

19 These were: (1) Prudential with £76 billion, (2) MAM with £72 billion, (5) Standard Life with £45 billion, (7) BZW with £34 billion, (8) Legal and general with £33 billion, (9) Hermes with £28 billion, (10) Gartmore with £25 billion.

exchange at Question Time over tax cuts or hospital closures as an economic and social event. It is a tragic myopia.

The benefit of corporate public relations to the corporate sector has thus slowly become clearer in chapters three to five. Corporate influence of journalists and the general public is only part of the equation. The main advantage that PR has brought to corporate elites has been to restrict access to the production and consumption of information about corporate activities. This is not generally achieved through covert control of, or organised conspiracy with, journalists. Indeed, corporate elites are in frequent competition and conflict, both with journalists and each other. Rather, business source advantages, business consumer needs, and financial journalist requirements have all combined to produce recurring patterns of corporate source dominance in the financial press. These patterns have resulted in significant financial and economic debates being confined to discussion amongst 'elite discourse networks'. Inside these networks there is little consideration of the consequences of decisions for the majority of the population. The example given here is takeovers but the implications for other forms of corporate activity and decision-making are quite pronounced. In all of this, corporate public relations has played a significant part. It has cultivated a financial media dependency on its steady supply of information subsidies and developed sophisticated techniques to encourage and block journalist access. PRPs have also identified the individuals and information that matter most to their corporate employers and have thus been an essential part of the process whereby closed 'elite discourse networks' are formed.

With the benefits of public relations for the corporate sector established, the question then becomes: can other groups acting in civil society also gain from the rise of public relations? Can 'resource-poor' and 'outsider' groups also use PR to increase their media access and therefore disrupt the elite discourse networks that form in news reporting? This is the question that occupies the third part of this book.

PART III

TRADE UNION PUBLIC RELATIONS

6

OUTSIDER AND RESOURCE-POOR GROUPS, TRADE UNIONS AND MEDIA–SOURCE RELATIONS

Part III asks: can 'outsider' and 'resource-poor' groups also use professional public relations as a means to achieve specific political and economic ends? Can they use PR to increase their media access, improve the quality of their coverage and, ultimately, influence 'elite discourse networks'? The focus for the research is the British trade union movement. Trade unions in the UK have been increasingly excluded from mainstream British politics, seen their resources decline significantly, and complained about negative media coverage for some decades. Thus, if unions can use public relations effectively, it is likely that PR would be useful to a variety of outsider and resource-poor groups attempting to influence media coverage and policy-making.

Chapter six therefore begins by evaluating the existing literature on industrial relations coverage, union communications, and media–source relations. The first section critically reviews the early work of the Glasgow University Media Group (GUMG) and other radical accounts of industrial relations reporting (from the mid-1970s onwards). Most of these studies concluded that the media were essentially hostile to unions and labour politics and, as a result, would only ever report unions negatively. Each therefore deduced that better union communications would not be particularly effective and that unions were better off pursuing other types of strategy to achieve their objectives.

In response, it is argued that the Glasgow Group's findings did not adequately explain the causes of media bias. While their claims of negative union reporting had some substance their explanatory frameworks tended to be flawed. Taking account of the more recent work on media–source relations, an alternative, and more optimistic, perspective emerges. In this it is suggested that the media were, and are, less inherently hostile to unions than previously suggested, and defamatory reporting was, in part, accounted for by the inadequacy of union communications. At a time when government and corporate sources were making increasing use of professional PR (see chapter two), poor union–media relations proved to be a significant cause of negative union coverage.

The second section returns to the debate by focusing on media–source relations literature – more particularly on research on 'resource-poor' and non-official sources. Even if the Glasgow Group's work offered an incomplete account, are unions still too disadvantaged as sources to make a meaningful impact on news texts? The findings of studies, from the 1970s to early 1990s, suggest that they are. A lack of economic resources and institutional legitimacy have been deemed to be almost insurmountable obstacles to such groups as they attempt to gain productive, long-term media access. As the third section concludes, while more recent research indicates that the potential for such groups to use professional communications is greater than hitherto acknowledged, they still suggest that that potential is limited.

Union communications and the Glasgow University Media Group thesis

Trade unions and the mass media: the Glasgow University Media Group thesis

Most radical research on industrial relations reporting in the UK has argued that (a) the national media is inherently biased against trade unions, and therefore, (b) union PR can make only a marginal impact on news production. These conclusions were initially formulated, and vigorously argued for, in the early work of the GUMG (GUMG, 1976, 1980, 1982, 1993, Beharrell and Philo, 1977). As several members of the group explained at the time (Philo, *et al.*, 1977, p136):

> there is little evidence to suggest that 'better communications' or closer working relationships between public relations departments and the media ever significantly change the character of media coverage … rendered meaningless in isolation within a framework of reporting that is fundamentally hostile to the aims which trade unions represent in industrial society.

The Group noted several trends during an extensive textual analysis of the 'contours' of news coverage. First, patterns of news coverage, which were remarkably similar across all channels, tended to focus overly on strikes and on particular industries (automobile, transport and public administration) at the expense of general industrial news and other industries. Second, strikes were always reported in a manner which undermined trade union positions. Images of unruly trade unionists, filmed on the shop floor and picket lines, were always juxtaposed with pictures of managers and ministers, giving interviews in calm and controlled office settings. The consequences of strike action for the general public were usually highlighted but the causes of the strike rarely explained. Third, management and government sources dominated the reporting of industrial and economic issues generally and therefore set the interpretive frameworks for news coverage. All these patterns meant that reports of strike action repeatedly gave the impression that powerful unionists were simply holding the country to ransom for personal gain. Similarly, in the wider reporting of the British economy, excessive wage claims and union obstructionism were to blame for, amongst other things, inflation and national economic decline. In contrast, government and/or management were rarely singled out as the cause of either industrial unrest or national economic difficulties.

These findings added up to a strong case of media bias against trade unions. The Group's explanations for this were based on a combination of 'cultural structuralist' and 'political economy' perspectives: the influence of 'dominant ideology' and the effects of corporate and state control over media organisations. According to the first of these approaches, as Walton and Davies explained (1977, p124), 'the general output of the mass media is ideological; but it is not consciously so. Rather, cultural assumptions of the dominant groups within our society are given privileged and central treatment.' As a result the ideas of 'dominant groups' tend to construct the normative frameworks through which journalists and consumers understand the world. Journalists, because 'they share a common culture with the most powerful groups and interests in society' (GMUG, 1982, p13), are further prone to reproducing those ideas. From a political economy perspective they also argued that dominant ideas were more consciously promoted by the direct control and ownership of the news-producing organisations. The BBC has never strayed too far from the reach of government control, and the press is owned and maintained by corporate conglomerates and media magnates pursuing free-market objectives. Ownership, coupled with advertiser pressure, dictates editorial appointments. Editors, in turn, employ journalists and take editorial lines favourable to corporate governing boards, advertisers and shareholders.

Whatever the explanation, the mass media appeared to be responsible for generating and perpetuating deep-seated prejudices against trade unions. The Group's core arguments were subsequently repeated and built upon by both media scholars and trade unionists. For example, reporting of the 1984–85 miner's strike in the UK was critically examined with the same conceptual framework advanced by the Glasgow Group (e.g., Curran *et al.*, 1986, Douglas 1986, Hollingsworth, 1986). Work in the USA (Puette, 1992, Parenti, 1993) produced very similar assessments about media coverage of unions. Studies by Winter (1990), Knight (1992) and Hackett (1992) also attempted to reproduce the Glasgow Group's findings in Canada. Winter, Desbarato, Waddell, and others (see Winter, 1990), looking at reporting of the issues pertinent to Canada's entry into the North American Free Trade Agreement (NAFTA), argued that coverage had strongly advanced the positions of corporate, free-trade advocates over those of unions and other pressure groups. Knight (1992) and Hackett (1992), looking more specifically at industrial reporting, concluded that union members were depicted as 'disruptive' and 'conflictive', whereas business sources were treated more neutrally, with greater authority and 'received more coherent treatment' generally.

In the UK in the 1990s, although the Group's work has been referred to less frequently, no major body of research has come to replace it. Indeed, its thesis is still periodically supported by similar studies of union reporting (see Seaton, 1991, Mitchell, 1997, Watts, 1997). As Seaton remarked (1991, pp256, 261), 'Union-bashing is one of the great conventions of the British media ... The "human interest" aspect of industrial affairs distorts real developments and changes to a kind of re-occurring moral fable, one in which unions are always the "baddies"'. The Group itself, in re-publishing much of its early work in a two-volume reader (Eldridge, 1995, Philo, 1995), has reinforced the standing of its thesis once again. Although offering a broader range of explanations for the causes of media bias, they still appear fairly sceptical about the ability of the left to influence the media with what Philo refers to (1995, p194) as 'the shallow science of imagistics'. Consequently, the conclusions about union communications also remain unaltered, i.e., any attempts to improve union reporting with PR are unlikely to be fruitful and precious resources are better employed elsewhere.

Re-evaluating the Glasgow Group thesis

While there exist many studies that document instances of anti-union media bias,[1] the Group's own empirical findings do not always support their interpretive frameworks. First, the trends noted in the content analysis reveal several things about news reporting, but do not concretely demonstrate that coverage is prejudicial. For example, similar patterns of news coverage across channels, and an overemphasis on strikes and certain industry sectors out of proportion to industrial activity in general, do not in themselves mean that journalists are antagonistic to unions. That managers are interviewed in their offices and union officials on picket lines, only indicates that individuals are interviewed in their natural surroundings – not a media attempt to de-legitimise striking workers (see similar arguments put in Harrison, 1985). That strikes are reported more than other industrial issues, and the consequences of action are covered more than the causes, indicates that 'news values' are driven by sensation and public interest rather than conscious attacks on the union movement. That trade unions are subject to negative and superficial reporting does not mean they alone suffer negative and superficial reporting (see chapter three, for example, on the reporting of businesses).

The claims that journalists were guided by dominant ideology were similarly vague and, at times, presented in a contradictory manner. At one point the Group accuses broadcasters of bias because industrial reporting is not an even reflection of reality; at another it demands that all minority opinions are reported equally. It rejects 'conspiracy' in favour of dominant ideology but then explains bias as resulting from the conscious acquiescence of journalists to owners and ministers. At one point it is suggested that management dictates to the media by maintaining its distance from journalists. At another, it is revealed that management views dominate because of greater media access.

Second, a closer examination of research on industrial relations reporting reveals that unions actually possessed distinct advantages in the news production process. As argued in chapter three, most journalists are, in general, not particularly pro-business. Indeed, as Philo *et al.* (1977, p140) noted at the time, 'people who work in the press and television are often themselves trade unionists'. More importantly, several

---

1 There are several accounts of the Thatcher government's close relations with editors of the predominantly right-wing press in the 1980s (e.g., Curran *et al.*, 1986, Douglas, 1986, Hollingsworth, 1986, Young, 1989, Curran and Seaton, 1997). Several 'liberal' and official studies of industrial relations reporting (Annan Report, 1977, McQuail, 1977, Weber, 1979) also offered muted support for the Group's claims about the way strikes were reported. There are also numerous political economy accounts of corporate and government influence over news producers and the dominance of institutional sources in reporting (see chapter one of this book).

studies (GUMG, and also Philo *et al.*, 1977, Annan Report, 1977, McQuail, 1977, Harrison, 1985, Jones, 1986, Seaton, 1991, Manning, 1998), have pointed out that industrial relations correspondents are closer and more sympathetic to unions than they are to business or government sources.[2] Additionally, a closer examination of the work of the Glasgow Group and others (GUMG, 1976, 1980, Annan Report, 1977, McQuail, 1977) reveals that, at the time, union sources actually gained more media access than business managers and government officials put together.[3] In fact, such was the media presence of union leaders in the 1970s, Hall *et al.* (1978) identified them as being amongst the nation's 'primary definers'. Such findings were also apparent in the data produced by several critical and institutional studies in Canada (see Tuchman, 1978, the 1981 Canadian Royal Commission on Newspapers in Ericson *et al.*, 1991, Hackett, 1992, Knight, 1992).

In effect, the Group's empirical evidence fails adequately to support its interpretive frameworks – regardless of whether its conclusions are accurate or not. The arguments about biased reporting patterns, vaguely accounted for by the notion of 'dominant ideology', are far too weak. Similarly, the influence of corporate owners and government officials over news production appear to have been countered, to a degree, by the closeness of reporters to unions at the time. Clearly, explanations for the negative reporting of unions, and for their poor public image[4] in the 1970s and 1980s, thus require further thought.

Trade unions and the mass media: a media–source relations perspective

An alternative, but in many ways complimentary, explanation can be developed by looking at industrial relations coverage from a media–source relations perspective. Subsequent to the publication of the Glasgow Group's early work, there has been renewed interest in the study of news sources (most significantly Ericson *et al.*, 1989, Hansen, 1993, Deacon and Golding, 1994, Miller, 1994, Schlesinger and Tumber, 1994). Much of this work suggests that a significant proportion of media bias is caused by uneven media–source relations and that those who are able to gain

---

2 For example: McQuail (1977, p139), 'It would seem as if reporters of industrial relations events are "closer" to local trade union officials than to Government or employers'; (Seaton, 1991, p263), 'Most industrial correspondents believe themselves and their colleagues to be politically on the left. They also argue that even journalists who enter the field for 'careerist' reasons develop an interest and respect for trade unionists'.

3 McQuail's study (1977, pp137–8), for example, offered the following results. Trades Union Congress officials/spokespersons and shop stewards accounted for 59 per cent of citations and 41 per cent of total 'mentions', 'reported statements' and 'quoted interviews'. Government ministers/Members of Parliament (MPs), CBI leaders/spokespersons, and managers/employers accounted for 24 per cent of citations and 38 per cent of the total category. Others, which included members of the public and workers, accounted for 17 per cent and 21 per cent respectively.

4 Between 1975 and 1984 MORI polls (Mori Poll Data, Sept. 1995) recorded that between 68 per cent and 82 per cent of people thought 'Trade unions have too much power in Britain today'. This included between 55 per cent and 73 per cent of trade union members. For the same period, between 60 per cent and 70 per cent thought 'Most trade unions are controlled by extremists and militants', including 55 per cent to 64 per cent of trade union members.

regular media access are also more likely to gain positive coverage and set news agendas. Applying this schema to the reporting of industrial disputes in the late 1970s and 1980s, it may be shown that most trade unions not only neglected the communications issue, they frequently took an adversarial approach in their deal-ings with journalists. Conversely, management and government devoted significant resources to managing the news (see chapters two and three). In effect, the anom-alies in the Group's findings, as well as much of the negative coverage of strikes and unions are, in part, explained by the unions' own communications failings.

For much of the twentieth century media hostility towards unions has been more than matched by union hostility towards the media.[5] As union membership grew, and industrial action increased through the 1960s and 1970s, mass media attention was further directed to unions and union leaders (see Manning, 1998, 1999). However, a mixture of union ignorance and hostility continued to inform union responses to media enquiries. Thus, when unions, in the mid-1970s, decided to address the problem of negative media coverage, they chose to attack the media rather than reor-ganise their public relations. The lead taken by the newly established TUC Media Working Group, one that seemed strongly influenced by the work of the Glasgow Group,[6] was that the media would always be biased against labour. Therefore trade unionists should monitor it, attack it and/or attempt to set up rival national newspa-pers controlled by unions (see TUC, 1977b, 1980a, 1980b, 1982, 1983).

As the last in a series of TUC publications (TUC, 1983) on the media explained: 'What this report sets out to do is discuss means of redressing legitimate grievances against the actions of the existing media – against abuses of their powers by particular newspaper articles and broadcast programmes.' In the early 1980s, much research was devoted to setting up and funding a new national newspaper – a project which was never realised (see McCarthy, 1984, Power and Sheridan, 1984). Several guides to the media were also produced, each aimed at educating union officials in media methods

---

5 For example, in 1923, a Labour Research Department pamphlet, entitled 'The Press' (p47) declared: 'Thus the sources of news are largely controlled by people who are closely associated with big capitalist interests and, like the proprietors of the newspapers themselves, are concerned to maintain the capitalist organisations of industry.' The combination of the BBC being forced to take the government's side in the 1926 General Strike and during the 1930s depression, coupled with the reactionary and dictatorial style of many 'press barons' in the interwar period (see Curran and Seaton, 1997), did not alter this view. In the post-war period, for example, the Labour Research Department declared (1946, p17): 'It is clear that the mere fact of the "independence" of a newspa-per may mean anything or nothing. A Tory newspaper representing big industrialists remains a Tory newspaper and, as such, hostile to the labour movement and the Labour Government'.

6 The output from the TUC Media Working Group (1978-90), and the statements supporting TUC Conference motions on the media, all bore close resemblance to the arguments expounded in the 'Bad News' series (see particularly TUC Congress Report, motion, pp552-3, 1975, Beckett, 1977, Griffiths, 1977, TUC, 1979b, Douglas, 1985, Myers, 1986). Philo, *et al.*, (1977, p136), clearly encouraged this approach: 'The severe limits of seeking improved communications with the media have driven some unions towards a "complaints strategy". This is a more positive and realistic approach to the problem in that it holds few illusions about the nature of "news" and journalistic practices within the media.'

(TUC, 1977a, 1979a, 1982, 1985, 1986). These were, however, minor efforts that drew far less interest than the more aggressive alternatives. None made mention of appointing experienced media professionals or of seeking outside advice. All explained themselves to sceptical unionists with the argument that 'the media is a nettle you must grasp – before it stings you' (TUC, 1979a, p5).

Continued union intransigence, at a time when government and businesses were increasingly employing professional PR techniques and personnel (see chapter two), resulted in a growing communication gap between unions and their opponents. The Glasgow Group's research into union communications (GUMG, 1976) revealed that the three largest unions, the Transport and General Workers' Union (TGWU), the Associated Union of Electrical Workers (AUEW), and the General Municipal Workers' Union (GMWU), had four media/press officers between them. Over a decade later, Manning's (1998) 1988 survey revealed that only seven of the thirty-seven largest unions had a full-time press officer. Verzuh's (1990) study of union communications noted that, in the 1980s, journalists had frequently experienced great difficulties in obtaining information and/or suffered personal abuse from union officials. These findings were corroborated by journalists (Harrison, 1985, Adeney and Lloyd, 1986, Hollingsworth, 1986, Jones, 1986, 1987) and even by the work of the Glasgow Group itself.[7] As Verzuh suggested (1990, p5): 'Significantly, the unions were unable to turn opinion around in their favour. Few had media relations officers with a mainstream media background. The tradition had been for the general secretary to make a call to a friendly reporter in a crisis. This lack of professionalism led to an increased deterioration in relations with the mass media.' In effect, hostility justified ignorance, and thus developed a vicious circle of declining media relations. The consequences were decreased access for unions, badly managed union images, poor presentation of union positions and weak communication with union members.

The communications imbalance between unions and their opponents was made abundantly clear during the National Union of Miners (NUM's) 1984–85 clash with the National Coal Board (see Adeney and Lloyd, 1986, Jones, 1986, Verzuh, 1990). While there is significant evidence that senior editors and proprietors kept abnormally close to Downing Street at the time (see Douglas, 1985, Hollingsworth, 1986, Young, 1989), the NUM's poor lines of communication were also a telling factor in the conflict. During the dispute the NUM had one press officer who also doubled as Arthur Scargill's assistant. The National Coal Board (NCB) began the dispute with six communications officers and ended it with twenty-five (COI, Sept. 1984, Sept. 1985). They also had the assistance of Tim Bell and Gordon Reece, advisers to the Conservative Party, advertising agency Lowe-Howard-Spink-Campbell-Ewold and

---

7 Hollingsworth (1986, p 242), 'One *Guardian* journalist described the situation as "excruciating … wherever you went you were told to fuck off and sometimes hit"'; Harrison (1985, p77), 'Whatever the failings of the broadcasters, few unions could at that time have claimed to honestly have had any sustained or concerted effort to meet the needs of television … a TUC survey in 1984 showed that in many unions internal and external relations remained a low priority'.

much of the output of the government's own communications machine. The NCB spent £4,566,000 on advertising (Jones, 1986), while the NUM rejected any attempt at a publicity campaign. Reporters were forced to use 'official' figures because the NUM had no reliable information on the activities of its own members.[8]

Clearly, there was some justification in claiming that there existed an anti-union consensus amongst official sources, and much negative coverage of unions during the 1970s and 1980s. However, union action during this period only encouraged more critical and/or ignorant reporting. Although unions had close links with industrial reporters, and they were widely reported and cited, they merely squandered these advantages. They were thus perceived to be a powerful force in British politics – but a force that had little sense of public accountability, and did not take the time to communicate its case to members or the general public. By the early 1990s, even industrial relations researchers had begun to notice that poor union communications had become a major obstacle to union campaigning.[9]

Unions as outsider/resource-poor sources

Even if poor union communications have played a large part in the production of negative news, will improved union PR make a significant difference? Past studies of the attempts of 'outsider' and 'resource-poor' groups to use the media have produced rather bleak prognoses. Research has commonly found that such groups are so disadvantaged, in terms of economic and institutional resources, that they are unlikely to make more than a minor or temporary impact on news production. Unions, meanwhile, have become considerably weakened over the last two decades – losing precious resources, institutional legitimacy and power. As marginalised and 'resource-poor' groups, much of the existing literature suggests that unions are now even less likely to make a strong impact on news texts – regardless of whether or not they improve their communications.

Resource-poor and outsider group media relations: radical pessimism

Early work in the USA (see Goldenberg, 1975, Gitlin, 1980) found that 'outsider' and 'resource-poor' groups, when attempting to gain media access, were severely

---

8 Jones explains (1987, pp6–8): 'The management had succeeded in dictating the pace and so exposed the weakness of Mr Scargill: his communications strategy was based on one person, himself ... Why did the media concentrate on the Coal Board's figures? The point was that the NUM had no figures of its own. In the big urban areas it did not even know the home addresses of its own members ... It was management that had the monopoly of that information. So during the strike the NUM could not even post its own members a copy of *The Miner.*'

9 Bassett and Cave (1993, p17), 'In part because their [trade unions'] overall organisation as public affairs lobbyists is so poor ... their effectiveness as a single-issue pressure group, advocating employees' interests, is now probably less than other bodies ... It is certainly considerably less than organisations such as the newly revitalised Confederation of British Industry'; Taylor (1994, p178), 'Britain's trade unions have not been very effective in recent years in presenting a public face to the world. Too many of them for too long were careless of what people thought about them.'

impeded by a number of factors. For Goldenberg (1975), the key disadvantage for smaller pressure groups was resources. Lack of finance hampered background research, promotional operations and a sense of official authority – all of which hindered attempts to form regular media contacts and gain long-term media coverage. Several other studies (Fishman, 1980, Gandy, 1980, Herman and Chomsky, 1988, Tiffen, 1989, Miller, 1994, Deacon, 1996, 1999) have also emphasised the correlation between economic resources and public relations efficacy. Greater resources mean more communications equipment and professional personnel which, in turn, mean more media contacts, greater production of news information subsidies, multiple modes of communication and continuous media operations. As each concluded, extreme variations in the possession of economic capital mean that well-resourced organisations can inundate the media and set agendas while the attempts of resource-poor organisations become quickly marginalised.

Miller (1994, pp132–3), for example, recorded that in Northern Ireland in 1989, Sinn Fein, with five voluntary press staff and a budget of £7,000, attempted to compete against official government sources with 145 communications staff and a £20 million budget. Herman and Chomsky (1988, pp20–1) make a similar point about the US military and its oppositions. In the early 1980s, the US Air Force produced 150 times as many press releases as its two strongest challengers combined (the National Council of the Churches of Christ [NCCC], and American Friends Service Committee [AFSC]) and held ninety-four times as many press conferences. During that period, the AFSC had eleven staff, compared to the last known figure for the Air Force of 1,305 (recorded in 1968). The differences take on greater significance in times of conflict – when companies and government departments rapidly employ more PRPs and/or hire consultancies to manage crises. Miller (1994, p78) found that, as tensions heightened in Northern Ireland, between 1968 and 1971, the British army increased its press staff from two to forty. Jones (1986) similarly observed that the National Coal Board was able to call on extensive communications resources in its conflict with the National Union of Miners in 1984–85.

Currently in the UK, even though smaller organisations are increasingly drawn to using PR consultancies and employing PRPs, most continue to be effectively deterred from operating large-scale professional operations. In 1997, the average fee per client for a small PR consultancy was £17,781. The larger firms averaged £72,629 per client (PRCA, *Year Book*, 1998). The PRCA also calculated that the costs involved in maintaining an in-house department in 1994 worked out at £42,000 per head (BDO Stoy Hayward Management Consultants, 1994). Thus the market determines that professional PR in Britain continues to be a service that is only affordable to large institutions and businesses.

The second factor that hinders smaller, outsider sources is their lack of legitimacy in the eyes of reporters. Gitlin (1980) and Goldenberg (1975) identified a strong link between an organisation's legitimacy and authority and its ability to gain regular and favourable coverage. It was thus clear to both that outsider sources struggled to gain regular media access, because they could never gain more than a fraction of the legitimacy that was naturally conferred on institutional and some corporate sources. Their research was echoed in the work of Hall *et al.* (1978) on media coverage of mugging in the UK. Hall *et al.* (1978) explained that journalists, in their search for 'objective' and 'authoritative' accounts, automatically sought out institutionalised sources. These sources, already legitimated by their power, representativeness and expertise, became the 'primary definers' of news agendas. Alternative sources, and journalists themselves, could only respond to those agendas and frameworks already determined. Thus, official source dominance resulted from the media's 'structured preferences' for the opinions of the 'dominant class'.

As many subsequent studies have shown, non-official sources find it difficult to maintain group consensus while simultaneously gaining media access and media legitimacy. What Cracknell (1993) called a conflict between 'commanding attention' and 'claiming legitimacy' has been repeatedly experienced by student groups in the USA (Gitlin, 1980), terrorist groups in Northern Ireland (Miller, 1994), international environmental groups (Anderson, 1993, 1997, Cracknell, 1993, Wykes, 2000), and by groups dealing with HIV and AIDs (Miller and Williams, 1993, 1998). In each case, certain strategies – demonstrations, acts of civil disobedience, the promotion of individual leaders, industrial action and terrorist acts – while achieving media coverage, were also prone to further de-legitimise particular groups in the eyes of the media and/or risked internally destabilising those groups in the long term. There is also the related difficulty of properly explaining a complex story and focusing media attention on the issues rather than the activities and personalities (see also accounts by Harding, 1998, Phillimore and Moffatt, 2000, Wilson, 2000).

A third, more general set of 'outsider' source disadvantages has been highlighted by the work of media sociologists. The state, many of its institutions and large corporations will always have the political, legal and financial means with which to apply pressure to journalists, influence their movements, and/or court them (e.g., Curran *et al.*, 1986, Herman and Chomsky, 1988, Nelson, 1989, Miller, 1994, Eldridge, 1995, Philo, 1995). Institutions also have a 'bureaucratic affinity' (Fishman, 1980) with media organisations, i.e., they attract journalists because they are usually physically accessible, well resourced, and provide a regular supply of information subsidies (Sigal, 1973, Fishman, 1980, Ericson *et al.*, 1989, Tiffen, 1989). As a result, of such political, legal and bureaucratic factors 'outsider' groups are further obstructed in their attempts to gain comparable media access.

Trade unions as resource-poor and outsider pressure groups

In fact, since the Glasgow Group's work was completed, unions have become both weaker and more excluded from the political process. They have lost funds and members, had the strike weapon impeded and links with government eroded, and lost what institutional legitimacy they formerly possessed (see accounts in Bassett and Cave, 1993, Millward, 1994, Taylor, 1994, McIlroy, 1995). They have thus lost their 'primary definer' status and increasingly come to resemble the 'outsider' and 'resource-poor' pressure groups discussed above.

Trade union memberships, finances and traditional methods of industrial action have all steadily declined. In 1979, at their post-war peak, unions had 13.2 million members and union density was 56.9 per cent nationally. By 1992, membership had dropped to 9.5 million members and density to 41.8 per cent – 34.19 per cent among TUC affiliated unions (McIlroy, 1995, pp20–6). Changing employment patterns have fractured and dispersed memberships across middle-class, service-sector professions – often leaving members working in small firms and on a part-time or temporary basis (Millward, 1994, Taylor, 1994). Legislation, in conjunction with changing patterns of employment and union membership, have combined to blunt the strike weapon severely and change the shape of British industrial relations. A series of ten employment and trade union acts, passed between 1980 and 1995, imposed extremely tight restrictions on union industrial action and, unsurprisingly, strike activity has declined rapidly since 1979. By the mid-1990s, the average annual number of stoppages and working days lost had returned to the levels of the 1950s, and 1993 recorded the lowest rates since statistics began (McIlroy, 1995, pp120–1). In Millward's view (1994, pp5–6): 'there were major and probably irreversible changes in employee relations during the 1980s ... Indeed so great were these changes that it is not unreasonable to conclude that the traditional distinctive "system" of British industrial relations based on collective bargaining is no longer characteristic of the economy as a whole'.

The institutional legitimacy of unions has also been denied by their steady exclusion from government and mainstream party politics. This process accelerated rapidly when the Thatcher government ended the tripartite post-war consensus – declaring the end of the commitment to full employment and war on unions (Young, 1989, Middlemas, 1991, Taylor, 1994). Ministerial communication with unions was immediately reduced. Government institutions, concerned with industrial relations – such as the National Economic Development Council (NEDC), industrial training boards, Arbitration and Concilliation Advisory Services (ACAS), the Manpower Services Commission and the National Enterprise Boards – were either abolished or had union representation reduced and/or cut altogether. Joining a union was no longer considered a 'right'. Indeed unions, and union activity in general, were denied legitimacy in the 1990 and 1993 Acts. After the collapse of the Wilson government, unions also came to be regarded as a liability for the Labour Party and connections were slowly cut there too (Minkin, 1991).[10] Labour also dropped its commitments to full employment and to reversing much anti-union legislation. As Taylor was to comment (1994, p164): 'In no other country in Europe have unions had to face such hostility from their government. Uniquely Britain also remains the one country where the role of trade unions in national life is still questioned.' With the decline of union power, reduced strike activity and a distinct lack of institutional legitimacy, the media have consequently lost interest in

---

10 By the mid-1990s more than 50 per cent of funding for the Labour Party was gained from sources other than the unions (reduced from 95 per cent in 1979) and, following the Nolan Report, union sponsorship of individual MPs was ended.

union activities. Indeed, coverage of unions and industrial relations has been wound down to the point of extinction (see Jones, 1987, Manning, 1998, 1999).

In effect, by the start of the 1990s, unions had become doubly disadvantaged as sources. On the one hand, poor union–media relations had become the norm and negative public images had become entrenched over decades. On the other hand, unions had lost many of the economic, political and institutional resources that would help reverse such trends. It was thus clear that, in the new public relations environment, they would have to struggle to get media access and favourable coverage. Under such circumstances radical observers appeared to have some justification for being sceptical about the value of improved communications for unions.

Radical pluralist optimism and non-official source strategies

This pessimistic prognosis, in the light of more recent work on media–source relations, now requires rethinking. As Schlesinger (1990, see also Schlesinger and Tumber, 1994, Curran, 1996) explained, such findings, left alone, risked repeating the mistakes of 'cultural structuralists' and 'radical functionalists'. In a critique of Hall *et al.* (1978), that was also applicable to the work of the Glasgow Group, Schlesinger put the following arguments. Primary definers, being often in conflict, did not speak with one voice; neither did they retain the same levels of access over time, let alone possess equal amounts of access. Similarly, journalists and non-official sources were not always relegated to positions of subordinancy and counter-definition, but did, on occasion, challenge official accounts. In effect, the work of Hall *et al.*, the Glasgow Group and other critical work on sources, gave an unduly determinist picture that did not account for change and the 'dynamic processes of contestation in a given field of discourse'.

Instead, work by Schlesinger and others, in the 1990s, not only produced an alternative radical pluralist perspective, but observed several instances of resource-poor and outsider groups successfully employing more professional communications. The elements of this alternative thesis have developed out of the following: (a) discussions of elite sources in the USA (Nacos, 1990, Hallin, 1994); (b) studies of environmental pressure groups (Anderson, 1993, 1997, Hansen, 1993, 2000); and, above all, (c) comparative studies of official and non-official sources in Britain (Miller and Williams, 1993, Miller, 1994, Schlesinger and Tumber, 1994). All three approaches have suggested means by which a 'more dynamic process of contestation' in given 'fields of discourse' takes place. As such, each offers an explanation of how sources such as unions may gain access to a media production process that was traditionally dominated by 'elite discourse networks'.

Anderson (1991, 1993, 1997), Miller (1993, 1994) and Schlesinger and Tumber (1994), have observed non-institutional source strategies for building up media contacts and attempting to develop authoritative media profiles. Each (see also Wilson, 1984, Hansen, 1993, 2000, Miller and Williams, 1993, 1998) documented cases of smaller pressure groups and charities successfully accumulating in-house media-relations expertise and sustaining journalist contacts over a period of time.

Additionally, they found that repeated positive appearances in the media brought long-term benefits. By providing a constant supply of information subsidies (news stories and research) to journalists, outsider groups managed to establish themselves in media discourses as legitimate sources. This process in itself encouraged a higher media profile and usually resulted in a further increase in institutional legitimacy. It was also observed that access, legitimacy, and the ability to set agendas could be further improved by collective action amongst resource-poor groups. If well co-ordinated, such groups could combine, seemingly to isolate a government or corporation in a particular media discourse.

These studies each presented examples of pressure groups developing quite sophisticated media strategies, which effectively identified them to the media as reliable and authoritative sources in particular subject areas. Miller and Williams (1993, 1998) observed such strategies being applied by the Terrence Higgins Trust. Schlesinger and Tumber (1994) found the same with trade associations/unions, such as the National Association of Probation Officers (NAPO), the POA and the Police Federation, and by pressure groups, such as the National Association for the Care and Resettlement of Offenders (NACRO) and the Prison Reform Trust. Cracknell (1993) and Anderson (1993) offered similar accounts of the development of media strategies by Friends of the Earth and other environmental groups. All these organisations have managed to establish positive media profiles without necessarily resorting to dramatic stunts or actions. Along with organisations such as Amnesty, Liberty, the British Medical Association (BMA) and the First Division Association of Civil Servants (FDA), each has shown that a steady accumulation of media capital may go some way towards overcoming traditional institutional advantages.

In effect, institutional legitimacy and authority is likened to a form of 'cultural capital' (Bourdieu, 1979, 1993) that is itself linked to, but not simply determined by, economic capital. In theory, such media/cultural capital can be accumulated and lost over time. Just as research indicated that non-official sources could use public relations methods to accumulate such capital, so studies have also looked at the ways official sources could lose it. Hallin (1994), for example, explained that news producers became more critical of institutional sources during the Vietnam War because of dramatic 'shifts in elite consensus' amongst official sources. In the UK, a number of studies have similarly highlighted tendencies for institutional conflict (either internally or with external allies) resulting in PR strategies becoming inconsistent and journalists becoming more critical. Schlesinger and Tumber (1994) noted differences between civilians and police officers engaged in public relations activities on behalf of the police services. Deacon and Golding (1994), Kavanagh (1995) and Jones (1995) observed frequent conflicts, involving professional PRPs, civil servants, advisers and politicians, taking place within political parties and governments.

More obviously, disparate departments or state institutions, like different corporate sectors, may have conflicting communications objectives. Miller (1993, 1994), Schlesinger and Tumber (1994), Deacon and Golding (1994) and Miller and

Williams (1993, 1998) have shown, in the continuing conflict in Northern Ireland, ongoing debates on the criminal justice system, opposition to the introduction of the community charge in the late 1980s, and in debates on AIDS/HIV respectively, that clear disagreements have surfaced between government departments. In these cases, individuals and institutions have come to be regarded as 'unreliable' by journalists and, on occasion, been seen to lose their standing as legitimate sources altogether. In effect, official sources frequently waste their economic and institutional resource advantages by engaging in conflict amongst themselves (see also part II of this book). At such times, outsider groups, if they have pursued clear PR strategies and built up legitimate media profiles, are able to challenge official media discourses.

As several studies have shown, such groups have indeed managed to achieve such interventions – occasionally to the point of managing to dictate agendas and affect government and corporate policy-making. The Campaign for Lead-free Air's (CLEAR's) campaign for lead-free petrol (Wilson, 1984), Greenpeace's success in halting Shell's plans for the Brent Spar oil rig (Anderson, 1997, Hansen, 2000), and the Snowdrop campaign that resulted in the banning of handguns (Thomson *et al.*, 1998) are three examples of government and corporate policies being altered as a result of skilled PR campaigns on the part of lesser-resourced organisations. Several other campaigns, while not necessarily achieving their ultimate goals, have similarly managed to embarrass governments and corporations – from the Greater London Council's (GLC's) successful 'battle for public opinion' (Curran, 1990a) to environmental groups obstructing the introduction of genetically modified foods. Thus, as some authors argue (Shoemaker, 1989, Blumler, 1990, Scammell, 1995) there appears significant potential for a range of interest groups, including unions, to use PR to gain a level of media access that was hitherto denied them. In Shoemaker's words (1989, p215): 'Journalistic routines (such as news-beats) result in media content that reinforces the status quo and limits media access to new ideas and organisations off the 'beaten' path. As a result, public relations efforts may be the only realistic strategy for a group to get media coverage.'

New unionism and new communication

In the last decade it has became apparent that unions, like many pressure groups, have indeed begun taking their communications more seriously. Many unions went through extensive restructuring processes and began employing more specialists and consultants (see Bassett and Cave, 1993, Jim Conway Foundation, 1993, Taylor, 1994, McIlroy, 1995) – including in the once ignored area of public relations.

The end of the TUC Media Working Group appeared to coincide with a new attitude towards the media. As Manning (1998, introduction) noted, indications are that unions have developed their public relations work quite considerably since he completed his fieldwork in the early 1990s. The TUC, for example, was relaunched in 1994 as a 'campaigning and public affairs organisation'. In addition to investing £300,000 in computer and communications technology, the newly created 'Campaigns and Communications Department' was expanded from six to ten with an annual budget of £260,000 (*PR Week*, 9.8.96, p9 and 23.8.96, p1) – all carried out at a time of general organisational cuts. Professional PR has been present at all stages, with Burson-Marsteller, Delaney-Fletcher-Bazell, Two-Ten and CARMA all providing consultancy services to the new department.

The external signs of improved union communications, more generally, are to be found in the recent increase in union advertising and the development of union journals. In 1970, the TGWU was the only union listed in the annual advertising records of Media Expenditure Analysis Limited (MEAL). During the 1980s, the TUC, the National Graphical Association (NGA), the National Union of Railwaymen (NUR), National Association of Local Government Officers (NALGO) and the BMA had all joined the TGWU as significant purchasers of advertising space (*MEAL Digest*). During the 1990s, the National Union of Teachers (NUT), Association of Electricians Union (AEU) and newly formed UNISON also became listed. Between 1990 and 1996, the largest union UNISON spent between £775,000 and £1,965,600 each year on advertising. Greater efforts have also been made to communicate with union memberships – as evidenced by the investment in union journals. A number of commentators have signalled the recent improvement in journal output as both content quality and circulation have risen (Marsh and Gillies, 1983, Rice, 1984, Labour Research Department, Aug. 1991, Aug. 1993, Taylor, 1994). Between 1981 and 1993, the ratio of journal copies to members, amongst the largest unions, increased from 1 copy/2.3 members to 1 copy/1.47 members.[11] Additionally, a far greater percentage of journals are now being sent direct to members' homes.[12]

Conclusion

Clearly, whatever their reservations about the media, indications are that unions have begun investing in their communications. How widespread and how effective new union public relations is has yet to be gauged. In fact, as already noted, there has been virtually no concentrated study on the use of professional public relations by 'outsider' and 'resource-poor' groups of any description. Almost all the studies of sources mentioned were produced prior to the very recent expansion of non-official professional PR and/or chose not to focus on the issue. Thus, research has thus far failed fully to explore the consequences for such groups of the recent arrival of the non-official PRP class, or relate this development to changing media–source relations.

At present, although several recent studies have noted the opportunities that exist for non-official sources to make an impact on media texts, the inferences are

---

11 In 1981, the sixteen largest unions had a combined membership of 8,512,555 and a journal circula-
    tion of 3,683,952 issues (Marsh and Gillies, 1983). In 1993, the twenty largest unions had a
    combined membership of 6,852,836 and a journal circulation of 4,664,500 (figures from Labour
    Research, Aug. 1993).

12 The signs of improved union communications appear to be taking place roughly a decade after
    similar transformations were recognised in unions in the USA (see Douglas, 1986, Puette, 1992).

that: (a) that impact is likely to be correlated with an organisation's overall accumulation of economic, cultural and institutional resources; and, therefore, (b) those impacts will still be of a limited or temporary nature. The reasons for this caution, in regard to unions, have been outlined in this chapter. First, even though unions are less 'resource-poor' than many pressure groups, they are still considerably out-resourced by institutions and corporations. Second, they lack institutional legitimacy and, more importantly, there is a distinct lack of media interest in their activities. With smaller union numbers, greater distance from the centres of power, and an unofficial elite consensus that marginalises union concerns, far less natural coverage is being generated. Third, unions are still suffering from negative images built up over several decades. This in itself greatly handicaps union campaigning and offers ammunition to opponents. Thus, if unions cannot persuade journalists and gain media access, how can they hope to break into the 'elite discourse networks' that dominate financial and political decision-making?

As yet there appears little to confirm or deny this overall outlook. The next two sections therefore attempt to gather new empirical evidence on the subject of trade union PR in the late 1990s. The research offers data on the rise of professional public relations within the union movement and attempts to evaluate how, and to what degree, it is helping unions overcome their communications disadvantages. As such it produces material relevant to wider debates about the prospects for 'outsider' and 'resource-poor' groups in the new professional public relations democracy.

7

TRADE UNION PUBLIC RELATIONS –
RESISTANCE WITHIN NEWS PRODUCTION

This chapter examines the state of 'new' union communications in the late 1990s and considers whether it has significantly raised the quantity and quality of union media access. As such it acts as an empirical focus for the evaluation of professional PR use by 'outsider' and 'resource-poor' groups. It is divided into three sections. The first of these describes the recent transformation of union communications and its current shape. It documents the widespread adoption of public relations by trade unions and attempts to gauge its level of professionalism. The second section asks: can trade unions overcome their various disadvantages and compete with corporate and government communications operations? What are the means by which they can gain sufficient access to the news production process, set news agendas, and ultimately come to influence decision-making processes within 'elite discourse networks'? The third section questions the effectiveness of new union communications. Is public relations a real alternative to traditional union methods or are precious resources better employed in other ways? Has better PR really aided union–media relations and improved public opinion of unions or have such trends been more the result of wider political and social changes?

The study was carried out using two methods: a survey[1] and a set of twenty-nine interviews.[2] Throughout this chapter, tables referred to in the text can be found in appendix II. During the research a number of specific campaigns were brought to light through a mixture of interviews and previously documented cases.

---

1 The survey questionnaire was sent out by post to all seventy-four affiliates (as listed in the 1997 'TUC Directory') in 1997. Fifty-four usable questionnaires, or 73 per cent of the total, were returned. Of the fifty-four respondents, twenty were Directors/Heads of Communication, seventeen were General Secretaries and seventeen had other titles ('researcher', 'communications assistant', etc.).

2 These included fouteen union PRPs, two union PR consultants, six general secretaries and seven (one ex) journalists with long experience of industrial relations reporting. In total nineteen different unions were visited (one in four). Theses were selected so as to be broadly representative of all types of union according to five criteria (including size, union density, private or public sector, and professional classification).

3 These include: the ambulance drivers' dispute (1989), the POA and Group 4/prison privatisation (1993), the General and Municipal Boilermakers' Union (GMB) and various 'fat cats' campaigns (1993–99), the UCW and its thwarting of Post Office privatisation (see chapter eight), Associated Society of Locomotive Engineers and Firemen (ASLEF) and the NUR's 'Save Our Railways' campaign against rail privatisation (1992–99) and campaigns against London Transport (1995–96), the TUC's relaunch (1994), attempts by teachers' unions to stop education cuts (1994–95), British

Several of the findings recorded here are related to data gathered on those cases – some successful, others not so.[3]

The state of union communications in the late 1990s

As this part demonstrates current union communications bears little resemblance to that observed in the 1970s and 1980s (in GUMG, 1976, 1980, Jones, 1986, 1987, Verzuh, 1990, Seaton, 1991, Manning, 1998). On all scales, from attitudes and approaches to resources and professionalism, union PR has been transformed in the last decade. Regardless of their uneasy relationship with the media, unions have made improved PR a priority of 'new unionism'. This has involved employing more people for PR work and increasing communications expenditure at a time of frequent staff and budget cuts. It has also involved the employment of former journalists and PRPs, media training programmes, and contracting work out to established PR consultants.

Media contact

Currently, the degree of union–media contact is high and union enthusiasm for public relations methods appears strong. Looking at figure 7.1 (chart of table A.1 in appendix II), over two-thirds (67.9 per cent) of unions are in contact with the media on at least a weekly basis. Large unions (100 per cent), professional/managerial unions (77.8 per cent) and public sector unions (75 per cent) all have more contact than small, private sector (53.8 per cent) and manual unions (63.2 per cent). Even small unions are likely to have contact a few times a year, and less than 2 per cent of unions said that they had no contact with the media at all.

Resources, expenditure and investment

Union restructuring has, in the majority of cases, involved the employment of more people to deal with communications (see figure 7.2). At the time of the survey only 9.3 per cent of unions stated that they had 'no PR function' – all but one of

Figure 7.1 Degree of union contact with the media

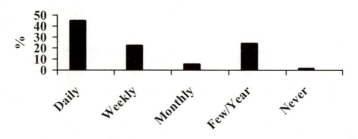

Airline Pilots Association (BALPA) and the TGWU's campaign against British Airways (1996 and 1997), the Banking, Insurance and Finance Union's (BIFU's) blocking of the Lloyd's takeover of Midland Bank (1992), and several smaller local campaigns led by UNISON, the GMB and NAPO, amongst others.

Figure 7.2 Numbers of people involved

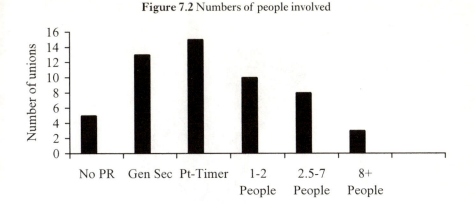

those were small unions. Thirty-seven per cent (75 per cent of large unions) had their own PR departments and 24.2 per cent employed an agency or individual (full or part-time) to carry out the union's public relations work. Only 29.6 per cent (57.2 per cent of small unions) left it to the General Secretary and/or an assistant to deal with PR – the norm a decade earlier. Looking at figure 7.2 (table A.3 in appendix II), the norm (66.7 per cent) is now to employ at least one person part-time to deal with communications. Just over a fifth (20.4 per cent) employ more than two full-time people in their communications departments. If General Secretaries are given a value of 0.25 and part-timers 0.5, then the total number of communications staff employed in the returning unions comes to 114.75 – an average of 2.125 people per union.

Investment in public relations operations has also been significant in the last decade. Few unions were able to supply exact information on communications budgets – thus making any summary of expenditure unrepresentative. Of those given, annual budgets ranged from £16,000, for a union with less than 3,000 members, to £3.4 million for one of the largest unions. More information was, however, forthcoming about changing trends in expenditure. Union investment in public relations began taking place in the 1980s and became more widespread in the 1990s. 47.8 per cent of unions increased their PR expenditure in the 1980s (table A.4 in the appendix II), while the rest remained static or decreased spending moderately. This rose substantially in the 1990s (see figure 7.3 – table A.5 in appendix II). Over this period 76.6 per cent of unions increased their communications resources – half of those 'greatly'. It appears that major investments were more likely to be made by large unions in the 1980s. More recently it has been medium (80 per cent) and small (88 per cent) unions that have increased their communications budgets. Public sector unions (93.3 per cent) have also increased their budgets more than private sector ones (69.6 per cent). Single sector unions (90 per cent), i.e. those with a clearly identifiable membership such as teachers or postal workers, have invested more than those with more mixed memberships (52.9 per cent). Future investment (see table A.6 in appendix II) is less widespread but still positive,

Figure 7.3 'In the 1990s, PR/communication resources have ...'

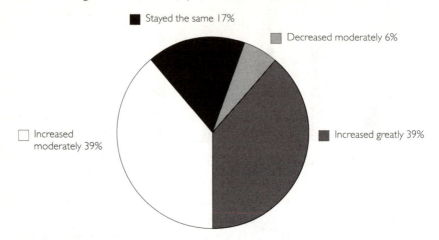

with 67.4 per cent expecting increases in communications resources over the next five years (80 per cent of public sector unions, 81 per cent of professional/managerial and non-manual unions), and only 2.2 per cent expecting a moderate decrease. Once again it was the medium and smaller unions which were most keen on making future investments.

Professionalism

Communications is one of many areas where the traditional practice of filling posts with career unionists has been altered in favour of employing professionals and specialists. Departments have more employees with a media and/or public relations background, and are more likely to offer specialist training for those without experience. As figure 7.4 (table A.7 in appendix II) shows, 63.4 per cent of unions

Figure 7.4 Background experience of staff dealing with communications/PR

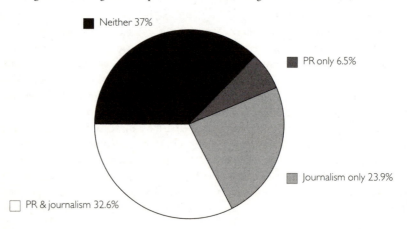

employ people with relevant skills. Size was an obvious factor separating unions here with 83.3 per cent of large unions, but only 35.7 per cent of small ones, employing people with experience. Significantly, although public sector unions tended to be amongst those unions most enthusiastic about PR, they had the least experienced staff. 66.7 per cent of them had staff with no PR or journalistic experience, while only a third of private sector unions lacked experienced personnel. Additionally, 55 per cent of unions offered training for those communications staff with no prior media/PR experience.

Prior to the survey, the research had already identified a number of examples of unions using PR consultancies traditionally more associated with the corporate sector. These included: work by GJW Public Relations for the ambulance drivers during their dispute in 1989; the NUT's use of Ian Greer Associates (*PR Week*, 24.5.96, p1); Lowe Bell's work for the Royal Maritime and Transport Worker's Union (RMT), NUT (*PR Week*, 28.4.95, p1) and UCW (IPR, 1995a); and Burson-Marsteller's contract with the TUC (*PR Week*, 23.8.96, p1).

The use of professional consultancy services was also very much in evidence in the survey. A quarter (25.9 per cent) of unions used PR consultancies. More than half (57.4 per cent) employed other types of agency/consultancy for communications work. The most commonly used suppliers of services were press cutting agencies (used by 31.5 per cent of unions), advertising agencies (27.8 per cent) and lobbying firms (27.8 per cent). Other agency services included media training, media distribution, media evaluation, design and publishing, and polling/market research. Several agency names came up frequently, thus suggesting a growth of union-PR links and the development of a consultancy sector specialising in union communications. Commonly named agencies were Union Communications (PR/lobbying), Westminster Communications (PR/lobbying), Rowlands/Lowe-Bell (Lobbying), GPC Connect (lobbying), Romeike and Curtice (press cuttings), MORI (market research), Landmark Publishing, Delaney Fletcher Bazell (advertising), and TM&D (advertising).

Attitudes

A positive union attitude towards the use of public relations had been experienced by most interviewees and was reflected in the survey results. As John Monks, head of communications at UNISON (interview, 16.10.97), explained:

> The union has carried on a commitment to put its money where its mouth is. It recognises that members want to be kept informed, and the importance of its external influence for the public image of the union. There have been cuts but any cuts experienced have been felt across the board. But the union recognises that without this sort of work, the union wouldn't grow, thrive or influence anybody.

Whether used as an accompaniment to, or replacement for, other forms of union action, PR is now widely regarded as an effective campaigning method: 66.7 per cent 'agreed' or 'strongly agreed' (table A.8 in appendix II) that 'Good communications/PR is now essential for winning strikes/pursuing industrial action';

18.8 per cent 'disagreed'. Seventy-five per cent 'agreed' or 'strongly agreed' (table A.9 in appendix II) that 'PR/Communications is becoming the key union method for achieving political and industrial goals' (including 86.6 per cent of public sector unions and 87 per cent of professional/managerial and non-manual unions). Only 16.7 per cent disagreed. These results thus concurred with Mitchell's earlier survey (1997, p158) in which most union respondents regarded public relations as the 'most effective' type of political activity (see table 3.1 in chapter three).

Despite a positive change, however, about a third of those interviewed complained of continuing negative attitudes towards the media, conservative memberships, and entrenched union bureaucracies. As one head of communications explained (interview, 1997): 'There has also been the difficulty of shaking off union attitudes of old ... When it comes to the final decisions on implementation the old trade unionism comes back. It's lots of little fiefdoms and castles built on every level and all interfering with the professional side of communication. It can be like tiptoeing through a minefield.' Such difficulties often resulted in PR that was 'more reactive than active', 'low profile on purpose' and 'more on an ad hoc basis'. Some, especially those from professional PR backgrounds, described 'the majority of current union operations' as being 'full of amateurs' and 'positively Luddite'. Such things had impeded the development and efficiency of PR operations and suggested more of an uneasy truce between the media and unions – rather than a working relationship.

Summary

Generally, cautious union attitudes have been superseded by the view that investing in communications is 'vital' to improve relations with memberships, the media, and the public. The state of union communications has much improved since Manning's (1998) survey, a decade earlier, and certainly no longer resembles that recorded by the Glasgow Group a decade before that. As *PR Week* (9.8.96, p9) was thus led to conclude: 'there's been much talk of unions moving away from perceived "strong-arm tactics" to a new era of corporate campaigning. For years American unions have been employing high-profile media campaigns to achieve their aims and more recently their UK counterparts have recognised that there's more than one way to skin a (corporate fat) cat'.

However, as a result of diminishing resources and, in some cases, continuing tensions between PRPs and older bureaucracies, the adoption of 'new union' communications has not been consistent across the union movement. Actual professional public relations experience was contained in less than a third of unions overall. Amongst small unions, public sector unions and manual unions, the numbers of experienced staff were extremely low. The cumulative result is that most unions have indeed modernised their communications but that that progress has not been as wholehearted and professional as in many rival sectors – for example, amongst large corporations, political parties, environmental pressure groups and state institutions.

Overcoming communications disadvantages

Can union PRPs overcome their own specific source disadvantages, as well as the more general ones encountered by 'outsider' and 'resource-poor' groups? The evidence accumulated in interviews with practitioners confirms that all the problems discussed in chapter six still exist. Unions, when compared to their corporate and government opponents, continue to be disadvantaged in certain communications respects. However, interviewees also indicated that unions are learning to overcome their disadvantages. This is because they have (a) particular resource advantages of their own which they may exploit, and (b) they have discovered ways of overcoming their resource deficits by developing alternative PR strategies. In an increasing number of cases such advantages and strategies have in fact proved decisive during media conflicts in the 1990s.

Union PR disadvantages highlighted once again

As expected, the most commonly cited 'disadvantage' of union communications was resources. Government and corporate resources far outnumber those of most unions. As Lawrie Harries of the RMT explained (interview, 7.10.97): 'We will always be at a disadvantage in terms of resources. They will always outspend us.'[4] These resources are telling in several ways. As interviewees explained, opponents with greater financial resources could afford to pay for advocacy advertising, expensive communications equipment, glossy publications with wide distributions, and make direct contact with all involved. Most importantly, greater finances enabled the hiring of expensive PR consultancies and the employment of several communications staff. For example, ASLEF and the RMT, with three communications officers between them, had to compete with forty-seven communications staff at British Rail before its privatisation. The POA, NAPO and other 'law and order' unions, each with minimal communications support, regularly had to take on the Home Office with its forty-three staff. The NUT, with one and a half communications officers, were competing with thirty-seven in the Department of Education (figures from unions and COI, 1970–99). More staff brought extensive contacts, more bodies to answer phones and respond to enquiries, twenty-four hour operations for media monitoring and contact, and extensive research and support facilities.

The other major communications problem, recorded in interviews, was 'media bias' – most especially in the tabloid press. Most unions, even if they had invested heavily in communications, regarded the media with suspicion. As Olive Forsythe, of the NUT, explained (interview, 19.5.97): 'We're always at a massive disadvantage

---

4 See also: Craig Ryan (interview, 30.7.97), 'Another disadvantage is resources. We are a small union covering a wide stretch of London and elsewhere. We have to justify every penny we spend on PR'; Noel Howell (interview, 2.9.97), 'Resources. We don't have the same resources. We use the technology to make up for the fact that there are so few of us. But we can't afford to book newspaper adverts putting our case'; Andrew Murray (interview, 9.10.97), 'Companies have more resources. Companies are much larger. If we were in for a long-haul dispute it would be a determining factor'.

because we are largely dealing with a right-wing press which sees unions as only being concerned with their own interests ... An individual journalist might see, but it is an ingrained prejudice that is real.' While many stated a respect for, and fair coverage from, industrial relations reporters, the numbers of such specialist journalists had rapidly declined during the 1980s (see also Manning, 1999). Other journalists, especially those from the tabloids, tended to have little knowledge of industrial relations and were frequently just looking for negative stories. Union PRPs often spoke of 'despicable hacks', who tried to catch out General Secretaries, looked for picket-line shots of unruly strikers, and attacked unions regularly for their politics and Labour party connections.[5] These attacks had consistently undermined traditional union campaign methods and had forced unions on to the defensive.

Some of the journalists interviewed agreed that unions still had to battle to overcome the prejudices of media organisations. As Seamus Milne of the *Guardian* commented (interview, 13.5.99):

> At one level unions can't [compete] because the media themselves are businesses. Some of the top companies fighting the employment relations bill were media organisations. During the late 80s and early 90s the media had greater levels of union derecognition than almost any other business sector ... When unions were more powerful – and still often now – it was the job of some journalists, like those on the *Mail* or the *Sun*, simply to go and bash the unions. If there were no strikes they looked elsewhere. There is a whole tradition of union-bashing stories.

However, a more general obstacle to union communications, from the point of view of journalists, was the fact that unions were no longer considered to be powerful organisations and were, therefore, less newsworthy. As Robert Taylor of the *FT* explained (interview, 20.5.99): 'Twenty years ago journalists were clamouring to talk to union leaders. Now union leaders are clamouring to talk to journalists ... Part of the reason is that the unions are no longer the national force they used to be. Therefore it's not a national rail strike but a strike on Connex South East – not something that's going to attract masses of media attention.[6] In effect, the

---

5 Other examples include: Chris Darke (interview, 3.10.97), 'Bias in the media clearly. The media are biased against unions and collective organisations. Things have got better, partly because unions have changed their attitudes and methods'; Lawrie Harries (interview, 7.10.97), 'You've got to distinguish between the industrial relations group of journalists who deal with front-line issues, who understand the industrial world and the broad framework in which unions operate; and the shifty side of Fleet Street who come out of the woodwork and attempt to run rubbish stories about you'; Chris Proctor (interview, 2.6.97), 'Part of it is the media input – because they're looking for stereotypes. For example, during disputes the media wanted to interview Alan Johnson on a picket line. I was adamant that it wasn't going to happen'.

6 See also: Barrie Clement (interview, 25.5.99), 'Now, because proprietors are not bothered about unions and they have less power, they are therefore less interested in covering them at all ... It's still an uphill battle for credibility for unions – although they are doing very much better than a few years ago'; Seamus Milne (interview, 13.5.99), 'There's much less reporting now. Industrial relations is hardly covered. It tends to be more covered as a consumer story. It's no longer political but a

interviews with journalists tended to confirm the difficulties encountered in earlier studies of 'outsider' media–source relations, i.e., that such groups were excluded because of a lack of media capital.

Several other more specific problems, relating to media strategy and certain types of unions, were also mentioned. For larger unions, which had expanded through mergers, the problem was having mixed memberships. Members had different political allegiances and came from a variety of professions, class backgrounds and geographical regions. This made it difficult to appeal to all membership sections and, at the same time, present the union coherently to the press and public. As Miles Weber of MSF asked (interview, 13.10.97): 'How can we campaign as a union if we cannot find a unifying theme? … Are we trying to become another TUC or a unified, branded, value-based operation?'[7] For smaller and less public unions, the problem tended to be a disinterested media, which brought back the problem of access generally. Another common problem mentioned by PRPs was the difficulty of turning complex disputes into 'sound bite' issues. This led either to oversimplified reporting or no coverage at all from journalists – both of which were counter-productive to campaigns.[8]

Union advantages and the overcoming of economic resource deficits

Many union officials, while recognising their disadvantages, were also keen to emphasise their advantages and that there were other means for achieving communication goals. Several insisted that good communications did not just rely on economic resources, connections and profiles, but also involved using alternative resources, playing to strengths, and developing media strategies accordingly. As Chris Darke of BALPA explained (interview, 3.10.97): 'To those against such [public relations] means, and those who argue the problem of resources you have to ask yourself "with the material you have, the members and the resources, how can you influence and move things on?."' In fact, a number of union PRPs had come to recognise their advantages and had tried to adapt their practices accordingly. Three

---

matter of how it affects the consumer. Most of the media report work as a consumer or lifestyle issue but not in other contexts. It's all got to do with the politics of the time; all to do with the ideology and power of the period'.

7 See also: Karen Livingstone (interview, 21.5.97), 'The disadvantage is that we are a general union which is hard to identify and with a lack of clear membership focus'; Craig Ryan (interview, 30.7.97), 'The biggest disadvantage is the very sensitive position our members occupy – the downside of the professional position. If we attack the government we can't look like we are supposedly the opposition and vice versa'.

8 For example: Rosie Eagleson (interview, 1.8.97), 'Often the issues are not really soundbite issues. It becomes hard to have a rational debate outside political posturing. It is a very complex issue. It's easy for politicians to wind up people's fears about crimes. But it's more complicated than that'; Chris Proctor (interview, 2.6.97), 'The dispute mostly concerned teamworking. But when I met with the industrial correspondents, they all said the story was all too complicated. The tabloid writers all suggested that we concentrate on the five-day week issue because that was what Mirror readers would understand. This emphasis was a PR decision'.

particular assets/advantages were repeated with some consistency: memberships, organisational speed and expert knowledge. Each went some way towards neutralising the shortfall in financial and professional human resources.

The first point to become established during the study was that unions were able to organise professional PR operations with very little initial outlay or ongoing expenditure. Unlike advertising, news coverage is free and, although the ruses used by PRPs to get media coverage may, at times, be expensive, the actual coverage is not. The main requirements for PR operations are work space, basic communications equipment and people. Basic public relations IT requirements include telephones and fax machines, postal services and access to printing facilities. It was evident that even the smallest unions visited had access to these. While many larger unions had purchased more expensive communications equipment,[9] several PRPs believed they could function well enough without buying anything too sophisticated. In fact, several interviewees from smaller unions, with memberships of between 5,000 and 30,000, appeared to have developed quite consistent media access and influence by just using existing union resources. These included NAPO, ASLEF, the POA, the FDA and BALPA. At both NAPO and ASLEF, experienced communicators had gained extensive national media coverage, amounting to several hundred 'hits' a year, with nothing more than a telephone and fax machine.

The most expensive part of any PR operation is in fact the employment of personnel.[10] However, PR is not a licensed profession, meaning that public relations can be practised without gaining specific qualifications, undergoing any long-term training or joining a professional association.[11] This suggests that unions (as well as other outsider and resource-poor groups) can make use of their sometimes extensive membership resources. In theory, one or two professionals can be employed to co-ordinate large networks of partially trained volunteers and thus unions can go some way to making up for lower PR staffing levels.

As most PRP interviewees explained, unions have indeed made great efforts in the last decade to improve communications and relations with their members; through better journals, ballots and consultation exercises.[12] To this end, 42.9 per

---

9   These included: (1) new computers and Internet facilities, (2) databases with information on media outlets, contacts and journalists – often used with advanced fax facilities, (3) in-house radio link-ups, (4) media training facilities, (5) advanced desktop-publishing software and in-house printing facilities.

10 In a breakdown of the PR consultancy industry (William Shackleman Ltd, 1995), human resources accounted for 54 per cent of total expenditure on PR. Most other significant costs are taken up by company services, space rental and financial incentives; all of which remain rather less relevant to non-profit organisations.

11 In fact, in the 1994 IPR membership survey (IPR, 1994) only 13 per cent were found to have a CAM certificate or other relevant qualification. In the 1998 IPR membership survey (IPR, 1998b), less than 5 per cent had a degree in public relations or journalism.

12 For example: John Monks (interview, 16.10.97), 'you obviously have to carry the support of individual members of the union … We are serious about keeping our members informed of what UNISON argues and why, and to understand why they are affected'; Karen Livingstone (interview,

cent of unions, who had 'communications priorities' (see table A.10 in appendix II), made internal and membership communications their first priority, with 61.1 per cent making it one of their top three priorities (table A.11 in appendix II). A number of unions had surveyed their members to gauge their concerns and had adapted journals and policies accordingly. Many had gone to great efforts to put out a range of new newsletters, magazines and reports. These were shaped and altered to fit the varying concerns of different membership contingents and branch activists. A number of commentators have accordingly signalled a recent improvement in journal output (see chapter six). The results have also been reflected in MORI polls of union members (MORI Poll Data, Sept. 1975–95).

The significance of members to union PR operations also became evident. Members were useful in two ways. First, they were regarded as an important source of information for campaigns. Even smaller unions often had branch networks covering broad geographical areas and containing members with specialist knowledge. Some unions even made requests in union journals and newsletters for possible stories on particular issues. Such information sources were instrumental in the POA's attempts to undermine Group 4 (1993) by feeding the press with escaped prisoner accounts. The National Association of Probation Officers (NAPO), the Manufacturing, Science and Finance Union (MSF), ASLEF, the GMB and UNISON all stated that they encouraged such information flows and used them to produce news stories on a regular basis. The second and more obvious use of members was during campaigns themselves. Media training for local members and branch activists had slowly become more common. The survey revealed that, of those unions with branches (30.2 per cent did not have local branches), 47.4 per cent gave 'media training' to branch members – 90 per cent in the case of large unions. Those who were not trained could still participate in local demonstrations and publicity stunts, letter-writing campaigns, etc. – activities which institutions and businesses could not organise so simply. The survey also revealed that 70.3 per cent of unions used branch members in media campaigns – 90 per cent in the case of large unions. Even in small unions (under 10,000 members) 30 per cent gave training and 40 per cent used branch members.

As well as providing practical campaign assistance, members were also often used to present the union in a positive light. The public popularity of teachers, postal workers and nurses appeared to be something that PRPs played on to improve the media images of their unions. The combination of practical networks and popular profiles in fact had proved invaluable to the prosecution of a number of large campaigns, including the ambulance drivers dispute with the government in 1989, the teachers against education cuts in 1994–95 and, above all, the UCW in its

21.5.97), 'We raised the role of publications for members and put a stronger emphasis on women members. The unofficial media strategy of much of our work is aimed at recruitment'; Chris Proctor (interview, 2.6.97), 'Last year we made the decision that the "Voice" was going to be more membership orientated. We decided to make the thing more user-friendly, to put in more local member stories and less committee reports'.

battle against Post Office privatisation in 1994.[13] For Seamus Milne, of the Guardian (interview, 13.5.99), all these factors made members an extremely useful resource for unions: 'So unions are now rather more powerful than people think. Before, when they were much stronger, people thought they had more power than they did. Now it's the other way round and people underestimate them. They have extensive networks and people everywhere, and with their people and their resources they can be very effective campaigners.'

Unions can also make up for their resource disadvantages in other ways. For example, more than half the interviewees believed that, due to bureaucratic factors, they could operate their communications with much greater efficiency than their larger opponents. As several explained, union PR departments are far more oriented towards campaigning than government departments and businesses. Although unions have fewer communications resources, they are more campaign-focused and normally have instant access to the general secretary. This means that they can respond to journalists with few delays. In contrast, government and business departments are set up for long-term communications opertions. They have small armies of staff, several layers of bureaucracy, extensive systems of checks and balances, and are often badly briefed on up-to-the-minute issues. Thus unions, if well organised, can respond faster, outmanoeuvre opponents and set agendas. As Karen Livingstone of the GMB explained (interview, 21.5.97): 'The main advantage is that we are quicker and faster than government and business because, ultimately, the general secretary gives us the authority to act. We are less bureaucratic and we have greater autonomy. We are closer to the top than in government or business.'[14] The speed of union PRPs was noted as a significant factor in several successful union campaigns, including: BIFU's battle against Lloyds Bank's takeover of Midland Bank (1992), ASLEF's disputes with London Transport over working conditions (1995) and the TGWU against British Airways over working conditions (1997).

---

13 See also: Lawrie Harries (interview, 7.10.97), 'Strong support from the members enabled us to keep going from June to October without any significant drop in support'; Karen Livingstone (interview, 21.5.97), 'We also make use of our breadth of membership. We use the information that comes to us from members and make use of national and regional officials'; Daniel Harris (interview, 18.6.97), 'The local members, once trained, were marvellous advocates. The local MP is very sensitive to the local press and therefore very responsive to the local campaign'.

14 Others include: Craig Ryan (interview, 30.7.97), 'Secondly, your government PR machine is very cumbersome. It's a big operation. They have to clear everything with ministers and so on. We are very nimble. We can get a press release out in an hour and don't necessarily have to check with the general secretary. In government you deal with the minister, junior ministers, senior civil servants, and the party also'; Andrew Murray (interview, 9.10.97), 'We are much less hierarchical and have more direct contact with the general secretary. Company people often have to go through five layers of bureaucracy to reach the top. Businesses are not often set up for disputes – they are not swift enough. They have huge communication departments but they are more used to dealing with the City of London, marketing issues, etc., but not disputes'; Keith Bill (interview, 19.6.97), 'We always run rings around them because we are freer to respond. We can give instant quotes – companies and departments just don't have the same freedoms'.

Union PRPs also believed that they usually had greater expertise than opponents and could exploit it accordingly. Union members are often closer to the industry than management and, especially in the case of professional/managerial memberships, have more specialist knowledge of the work sector. When companies bring in consultancies, they may have communications expertise but they are often lacking detailed knowledge of the business, relevant legislation, the dispute, etc. Once again, this improves the speed and consistency of union messages in relation to their oppositions.[15]

Interviews with journalists tended to confirm these two union advantages. As Barrie Clement of the *Independent* explained (interview, 25.5.99):

> The advantages of a union are that they can be leaner and meaner, especially in a fast-moving situation like a strike. That's because the media person can speak to the general secretary immediately and then go back to the journalist. It's different in a big corporation with a big bureaucracy where they have to report to the head of communications and check with the heads of departments and then the secretary of the chief executive. If you compare the ability of the press person in a union, who knows what the general secretary is thinking and doing, with the press person of a large organisation, who has no idea of what the chief executive is doing and thinking, you can see the differences.[16]

Union strategies – overcoming institutional disadvantages (media/cultural capital) and a hostile media

Union PRPs are also managing to overcome poor media relations and profiles by developing sophisticated media strategies which exploit particular union strengths. Not only have they established their own networks of media contacts, they have discovered ways of presenting their unions more favourably – both during short-term disputes and in long-term image-building exercises. As such, they have shown that there are several ways of making up for a lack of institutional authority (or media/cultural capital) that do not require large financial outlays.

---

15 As a number explained: Chris Darke (interview, 3.10.97), 'We are a lot smarter at understanding how to influence the media in our particular area. We know a lot because we are a niche organisation'; Joe Marino (interview, 14.10.97), 'Also, food hygiene is a good news story that will hit the headlines. It is a specialist area and we have strengths in the industry – although disadvantaged outside'; Hannah Jeffries (interview, 31.7.97), 'We have better inside knowledge, especially if the company is using outside PR'.

16 Seamus Milne (interview, 13.5.99), 'They [unions] are that much quicker to respond. They have no bureaucracy and no hassle. They just have to get through to the general secretary. But businesses have to go through layers of bureaucracy to get approval – secretaries, department heads, the head of communications, all the way up to the chief executive. That's how the T&G [Transport and General Workers Union] ran circles round British Airways – one man and a mobile phone. Things move fast in a dispute and you have to be quick'; Christine Buckley (interview, 1.6.99), 'I think government and business can be quite impeded in their communications ... Many of the government press officers who work for the various departments are not particularly good. They have a reluctance to talk about issues and won't comment. Many of them are generally not very communicative ... They take forever to go down and answer the most basic questions'.

Many of the unions, small as well as large, successfully operated an active policy of acquiring and maintaining media contacts and demonstrated that they could also become established sources for journalists. As several explained, a steady supply of newsworthy stories to a range of correspondents, ensured that those journalists: (a) took up a greater proportion of information supply from union sources; (b) came to established union sources in search of stories, and; (c) automatically returned to those sources for quotes and information to balance out that obtained from government and business sources. As one experienced communicator in a small union explained (interview, 1997): 'I offer a high number of stories, and can deliver something every week or at least every third week. That also means they come back to me for comment. The quid pro quo is that they will come back to me for a story that isn't mine. Journalists are more likely to use my stuff because of past rewards and favours.' Interviewees at the POA, NAPO, UNISON, the CWU, the NUT and ASLEF all outlined similar long-term operations, each designed to cultivate journalist contacts at all levels.[17]

Many unions, large and small, have also avoided the difficulties of getting national media coverage by focusing on local and community media. Local media are less politically hostile to unions, more in need of information subsidies, and interested in covering local issues.[18] Unions, with their local branch networks, strengths in particular industry sectors, and community roles, have been well placed to take advantage. Some, such as the Bakers, Food and Allied Workers' Union (BFAWU) and Association of Magistrates Officers (AMO), only concentrated on local industries and institutions. The TUC and CWU, although they had national networks and appeal, often campaigned on the local level – supplying the same arguments but with regional-specific information, across the country. Others, such as MSF, the GMB and UNISON, offered central expertise to local branches with different campaign interests. Sometimes the larger unions managed to achieve blanket coverage in the local press, radio and television, which then led to the national media picking up the story.

As well as improving access through the regular supply of information subsidies, PRPs have worked hard to develop media-friendly union images. As Andrew Murray of the TGWU (interview, 9.10.97) explained:

---

17 For example: John Monks (interview, 16.10.97), 'Our press officers are forever in contact with their sources, so we have become a source of expertise for newspapers. So when you've got a story to relate the contacts are established and we have a fighting chance of getting a say in the press'; John Richards (interview, 20.5.97), 'A sea-change happened during the miners strike of 1984–85 – the necessity of maintaining good contacts. The secret is not to worry them unnecessarily – wait for a good story and present it well and at the right time'; Daniel Harris (interview, 18.6.97), 'When the story finally broke those contacts came flooding back to me. I built up a long-term rapport with the media … For three years I was putting out press releases and talking to people.'

18 Rosie Eagleson (interview, 1.8.97), 'They [local media] are always desperate for stories, and local radio in particular'; Andrew Murray (interview, 9.10.97), 'Local radio are always looking for stuff. You can be very effective by hitting a number of small stations. You can line up several, with different local radio stations, all through Broadcasting House'; Joe Marino (interview, 14.10.97), 'You've got more chance when you're using the local media – if it's of local public interest. The local media are very interested in arguments about the effects on the local economy'.

Over a period one can reposition the union's image in the media. This is done grad-
ually over time. We promote the union's services more publicly, co-operation with
employers and the non-conflict side of the union. We are moving away from the
image of a dinosaur to something more modern. We are not completely transformed
but one has to be realistic – generally the negative image of unions has been dissi-
pated. That's not just down to the T&G. A number of unions, including the TUC,
have put a lot of effort into improving the image.

In the survey, work on the 'union image' was a campaigning priority for a quarter
(25.9 per cent) of unions (table A.12 in appendix II). It was thus one of the two
most commonly mentioned communications campaign priorities (along with
campaigns to influence politics/legislation).

The strategies involved in improving union images and media access varied
according to the type of union involved. The most commonly applied technique, as
revealed in interviews, was what might be referred to as the 'public service
approach'. Instead of campaigning on wages and personal employment issues,
union PRP strategies were designed to appeal to the public and escape the common
accusation that 'they put their own interests above those of society at large' (Seaton
1991, p256). Unions increasingly focused on issues such as safety, healthcare,
educational standards, prejudice and social inequality. For example, the ambulance
drivers' dispute in 1989 ensured that its campaign put the public first and, consequently, drivers gained considerable popular support. As Kerr and Sachdev
observed (1992, p140, see also Philo, 1995, Manning, 1998), 'By conceiving an
industrial and public relations strategy that built on public support and media
attention, the ambulance unions were able to avoid the pitfalls of 1979'. This strategy has also been successfully repeated by the UCW, the NUT, the NUR,
NALGO, and the RMT.[19] In each case the unions worked hard to demonstrate a
united front with service users, feed the media and set the agenda for the dispute.
As interviewees acknowledged, public sector service unions clearly benefited more
from this approach than private sector and industrial unions.

For unions such as the FDA and BALPA, strategies have combined the public
service angle with a carefully cultivated image of 'professionals' doing a job with
great skill and expertise. Their spokespersons have therefore found themselves in
the role of 'official' and/or 'expert' source. As Craig Ryan of the FDA (interview,
30.7.97) explained:

Our strategy, basically, is to use media and PR to promote our standing and profile.
The media are not interested in how badly paid we are … Professional concerns to

---

19 Rosie Eagleson (interview, 1.8.97), 'The principles of fairness and equality underlie cuts and job
losses. It's always about the public and the impact on the public – the public service angle'; Lawrie
Harries (interview, 7.10.97), 'We won the argument over the signal workers dispute in 1994. We
held the moral high ground from day one. We continued to argue an easily understood case'; Olive
Forsythe (interview, 19.5.97), 'The NUT emphasises educational improvement over and above
wage rises … We also have to have parents on our side and the public definitely. Without them we
are lost'.

our members – that's what gets us coverage. It also impresses management because they take us seriously. We are speaking with authority – more than an organisation of 10,000 members should normally have.[20]

Two other strategies avoided the union image problem altogether and, in fact, question the importance of acquiring more than minimum levels of institutional legitimacy and/or media capital. The first of these involved attacking oppositions and guiding journalists to negative stories. Rather than campaigning on wages and conditions, some unions had gained more by attacking executives and politicians for their salaries, intransigence, and for financial, legal or sexual irregularities. Such attacks diverted the media spotlight away from unions and made their oppositions appear unreasonable and untrustworthy. According to Kerr and Sachdev (1992) and Philo (1995) this worked extremely well in the ambulance drivers' dispute in 1989. This strategy was also successfully employed by: the POA against Group 4 in 1993, by the NUT against education cuts in 1994 and 1995 and, most dramatically, in the GMB-inspired 'fat cats' campaigns.[21] On each occasion it was a company or government department that was made to look incompetent or intransigent.

Negative information supply also appeared to play a part in several low-key, long-term PR campaigns. For some smaller unions, such as AMO or NAPO, such means were the only hope of promoting particular approaches to policy-making

20 See also: Chris Darke (interview, 3.10.97), 'We have a single identity clearly associated with all issues of civil aviation. Pilots are still looked at with a bit of mystique. So to some extent we are able to say things with greater authority ... We have a very high input into the ways those jobs are done. But we are seen as professional, which, we use to influence decisions – not just to raise wages'; Miles Weber (interview, 13.10.97), 'We have a perceived political muscle because we represent many wealthy professional people, many of whom work at a high level of the production chain. So the government understands the implications of our real strength'.

21 Kerr and Sachdev (1992, p141), 'Perhaps their most striking finding was the dramatic role reversals of normal media images: namely, the contrast between the popular, respected trade union leaders and the aggressive, intransigent minister'; Lawrie Harris (interview, 7.10.97), 'The message was "the railways were treating their staff in the same contemptible way that they were treating their passengers ... we were the victims of the cuts in the same way that the passengers were"'; Mary McGuire of NALGO (quoted in Verzuh, 1990, p30), 'we concentrated on ... the fact that the services they [union members] provided to the public were being placed in jeopardy ... Employers were always made to look like the bad guys'.

22 For example: Harry Fletcher (interview, 13.10.97), 'Up to May 1997, the policy was to use the media to criticise government policies wherever possible ... The attitude was that the chances of getting change were remote and we therefore had to criticise the administration and work through the media as a means of getting change'; Craig Ryan (interview, 30.7.97), 'Where we run the more proactive campaigns it tends to be a very long-running theme. For example the 'freedom of information' campaign, which has been running for fifteen years. We have a very long view of that kind of thing. We are looking for media opportunities to get our message across all the time'; John Monks (interview, 16.10.97), 'We have continued to campaign against privatisation in one or other of its various forms. Although campaigning is not on the streets we are campaigning as hard as ever for pay, versus cuts, and against PFIs [private finance initiatives]'.

during the years of Conservative government.[22] Issues, such as inequality in the legal system, the minimum wage, privatisation, health and safety conditions, cuts in health and education, multinational monopolies and freedom of information, have all been integrated into long-term union campaigns over the last decade. All similarly found their way on to the legislative agenda of the new Labour government. As Barrie Clement of the *Independent* pointed out (interview, 25.5.99):

> Press officers see it as their job to get union issues into the media, so that they are seen to be working behind the scenes despite the fact that nothing much newsworthy is happening and there are less strikes. So they campaign on fairness at work, sexual equality, the minimum wage, and so on. For example, they put a lot of pressure on about the introduction of the minimum wage and they have also had a hand in the Employment Relations Bill ...

The second means by which unions had bypassed the need for institutional legitimacy/media capital was by using third-party endorsement. As Keith Bill of Union Communications (interview, 19.6.97) advised: 'The way for unions to do anything is not to do it themselves. The trick from now on is to get other people to do it.' For many unions, greater media access and more positive coverage had been achieved by putting their case through MPs, scientists, charities, pressure groups, poll organisations and public figures – each of which had been able to speak out on the union's behalf. The information was then presented by journalists as information produced by more objective sources instead of merely the opinions of self-interested unionists. For the teachers' unions, parents associations often become third parties; for the communications and rail unions it was charities and pressure groups working under general campaign banners; for unions such as MSF it was often scientists and MPs.[23]

Clearly, unions are adopting the professional PR methods of business and government – but with a difference. They are identifying and exploiting their own natural resource advantages and personalised PR strategies – all of which go some way to making up for their disadvantages. As they have made a greater impact on news producers and 'elite discourse networks', so the overall images of the union movement have improved, long-term campaign goals are being reached, and short-term victories achieved. That small and medium-sized unions are increasing investment in PR much faster than large unions (see back), indicates that PR is indeed one area where it is possible to overcome a lack of economic resources. As Chris Darke of BALPA (interview, 3.10.97) explained:

> But strikes are not a necessary weapon of current-day deterrents. A lot more is going to be about how you influence the market and players in key positions and that is central ... It's influencing the power game of those that have the power – it means using professional help and the use of consultants – business consultants and

---

23 Third-party endorsement is also a strategy strongly advocated by Wilson (1984) and described by Cracknell (1993), Miller and Williams (1998) and others writing about pressure group activity.

management consultants. What we've got to do is look at and say the way in which certain companies behave is not right and we can look at these companies using management consultants who can say it that much better. In today's game you are looking to influence in all directions and there should be nothing that isn't open to us to influence and thus ultimately help our members. So you can use consultants, strategists, and you can actually take some action that collectively solves it ...

Evaluating the effectiveness of new union communications

This section attempts to evaluate the effectiveness of union communications. It is clear that unions have made large investments in their communications operations. It is also clear that they have developed media contacts, reduced negative coverage and raised their approval ratings with members and the general public. But for many observers, such changes have resulted less from improved communications and more from such factors as reduced union militancy and a shifting political environment. To determine comprehensively which factors are more influential is, in fact, a near impossible task – as scholars and practitioners have found in numerous studies of communication. However, the findings of this survey do suggest that improved union PR has played a significant part and that unions, whatever their misgivings, will continue to invest in public relations.

Improved relations, access and favourability

The evidence accumulated from the survey and interview responses suggests that there have been considerable improvements in union–media relations – even for those unions with more militant reputations. Despite a continuing union belief in media bias, hostile relationships have now been replaced by uneasy truces and a commitment to keep talking to the media. As Laurie Harries of the NUR (interview, 7.10.97) commented: 'you can't call them [tabloid] journalists, quite frankly they're despicable ... But we are conscious of the need that the media understand what our case is. We are more media-conscious now than we have ever been – even on local disputes. The union is very much aware of the need to use it to the best advantage'.[24]

As table 7.1 (table A.13 in appendix II) shows, survey respondents' impressions were that relations deteriorated from the 1970s to the 1980s but, in the 1990s, they appeared to be approaching a post-war high. In the 1970s, just over a quarter of respondents thought relations were 'bad' or 'very bad'. In the 1980s, 45.3 per

---

24 For similar examples: Hannah Jeffries (interview, 31.7.97), 'It's still a bit cynical even if more open to persuasion ... There is an understanding between the media and trade unions. It's not based on trust but on an understanding of each other's motives. Previously we were scared because we didn't understand where they were coming from ... Things are different now'; John Richards (interview, 20.5.97), 'ASLEF always had a guarded attitude towards the media – the media are always out to get us ... Sometimes in the past, relations were non-existent and we refused to talk to the press if we could ... We get a better press [now] but it does depend on how we handle our media relations. We take a very professional view'.

Table 7.1 Individual union relations with the media,
1970s–1990s

Union–Media relations	1970s percentage	1980s percentage	1990s percentage
Good/very good	33.4	19.1	56.0
Neutral	38.9	35.7	34.0
Bad/very Bad	27.8	45.3	10.0

cent of respondents classified relations as 'bad' or 'very bad'. In the 1990s, a clear majority (56 per cent) thought them 'good' or 'very good', with only 10 per cent describing them as 'bad' or 'very bad'. Breaking down the figures in terms of size, small unions had the best relations throughout the 1970s and 1980s, but large unions did so in the 1990s. In fact the most dramatic improvement came for large unions whose respondents believed that their good relations went up from 20 per cent, in the 1980s, to 72.7 per cent in the 1990s. Public sector union respondents also believed they had better relations (81.3 per cent) in the 1990s, while only 38.5 per cent of private ones did.

As figures 7.5 and 7.6 (tables A.14 and A.15 in appendix II) indicate, good relations have been followed by better access and more favourable coverage. Despite the decline in industrial relations reporting and media interest, 65.3 per cent of respondents thought access had improved since the 1980s, and 79.1 per cent thought media coverage was more favourable. This compared with only 17.3 per cent who believed access had become worse and 2.1 per cent who thought coverage was less favourable. Large and medium-sized unions had improved their access and favourability significantly more than smaller ones. In fact, 75 per cent of the respondents of medium-sized unions believed their access had increased. For

Figure 7.5 'Compared to the 1980s, has union access to the media in the 1990s …'

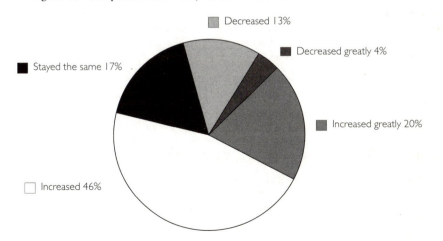

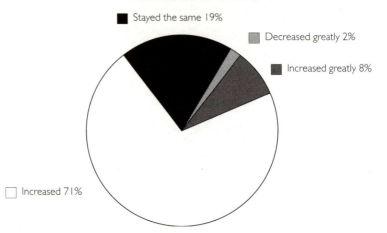

Figure 7.6 'Compared to the 1980s, favourable media coverage of unions in the 1990s has …'

larger unions, with regular access, favourability was more important. Significantly, 90 per cent of respondents in large unions reported an increase in favourable media reporting. Public sector union respondents (92.8 per cent) thought they had more favourable coverage than respondents in private sector unions (75 per cent), and professional/managerial unionists believed they (68.8 per cent) had done better than those in manual unions (52.9 per cent).

All journalists interviewed also believed that union communications had improved and that union–media relations were far better in the 1990s. Indeed, some were very positive about the increased professionalism of union communicators. As Seamus Milne of the Guardian observed (interview, 13.5.99):

> One, they are no longer so antagonistic to the media, and two, they have broader contact with different kinds of correspondent. So they go for transport or the environment or politics … It's changed a lot since the NUM in 1984/85. Then it was a state of open warfare. All unions were covered in a very hostile way. There were lots of very political negative stories and this led to increased conflict between the two. Very few correspondents could get access. Now everyone, even the most negative tabloids, can get some sort of access.[25]

25 Robert Taylor (interview, 20.5.99), 'As the unions get less and less powerful they have tended to put more into their communications … There's more professionalism in some of the unions – not all. You can see that just by looking at some of the journals they put out'; Barrie Clement (interview, 25.5.99), 'ten or fifteen years ago most unions were very suspicious of reporters because they regarded the press as a Conservative, with a big C, press. And to some extent that's true … At some point they decided to use the press rather than avoid them and it worked. It certainly helped to get unions into the media in a more positive light … People are on mobiles these days. It's far easier to get hold of union officials now. When I started it was almost impossible. There were no press officers, the union officials were reluctant to speak and hard to reach, and it was virtually impossible tospeak to anyone.'

Media coverage is not the only thing to show significant improvement. Memberships are more positive about their union leaderships and the general public is more positive about unions generally. In September 1995 Gallup found that 67 per cent of people thought that trade unions 'Generally speaking ... were a good thing', compared to 51 per cent in 1979. Only 17 per cent thought them 'too powerful', next to 84 per cent in 1979. MORI polls also showed that some faith in union leaderships had been restored to union members. Between 1975 and 1984 MORI polls (Poll Data) recorded that between 55 per cent and 73 per cent of trade union members thought 'Trade unions have too much power in Britain today', and between 55 per cent and 64 per cent thought 'Most trade unions are controlled by extremists and militants'. By 1995 only 14 per cent thought them 'too powerful' and only 23 per cent thought them 'controlled by extremists and militants'.[26]

Other factors involved

There are of course many other factors which have contributed to the improvement of union profiles. To date, many union observers (Edwards and Bain, 1988, Marsh, 1990, Seaton, 1991, Taylor, 1994, McIlroy, 1995) have suggested that union (un)popularity is more closely linked to union militancy and/or changes in the socio-political environment. A study by Edwards and Bain (1988) concluded that union popularity declines as inflation and/or levels of industrial action rise. Marsh (1990) and Manning (1999), amongst others, have suggested that the Thatcher government was a greater determining factor of media hostility towards unions in the 1980s – a conclusion not too dissimilar from the one supported by the Glasgow University Media Group. In effect, an elite consensus developed in the 1970s and 1980s – one that regarded unions as the greatest cause of British economic decline and social disruption. Such a consensus came to be reflected in the media.

All the external conditions which made unions unpopular have now changed. Unions are smaller and no longer perceived as a threat to the establishment. The average number of stoppages and working days lost to strike action have declined significantly. It is also clear that the last Conservative government (1992-97) was deeply unpopular with both the media and public. Although Labour and the union movement have kept communications discreet, business and political opinion is generally less antagonistic towards unions, and they have once again been granted access to government policy-makers. Elite consensus currently agrees on two things: the economy is strong and, following Conservative legislation, unions can no longer be singled out as a hindrance to sound economic development. Thus, all the external conditions which made unions unpopular have now been transformed and unions should, by default, have an increased level of popularity once again – regardless of their PR activities.

---

26 However, problems do remain. According to Gallup, in September 1995 only 32 per cent of people thought union leaders 'representative of their members'. MORI (Poll Data, 1995) also found that only 35 per cent of members disagreed with the statement 'Trade union leaders are out of touch with their members'.

Interviews and the survey asked respondents to reply on this matter. The results were rather inconclusive. Although almost all interviewees believed union communications had made a very real impact, a significant minority were inclined to give more support to the political climate argument. As Andrew Murray of the TGWU (interview, 9.10.97) explained: 'It's all part of the political climate – also because unions are not seen as the threat they were in the 1970s. Instead there has been a change of attitude against macho or greedy management. How trade unions are seen does fit into a larger matrix.'[27]

Survey respondents were also divided over whether improved PR or changing political and economic circumstances were more responsible for improved media coverage and increased public approval. In response to the statement 'Improved public opinion of unions is due more to unpopular government and a decrease in strike activity – *NOT* public relations', as many respondents 'agreed' as 'disagreed' (see table A.16 in appendix II). Doubts about the usefulness of public relations more generally also surfaced. Only 45.8 per cent disagreed or strongly disagreed with the statement 'PR/Communications tactics are limited and will never really replace other union strategies and campaigning forms' (table A.17 in appendix II). 35.4 per cent agreed or strongly agreed and 18.8 per cent did not know. There was some variation across types of union and further efforts were made to cross-tabulate financial investment data with the tables on media relations, access and favourability. Although greater investment did equate to better relations, etc., the increases were not significantly higher than the averages – being only a few percentage points better in most cases.

Improved communications a substantial part of change

However, other survey responses, combined with the replies of most interviewees, indicated that unionists believed improved communications had played a key part in better media relations and access. To begin with, trade union reporting has declined. Unions are smaller and less involved in 'newsworthy' industrial action, and media outlets have cut down on industrial reporting (see Manning, 1998, 1999). Despite this, a clear majority of respondents (see figures 7.5 and 7.6) believe access and favourability have increased. Unions may not be the central focus of stories but they certainly get their arguments reported in the media. This is most likely to be explained by the increased proactivity of union PRPs.

---

27 Seamus Milne (interview, 13.5.99), 'Generally you can't separate industrial reporting from the social and political context. The unions were more powerful in the 70s and 80s and that meant that they were over-covered ... Now they're under-covered. There are very few labour correspondents left. If you think that the unions still have seven million members they are some of the largest voluntary membership organisations. And by whatever measure they should have more coverage than they do. The fact that they don't has got to do with the political climate'; Barrie Clement (interview, 25.5.99), 'In the past I have worked with people whose only idea of a union story was a negative story. They were looking for disruptive strike action, for militants and Trotskyists taking over. But there's a lot less of that now and that's because there are less strikes and less militancy'.

Second, a number of union victories have clearly been gained, or at least aided, by the use of PR. This growing list includes: the ambulance drivers in 1989 (see Verzuh, 1990, Kerr and Sachdev, 1992, Manning, 1998); the NUR in 1989 (Verzuh, 1990); the POA in 1993; the UCW in 1994 (see IPR, 1994, Cockerell, 9.1.97, and chapter eight in this book); BALPA and the TGWU against British Airways in 1996 and 1997. Other union campaigns, although failing to achieve their objectives, were extremely damaging to the government and/or particular corporations. These have included the TUC against pit closures in 1993, the NUT against education cuts in 1995, the railway unions against privatised railways, 1993 to present, and ongoing 'fat cats' campaigns against corporate pay, 1992 to present. Each of these might also be said to have contributed to a shift in the political climate itself – thus aiding the election of New Labour in 1997 and forcing several welfare and industrial relations issues onto the political agenda.

Proactive long-term communications also appear to have benefited general union–media relations to a degree that appears too large to put down to other circumstances. For example, it appears quite significant that larger unions, which invested more for longer periods (see back), have also had the largest improvement in media relations in the 1990s. In the 1980s only 20 per cent had 'good' media relations; by the 1990s, 72.7 per cent claim to have 'good' or 'very good' relations. Similarly 90 per cent of large unions believe that media reporting has become more favourable to them. The same story can be applied to public sector, professional/managerial and non-manual unions, which also invested more and gained better coverage. For example, 93.3 per cent of public sector unions increased communications expenditure in the 1990s; 81.3 per cent believe they have had more positive media relations and 92.8 per cent increased media favourability.

Third, the overall impression given by respondents to the use of PR is more than favourable. Figure 7.3 (see tables A.4, A.5 and A.6 in appendix II) showed that large majorities had invested, and expected to make further investments in, their communications. Similar majorities (see tables A.8 and A.9 in appendix II) believed that communications methods were essential for pursuing industrial action and other goals. Additionally, 70.2 per cent 'disagreed' or 'strongly disagreed' (see table A.18 in appendix II) with the statement that money was 'better spent on other union priorities' and only 8.5 per cent 'agreed'. Whatever union leaderships believe are the reasons for improved media relations, they obviously think improvements in PR are a necessity – if only because the opposition are investing heavily in communications. This suggests that PR has had, and will continue to have, a leading role in union activities.

Finally, the view of the majority of journalists interviewed was that union public relations had made a significant difference to union campaigns and had now become a vital campaigning tool. For Robert Taylor of the *FT* (interview, 20.5.99):

> The success or failure of an industrial dispute now depends on whether the union concerned is able to satisfactorily put over their case to the journalists and to the general public. They have got more sensitive in the way they approach things. And

they have been quite influential in changing opinions on other issues such as race or gender or the minimum wage. They have been quite effective in recent government policy-making.[28]

Conclusion

Evidently, a majority of unions have made a clear organisational decision to use public relations as a means of achieving a number of political and economic objectives – from increasing and maintaining memberships to influencing legislation. Minimal public relations operations are now considered a standard requirement for medium and large unions, and many small unions are attempting to expand their own communications operations. Like other organisational sectors, unions are employing professional consultants, using specialist equipment and services, adopting professional PR strategies, and focusing their campaigns on those who count – corporate and political elite decision-makers.

In the new public relations environment, unions are quite clearly disadvantaged in terms of the economic and cultural resources they have at their disposal. The study did tend to confirm a general correlation between the size of a union and its investment in public relations personnel and equipment. It also suggested that, on the whole, those unions that had invested more had gained greater media access and more success in their campaigning. The findings then offer some support for previous work that linked economic resources to PR efficacy (e.g., Gandy, 1980, Herman and Chomsky, 1988, Miller, 1994, Schlesinger and Tumber, 1994, Deacon, 1996, 1999). All of which indicates that corporate and government elites, which employ the majority of PR resources and personnel, have a significantly stronger influence over the norms and values established in long-term media discourses.

However, this chapter has also suggested that, contrary to the assumptions of many earlier source studies, public relations is not just another economic resource to be monopolised by those with more economic and media/cultural capital. The fact that public relations coverage is free and reliant on human resources, leaves much scope for 'outsider' and 'resource-poor' groups, such as unions, to make an impact. Clearly, several other factors can also affect an organisation's ability to use

---

28 Seamus Milne (interview, 13.5.99), 'I can't think of a recent dispute in which the majority of the public were not behind the unions. It all came out in polls. In that respect the media are behind the times in their coverage – very outdated … Unions have had a number of successes in the 1990s'; Barrie Clement (interview, 25.5.99), 'It's not necessarily likely to achieve a victory. But there have been notable examples where unions, which have been taking industrial action, are favourably reported even when causing considerable inconvenience to the public. For example the ambulance drivers dispute (1989) or the signal workers (1994). In each case it was about having a strong grip on press relations and having a positive attitude towards it'; Keith Harper (interview, 20.5.99), 'Their [unions] PR improved as their power declined and they realised that they needed a forum, a conduit, with which to communicate … since the 1980s … the unions have learnt, from a point of low popularity twenty years ago, to improve their communications. And so they have improved despite the drop in power and direct coverage … In some respects union PR has become very effective and sophisticated'.

PR effectively. One of these is human resources – something that outsider and resource-poor groups can take advantage of if they are well organised. Another is the speed with which an organisation can operate its communications. Yet another is the malleability of journalist routines and of what is considered 'newsworthy'. Knowledge of journalist routines, patterns of coverage and 'news values', has enabled union PRPs to become regular suppliers of information subsidies. It has also enabled them to devise skilful PR operations that can overcome a lack of institutional authority and/or negative union images. Indeed, in at least two examples, extremely small unions, operating with one part-time practitioner and household communications equipment, have managed to get more annual coverage and/or influence than organisations a hundred times larger. Some union operations have been so successful that they have had major impacts on long-term media discourses and short-term policy-making – often while unions themselves barely registered in the media at all.

It might therefore be concluded that outsider and resource-poor groups can effectively use PR to influence news producers and, ultimately, to gain entry into the 'elite discourse networks' described in earlier chapters. Dominant media discourses, largely chartered by governments, institutions and businesses, can thus be knocked off course. Clearly, pressure groups, charities and trade unions can become 'primary definers' too – and without the general public necessarily being aware of their presence.

8

THE UNION OF COMMUNICATION WORKERS VERSUS POST OFFICE PRIVATISATION IN 1994

This case study illustrates the findings of chapter seven. It looks at how a very successful PR campaign, run by the Union of Communication Workers, contributed to the failure of the government to privatise the Post Office in 1994.

Events were set in motion on 15 July 1992, when Michael Heseltine, President of the Board of Trade, unexpectedly announced that Parcelforce would be privatised. Two weeks later the government declared it would be reviewing all postal services and thus signalled its intention to privatise the whole of the Post Office. After two years of delays, Heseltine announced (19 May 1994) the forthcoming publication of a green paper – 'The Future of Postal Services'. This presented three options: greater commercial freedom for the Post Office within the public sector, a complete privatisation, and the government's preferred option of a partial (51 per cent) privatisation. The paper, published at the end of June, gave a three-month consultation period, after which the government would announce future legislation. Prior to the May announcement several interested parties had begun campaign preparations and, with the publication of the green paper, the campaigns began in earnest. Apart from the DTI, Post Office management had a significant interest in the issue. Led by Bill Cockburn (chief executive) and Michael Heron (chairman), it had been campaigning for two years for more freedom from government.[1] Management now made the strategic decision to follow the DTI and campaign for the 51 per cent privatisation option.

The unions' campaign, led by the UCW,[2] had begun preparing to defend the Post Office's public-sector status even before the 1992 announcement. Their campaign began to accelerate during the early months of 1994 and gathered momentum over the summer. Since no union campaign up until that time had succeeded in halting a privatisation, the prospects were not good. On 12 July, when MPs voted by 305 to 273

---

1 As well as dealing with DTI restrictions, Post Office profits had been increasingly used to reduce the Public Sector Borrowing Requirement (PSBR) of the Treasury. Such demands had led to a fourfold increase in taxes paid to the government since 1991, therefore leaving little for new capital investment.

2 The principal union involved was the UCW, whose membership included the majority of Post Office staff. The National Communications Union (NCU) and Communications Managers' Association (CMA) played supporting roles. Together, they made up POUC – the Post Office Unions Council. All three were represented on the sub-group committee that met to plan the campaign.

in favour of a motion supporting the 51 per cent privatisation option, the government's long-running privatisation programme looked set to continue.

However, after a summer of media campaigning and lobbying, in which the Labour Party and many other interest groups entered the debate, the government's plans suddenly began to look doubtful. Between the end of the consultation period (30 September 1994) and the start of November, when legislation was being finalised for the Queens Speech, Heseltine and the DTI looked increasingly desperate. On 2 November, with the cabinet divided, Ulster Unionists refusing to support the government, and up to twenty Conservative MPs threatening rebellion, plans for the Post Office were shelved. The strength and ingenuity of the union's campaign was cited as being the main reason for the government's retreat in a series of articles in the *FT* (Taylor, 1994a, p8), *Independent* (Brown, 1994a, p19), *Guardian* (Harper, 1994, p5) and *PR Week* (3.11.94). Robert Taylor (1994a, p8) described the union's campaign as 'the most effective and professional campaign by a British union for a long time'. *PR Week* (3.11.94, p1) described the UCW communications team as: 'prime examples of a new generation of union professionals using communications tactics more familiar to big business … a devastatingly effective team galvanising the union's most useful weapon – its 160,000 members – and in the process becoming the first union ever to defeat a government privatisation'.

The research involved the accumulation of information on the activities of sources – through documents and interviews with participants.[3] The second stage was a content analysis of the national press, during the six-month period in which the campaigns were most intensive, plus further interviews with journalists.[4] The two sets of evidence were then compared to look for patterns and correlations.

Union communications or force of circumstances?

Although the pro-privatisation camp lost the campaign, commonly used types of analysis, when applied to this case, suggest that union activity had little to do with the eventual outcome. The distributions of economic and cultural capital of the different parties, combined with a conventional content analysis of news coverage, indicate that corporate and political elites dominated as news sources. At the same

---

3 The principal source of documentation, records and news cuttings was the research archives of the UCW. Documentation included: all records of the union campaign and correspondence; press releases, promotional material and submissions from the unions, DTI, their respective allies and opponents. Eight interviews were also conducted: three (ex) union staff who had worked on the campaign, two PR consultants who had worked for the UCW, two DTI officials and a Post Office head of communications.

4 The newspaper analysis looked at a total of 285 articles appearing in ten national daily newspapers. The analysis was applied to all articles appearing in these newspapers between 18 May (the day before the initial cabinet meeting) and 2 November 1994 (the day the cabinet rejected all options) – a twenty-five week period when coverage was heaviest. The breakdown between papers was as follows: the *FT* – 51, *The Times* – 51, the *Guardian* – 45, the *Telegraph* – 40, the *Independent* – 34, *Today* – 15, the *Mirror* – 15, the *Daily Express* – 11, the *Daily Mail* – 11, the *Sun* – 10. A further seven interviews took place with journalists who covered the story.

time, the Conservative government was extremely weak and divided. It could thus well be argued that negative coverage of the DTI and Heseltine, and the eventual collapse of their proposals, resulted from a breakdown in elite-source consensus and subsequent elite conflict.

Elite source advantages and media dominance

In terms of economic and professional PR resources, the Post Office and DTI were greatly advantaged. The Post Office had a turnover in 1994–95 of £5.88 billion and 190,000 employees, and a network of some 460 'communications staff' (Post Office, Feb. 1997a, Feb. 1997b). As several newspapers observed at the time (Rudd, 1994, p10, Tieman, 1994a, p19, Gribben, 1994), its campaign was extremely thorough.[5] Roland Rudd, of the *FT* (Rudd 1994, p10), called it a 'campaign that was impressive by the standards of any professional consultancy'. Articles in the *Telegraph* (Goodman, 1994) and *The Times* (Bassett and Pierce, 1994, p10) estimated that £1.8 million had been spent by August 1994 – although the total figure was probably half that (over and above the fixed costs of the Post Office).[6]

Heseltine and the DTI had the might of the GIS (Government Information Services) and Conservative Party press machine. The *IPI Directory* for January 1994 (COI, Jan. 1994) lists sixty-seven communications staff at the DTI. Ministers and government departments already benefited from the 'Hansard advantage', ensuring that government statements and select committee evidence gained coverage in the 'quality' press. In November 1994, in answer to a Commons question (Hansard, 12.2.97, pp223–4), the DTI declared that £1.6 million had been spent on consultancy for the project alone. Heseltine and other ministers (notably Edward Leigh, Patrick McLoughlin and Tim Eggar) attempted to promote the privatised options vigorously. The full costs of the DTI campaign are, however, not determinable. In contrast, the UCW had a total staff of 120 and an annual turnover of £12.5 million. The unions had a handful of 'communications staff' in total. They claim to have spent £500,000 on their campaign – most of which went on printing and distributing campaign material (including over 7 million assorted cards and leaflets) over a six-month period in 1994. This amount was far beyond the means of most unions, but still considerably less than that spent by the combined pro-privatisation lobby of the DTI and Post Office management

---

5 The campaign involved: private meetings with 150 MPs; at least three mailouts to all 190,000 postal workers, explaining events and putting the case for privatisation; monthly front-page spreads in *The Courier*, the Post Office staff magazine; regional briefing meetings and weekly updates for 12,000 managerial staff; a hotline number for employees and members of the public to call; a glossy document arguing the case for privatisation – sent to all main offices, 'opinion formers' and 'decision makers'; a promotional video distributed to post offices and sub-post offices; a high-profile media campaign; and advertising in the national press (interview with James Lindsey, 24.6.97).

6 This figure was actually estimated by the UCW (according to UCW Sub-Group Committee minutes, 25.8.94, and interviews with union staff) and probably an exaggeration. The Post Office itself, claimed that it had only spent £38,000 – a figure that would not have covered the printing and postage of one letter being sent to all employees. The exact figure remains unknown.

Table 8.1 Actors cited in press coverage

	Pro-privatisation %	Anti-privatisation %	Others %
DTI/Heseltine	10.4		
Government			5.2
PO management	18.7		
Unions		14.0	
Labour		16.5	
Other organisations			12.1
Conservative rebels		18.7	
Public/postal workers			4.4
Total	29.1	49.2	21.7

Note: Sample, 364 citations in 283 articles

The content analysis also suggests that government and business sources did generally dominate. While the unions and Labour Party were widely cited in articles, their overall contributions to news content were rather smaller than those of Post Office management and Heseltine/the DTI. Unions and other anti–privatisers did appear to do well in terms of being cited in articles (see table 8.1). The Labour Party (16.5 per cent) and the unions (14.0 per cent) figured rather more than members of the DTI (10.4 per cent) and other government figures (5.2 per cent). The most cited groups were in fact Post Office management (18.7 per cent) and Conservative Party rebels (18.7 per cent). However, the focus on source quotations is somewhat misleading. The contributions of the Labour Party and the unions were, more often than not, reduced to a single quotation in the middle or end of the article. In other words, they were simply used to offer 'journalistic balance' within articles framed by the contributions of other organisations.

Table 8.2 Sources contributing to press coverage

	Pro-privatisation %	Anti-privatisation %	Others %
DTI/Heseltine	20.7		
Government			19.0
PO management	15.6		
Unions		12.6	
Labour		11.0	
Other organisations			11.3
Conservative rebels		8.5	
Public/postal workers			1.2
Total	36.3	32.1	31.6

Note: Sample, 564 contributions in 283 articles

Indeed, if the same articles are looked at in terms of article content and actors' contributions (see table 8.2), the results are strongly skewed in favour of the DTI (20.7 per cent), other government sources (19.0 per cent), and Post Office managers (15.6 per cent). Labour (11.0 per cent) and the unions (12.6 per cent) are some way down, with Conservative 'rebels' (8.5 per cent) contributing least. This picture becomes more skewed still when looking at the number of times groups are not mentioned at all. The views of Heseltine and the DTI are discussed in, or contribute to, 89 per cent of articles. Post Office management are included in 56 per cent of stories. The unions are only mentioned in 37 per cent. The public and postal workers have negligible input, with 4.4 per cent of citations and 1.2 per cent of contributions.

From the point of view of the journalists covering the story it was also the institutions and their spokespersons – the Post Office and DTI – who were responsible for placing the issue on the political and news agendas. According to Roland Gribben of the *Telegraph* (interview, 21.5.99): 'It was a combined effort. The government effectively brought it in. The Treasury and the DTI had had it sitting on the back burner for some time. But it really came to the fore when Hezza decided to bring it in. At the same time Post Office management had been pushing it behind the scenes – they wanted their freedom from government.'[7] Thus, as demonstrated in virtually all earlier studies of media content (e.g. Sigal, 1973, Hall *et al.*, 1978, Gans, 1979, Herman and Chomsky, 1988, Tiffen, 1989, Hallin, 1994), the substance of coverage proved to be very much guided by institutional sources.

At the same time, an examination of the media profiles of the principal organisations involved (see figure 8.1) demonstrates that the content of coverage was significantly more unfavourable to Heseltine and the DTI. For most of the period the unions were presented quite neutrally, scoring a small positive average for all papers except the *Daily Express*. The overall rating for Post Office management was slightly negative, with only the *Daily Express* and *Sun* newspapers offering positive overall coverage; its least favourable exponents were the *Mirror* and the *FT*. The DTI and Heseltine had the most negative coverage with an overall weekly average below -0.5. Their main detractors were the *Mirror* and *Today*; their least critical were *The Times* and the *FT*. This picture was not uniform throughout the period. For the first ten weeks of the campaign, until late July, the DTI/Heseltine appeared to be struggling but in contention. After that they rarely managed to obtain neutral coverage and came out extremely badly in the last seven weeks. Post Office management had fairly neutral coverage during the first fourteen weeks, faced a negative barrage at the start of

---

7 Roland Rudd, then at the *FT* (interview, 23.11.98), 'I'm not taking anything away from the union but the Post Office itself did a remarkable job of getting it on the political agenda … That it became possible was down to Heseltine, who was in favour when he came in and he had large Tory backbench support for it. But it got on the agenda because of the efforts of Bill Cockburn and the Post Office'; Keith Harper (interview, 20.5.99), 'The government brought it on to the agenda because they wanted to privatise the Post Office. It was one of the big things that Heseltine wanted to do. Post Office management were very much in favour of it, because firstly it would commercially free up the Post Office, and secondly, because they personally stood to gain quite a lot of money in the long run'.

Figure 8.1 Cumulative favourability of coverage for organisations in the broadsheet press, 18 May to 3 November 1994

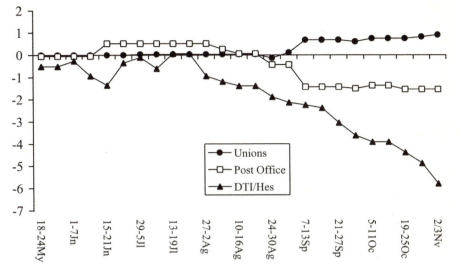

Note: sample, 283 articles. For an account of how favourability ratings are obtained see figure 5.1.

September, and never recovered thereafter. The unions maintained neutral coverage and gained some positive coverage after week 15.

What becomes clear from these findings is that less access to the media does not necessarily mean poorer presentation of an organisation's case or profile. One might even conclude that 'news values' tend towards negative coverage and that more coverage of a powerful but poorly communicating source harms an organisation's cause. In this respect it might be argued that the coverage and outcome of the campaign was less related to union communication activity and had rather more to do with the general divisions and tactical errors of their high-profile oppositions – an explanation suggested in several other studies of institutional sources (Hallin, 1994, Miller, 1994, Schlesinger and Tumber, 1994).

Institutional divisions

The pro-privatisation sources were indeed divided and, consequently, their communication campaigns were erratic. By 1994, the Conservative government was already deeply unpopular and holding the smallest majority since it came to power. On the issue of Post Office privatisation, the cabinet was profoundly split between 'consolidators' and 'radicals'. While Heseltine and Clarke had managed to resolve their differences in favour of privatisation, Major was unsure, and several cabinet members – notably Hurd, Newton and Hunt – were opposed to it. Major's own position was so weak that speculation was rife about his immediate survival as Prime Minister. Press coverage at the time highlighted the level of public opposition and pointed out that it was a privatisation that not even Margaret Thatcher had dared to attempt. As a memo to the UCW, from Connect in April 1994, commented (Connect Public Affairs Ltd correspondence with UCW, 21.4.94): 'The consolidators in the Cabinet believe that after an impossibly difficult legislative year, it would be best not to proceed with what could well be highly controversial legislation which would leave ministers vulnerable to pressure from potential rebels.'

The ambivalence and fears of the party were reflected in a confused and inter- mittent campaign. Divisions and anxieties resulted in a green paper being delivered rather than the government pressing ahead with a White Paper. As the whole issue was then technically 'under review', neither the government nor DTI could actively campaign for their preferred option. Guy Black (interview, 18.6.97), commenting on the government campaign, said:

> I don't think it existed in any great way. To some extent, my instinct was, that the DTI lamentably failed ministers in this matter. Over the summer there was a lot of opposition and by the time it got to the party conference, the game was almost up. During these three months (July, August, September) the government was making absolutely no effort to sell their proposals to anyone – the back-benchers, the public, or whoever.

Whether it was ministers or civil servants, the case was not put across.[8] It was also apparent that Post Office management, ministers in the DTI and Treasury, and their allies in the IoD and CBI, were not in accord. Post Office management wanted freedom but as a whole organisation. For Heseltine freedom meant privatisation, but he knew that full privatisation would be politically impossible. To complicate matters, the Treasury was only going to be happy if it could either continue to tax the Post Office each year or gain the revenue from a sale of 50 per cent or more of it. Heseltine's final compromise of a 51 per cent sell-off left none of the supposed allies for privatisation happy and no more likely to co-operate than before. When the IoD and CBI began calling for a 100 per cent privatisation, this only served to heighten opposition and upset a shaky compromise.

Thus, one could convincingly argue that the divisions amongst the pro-privati- sation lobby caused their campaign to implode at an early stage. If any credit is to be given to the unions' communications campaign several questions need to be answered. How did they: (a) overcome their economic and communications resource deficits; (b) manage to put across convincing and authoritative arguments with little institutional authority or legitimacy; and (c) manage to set news agendas and exploit elite-source conflicts with little obvious media access?

---

8 These views were echoed in the press and in interviews with DTI civil servants. A 'ministerial source' was quoted in the *Guardian* (Bates, 1994, p4) as saying 'It is not a question of opposing the sell-off but of having a clear strategy for winning public support … The feeling is that not enough attention has been given to promoting the idea.' As a DTI official recalled (interview, 16.6.97), 'The way it came out in the end – there was not a clear government proposal for privatisation. Although there was clearly a preferred option, the government had to appear to remain judiciously open – it couldn't simply come out and lobby for the one they preferred. In the end, the government as a whole was just that much more ambivalent … One might even reach the conclusion that not enough was done against the campaign to stop privatisation'.

Overcoming the economic and media deficits

PR expertise, media contacts and insider information

While the unions, led by the UCW, did not have the PR and economic resources of their rivals, they found several ways to overcome their shortfall. This began with an accumulation of in-house and consultancy expertise. Since 1990 the UCW had begun to build up its communications capacity with the employment of its first full-time Media and Campaigns Officer (Daniel Harris). With the arrival of the new general secretary, Alan Johnson, the emphasis on media relations grew as the communications budget increased (Chris Proctor interview, 2.6.97). In 1993, Julia Simpson was thus recruited as head of communications. By 1994 there was an established core team of four, plus other union representatives, meeting on a regular basis. As preparations developed, the unions made up for their lack of professional communications staff by hiring a number of consultants. Connect Public Affairs Ltd was taken on in August 1992 – to lobby, advise on strategy and keep the unions updated on parliamentary and government activity. Keith Bill of Union Communications was employed to run PPS (Protect our Postal Services) in March 1993.

As the campaigns got under way in the summer of 1994, in addition to pulling in more union support staff, further consultants were recruited. David Lane, an ex-director of Royal Mail International, was hired. The most widely publicised alliance, however, was with Lowe-Bell Political, headed by a principal adviser to Margaret Thatcher and the Conservative Party – Tim Bell. Lowe-Bell supplied a team of four to work part-time on the campaign for a six-month period starting in July 1994. Both sets of consultants brought contacts and access to the business community and Conservative Party. The overall costs of all these consultants ate heavily into union funds but were substantially less than many press estimates claimed. Consultancy fees accounted for approximately a fifth of the £500,000 campaign bill.[9]

Although the unions did not have the media profile of their opponents, the core team had spent a lot of time building up media contacts. As Daniel Harris explained (interview, 18.6.97):

> I built up a long-term rapport with the media … This filtered through to the national press. For three years I was putting out press releases and talking to people … Throughout the period, from a very drip drip drip approach we were getting good stories about local postmen in … It was a long slow build-up of quotes and stories, always giving the union the moral high ground.

---

9 Bills for Connect varied from a few hundred pounds up to £2,000 per month. The London Economics report was billed at £20,047.62 (London Economics correspondence). Desperate to win the contract, Lowe-Bell offered its services at very reduced rates (recorded in UCW Sub-Group Committee correspondence, 29.6.94). Two interviewees put the costs at less than £40,000 in total. Total costs in consultancy fees are thus estimated to have been in the region of £90,000.

Lowe-Bell's arrival also brought in its contacts with the right-wing press.[10] Thus, by the summer of 1994, the UCW had built up, or purchased through hiring PR consultants, regular media contacts across the national media. In effect, it had accumulated large amounts of media capital as sources – enough to begin competing with the Post Office and DTI. Keith Harper, then industrial correspondent for the *Guardian*, confirmed the level of union information subsidies being supplied at the time (interview, 20.5.99):

> They [the UCW] were a big source for journalists. They provided surveys and polls and documents and provided stories through their members ... the UCW played it so well, there's absolutely no doubt. By a succession of polls and surveys and political activity, from meetings to demonstrations in local town centres, the unions led a very successful campaign

The consultants also delivered vital inside intelligence on their opponents' actions. This allowed the unions to time their activities, outmanoeuvre their opponents, and make best use of their resources. As Mario Dunn of the UCW (interview, 23.6.97) explained: 'We were aware when pressure was needed most – timing was the key element. You can write to an opinion-former or policy-maker, but if you do it two weeks too early it's useless.' Connect Public Affairs Ltd, the CMA union and David Lane all provided detailed information on Post Office and DTI plans for privatisation. Connect Public Affairs Ltd was the eyes and ears of the unions in Parliament. As its initial correspondence with the UCW stated (Connect Public Affairs Ltd correspondence, 21.8.92): 'Connect is in a very good position to provide the union with political intelligence. We have excellent contacts with the Department of Trade and Industry, including with ministerial private offices. We can provide the union with an early warning system on developments on Post Office privatisation'. Advance warnings enabled the unions to begin initial preparations as early as January 1992 – six months before Heseltine's first announcement of a parliamentary review. This continuing flow of information also kept the unions up to date with every important committee or cabinet meeting, thus allowing media exposure and public campaigns to be timed appropriately.

The use of union membership

While the UCW could not match its opponents' economic, professional PR and media resources, it did have a very significant resource in its 160,000 members. The UCW had over 100 branches spread across the UK – possibly the best network of any union in the UK and far superior to many businesses and government departments. In addition to the UCW's membership, the CMA had 14,000 members in Post Office management positions. The unions identified this potential campaign-

---

10 Guy Black (interview, 18.6.97), 'Rather then just getting articles into the *Guardian*, the *Mirror* and the *Independent*, we thought of ways of getting stories into the *Sun*, *The Times* and the *Telegraph*. The UCW was doing a brilliant job in the local and national press – we could only refine this and help in placing them in non-pro-union newspapers'.

ing resource early on and the membership became a vital part of the campaign. Media training was given, and campaign packs circulated, to all local branch representatives. Branches worked hard to promote the union message in the regions – through the local media, town councils, local events and in letter-writing to local MPs. Every union postman and postwoman was given information cards and encouraged to discuss the issues with customers on their doorsteps. In fact, in Keith Bill's estimation (interview, 19.6.97), one widely supported by other sources:[11] 'The real credit should go to the members – they were the ones that won it – not Lowe-Bell. They sent ten times as much mail to MPs as the railways campaigners.'

At the same time, this network was carefully co-ordinated and kept uniform by campaign headquarters. Communication was maintained with branches through regular 'Special Branch Circulars'. As a UCW campaign brief explained:

> Using the media will be an important factor in these campaigns. Political Officers and Regional Secretaries are already receiving news releases and election information. Headquarters can also send out prepared news releases to blanket over 850 titles nation-wide. This has the effect of ensuring the same message reaches everyone at the same time ... In conclusion, we need tight co-ordination from the top and a lot of activity on the ground.

This closely co-ordinated media and letter-writing campaign worked consistently over the summer and was used to maximum effect at particular pressure points.[12]

Clearly the unions made up for their lack of professional and economic resources in a number of ways. The unions had tighter and more direct lines of communication – all focused through a small and fast-acting committee. They bought in consultants to provide specialist knowledge and greater media and political 'insider' access. This was combined with a large and extensive network of voluntary labour that remained tightly co-ordinated from the top. What also becomes apparent when comparing the three sides was that the UCW's communications structure was also better suited to fighting the campaign. The DTI and Post Office, while having much larger networks of communications officers, were more likely to be slowed down by their extensive bureaucracies. While each maintained consistent channels of communication with the media, those channels were structured to produce an even, steady and long-term form of output. They were thus not set up for the speed and adaptability of a fast-moving campaign.

---

11 Interviews with Daniel Harris (18.6.97), Guy Black (18.6.97), Roland Rudd (23.11.98) and Keith Harper (20.5.99), and in articles in *FT* (Taylor, 1994a, p8) and *PR Week* (3.11.94, p1).

12 For example, a UCW Sub-Group Committee letter commented (1.7.94): 'In one part of London alone, 70 postmen and women are preparing to deliver leaflets at weekends in their own time.' Another reports (25.8.94): 'Activity by branches is frenetic. Millions of leaflets have been distributed. Rallies are being organised every weekend and countless initiatives are being pursued in relation to local petitions.'

Overcoming the limits of institutional authority with third-party endorsement

One of the most significant factors in the media campaign was the unions' use of third-party endorsement. As Lowe-Bell strategists explained (Lowe-Bell Political, presentation, 1994): 'Winning is all that matters – not how much the UCW is in the news ... the campaign must encourage submissions independently of the unions' case but which support its central arguments. It is vital that this process does not look like a union inspired lobby.' The unions developed their strategy accordingly. Through a mixture of lobbying, public campaigning and polling, they galvanised a range of opposition sources and helped feed third-party opinions to the media. In effect, they bypassed the need for institutional legitimacy and direct access. Instead they gained a voice by using the legitimacy and access possessed by other sources: the public, 'economic experts', politicians and assorted 'neutral' user groups.

Public opinion and economic experts

The 'voice of public opinion' was aired frequently by the commissioning and publishing of opinion polls – a common PR ruse for getting coverage in the national press. A series of polls, conducted by Gallup, Access Opinions and MORI, were conducted – usually on behalf of the UCW. The polls, of the general public, Conservative voters, constituency chairpersons, sub-postmasters, Post Office managers and MPs, found their way into the national press with some regularity – often providing the basis for a headline story. In the content analysis, sixteen articles featured a MORI poll in the story, and poll results were mentioned with great frequency by all anti-privatisation campaigners. 'Sub-Postmasters Oppose Sell-Off' (Timmins, 1994, p2), 'Post Office Managers Reject Sale' (Whitfield, 1994, p7), 'Tory MPs "Oppose Sell-Off of Royal Mail"' (Wynn-Davies, 1994, p6), were some of the MORI-inspired headlines in the *Independent*.

The unions also set up Protect our Postal Services, in March 1993, to organise and promote localised public responses that were 'not under the UCW banner'. The group was made up of a number of charities and pressure groups with an interest in postal services.[13] Although the unions had minimal representation on the PPS board, the two were closely connected. Keith Bill simultaneously acted as secretary of PPS and sat on the UCW sub-group campaign committee. Protect our Postal Services press releases refer enquirers to Guy Black or Bill Hamilton – both of whom were working for Lowe-Bell on the UCW campaign. The demands of the organisation were never particularly different from those of the Post Office Unions Council. As a UCW Sub-Group Committee letter (1.7.94) explained: 'Once they [PPS] have seen

---

13   These included the National Federation of Women's Institutes, Action with Rural Communities in England (ACRE), Royal Associatiion for Disability and Rehabilitation (RADAR), Help the Aged, the National League for the Blind and Disabled. The inaugural meeting took place in March 1993. The official launch, with cross-party support, took place at the House of Commons in June 1993.

the Green Paper they will adopt a position and campaign vigorously on what is likely to be a platform remarkably similar to our own (aimed at keeping the Post Office together).'

One of the most skilful PR moves by the UCW was to get free-market econo-mists to argue its case for it. In advance of June 1994, the unions had already put forward alternative proposals in the shape of an Economists Advisory Group (EAG)-commissioned report (EAG, August 1993) and a submission to the Trade and Industry Select Committee. Advice after June, from all the consultants concerned, was for the union to present a credible 'alternative White Paper' at the end of the consultation period. According to Lowe-Bell Political (presentation, 1994), this would come from 'a reputable Business School, preferably using a consultant that is a known Tory sympathiser' and would be an 'independent and authoritative study on the case for greater commercial freedom within the public sector'. Eventually London Economics was commissioned to produce a report at short notice. Although Bill Robinson, the principal author, had been an adviser to Norman Lamont, and the consultancy was generally recognised to be a Thatcherite think tank, the report argued the unions' case. The conclusions of the report (London Economics, September 1994, p79) stated: 'evidence suggests that there is no reason to believe that, simply by transferring the Post Office to the private sector, the company and the public will benefit from significant gains than would be the case if the Post Office remained publicly owned ... We propose an alternative model of a publicly-owned, commercially free Post Office'. Predictably, the report was taken up and given wide coverage.

Supplying information subsidies to politicians

Just as sources supply an information subsidy to various media outlets, so they do the same for supportive MPs. In this case, the unions and their hired consultants provided detailed briefs, ready-drafted speeches and motions, and a communica-tions network for Labour, the Ulster Unionists and rebel Conservative MPs. Although running its own campaign, the Labour Party was in close contact with the unions throughout. Both set up national petitions and paraded over-sized letters, surveyed sub-postmasters, referred to the same MORI polls and argued for increased 'commercial freedom within the public sector'. The arguments on Value Added Tax (VAT), closure of rural post offices, loss of the second delivery and international comparisons, all argued in Labour campaign materials and in parlia-mentary debates, each appear remarkably similar to campaign materials, strategy and research documents produced by the UCW. Peter Hain MP, the most vocal Labour critic after Robin Cook, had previously worked for the UCW. He remained in regular contact with the union and asked parliamentary questions in accordance with union strategy.

The battle for the support of dissident Conservative MPs and Ulster Unionists employed much of the time of local branch members and Lowe-Bell. A combina-tion of lobbying, local media campaigns and letter-writing pushed wavering Conservatives towards very public rebellion. The unions were in frequent contact with Nicholas Winterton and other Conservative rebels. Right up until Heseltine's final meeting with rebels on the 1 November, the unions were briefing them and organising their resistance (Lane, correspondence 30.10.94). Jim Lester, a prominent rebel and proposer of a well-publicised Early Day Motion, was sponsored by the CMA union. The motion, immediately signed by seven Conservative rebels (with up to twelve more to follow), was itself penned by the UCW (Mario Dunn, interview, 23.6.97) and simply supported the unions' position (Hansard, 19.10.94): 'This motion ... welcomes the publication of a report by London Economics ... and therefore supports the parts of the Green Paper which retain the Post Office as an integrated organisation in the public sector, endowed with greater commercial freedom.' The Ulster Unionists were also lobbied regularly and directly. A meeting at the Commons was arranged for the MPs in July and a special briefing document, spelling out the problems of privatisation for Northern Ireland, prepared for them by the UCW (UCW, July 1994).

Alliances with assorted user groups

A third conglomeration of third-party endorsement was built up from user groups and other interested parties. The main targets were the Mail Users Association (MUA), the Post Office Users' National Council (POUNC) and the National Federation of Sub-Postmasters (NFSP). All three were lobbied and had informal talks with the unions. As a UCW Sub-Group Committee circular (25.8.94) explained: 'As already reported, the Mail Users Association are on course to produce a helpful response to the Green Paper ... We are also working hard to influence the POUNC response ...'. After a closely fought lobbying battle for the support of the National Federation of Sub-Postmasters, which included a UCW survey of sub-postmasters, Colin Baker of the NFSP agreed to meet with the union. It was subsequently reported (USW Sub-Group Committee letter, 14.9.94) that: 'following our discussion we are now guaranteed a positive message from the NFSP nationally'.[14] All three, plus the Periodical Publishers' Association (PPA) and Reader's Digest, eventually adopted positions that, if not entirely in accord with the unions, were critical of the government's attempts to break up the Post Office.

The degree of accord between the UCW and its allies becomes apparent in the press releases and submissions to the DTI that followed. The union response to the Green Paper (POUC, Sept. 1994, p3) reads: 'Ownership is itself not the most important issue facing the Post Office ... (p29) If the government is genuinely committed to ensuring that the whole of the Post Office remains a British success story, it will keep it together and give it genuine commercial freedom in the public sector.' These can be compared to a number of allied organisational press releases at the time. David Rogers of the MUA (press release, 17.6.94) 'Privatisation is but a

---

14 Similar lobbying efforts were also reported in correspondence with David Lane (12.7.94) and in a
    UCW Sub-Group Committee memo (25.8.94).

political option and not necessarily the best option available'; POUNC (press release, 30.9.94) 'The postal users watchdog has told government that it is unable to endorse any of its proposals and it has urged that consideration be given to keeping all three post office businesses together'; the National Consumer Council declared (press release, 19.10.94) that it was 'critical of the Green Paper for failing to consider the option of keeping the three parts of the Post Office together, either privatised or in continued public ownership'; Colin Baker of the NFSP (press release, 30.9.94) 'It [the Federation] does not see ownership as a critical issue. However should separation and privatisation take place, the Federation has many concerns'; PPS (1994, 'Freedom to Deliver') 'the natural synergy of common ownership. Protect our Postal Services believes now is the time to examine in detail the mechanisms required to give the Post Office the financial freedom it needs as an integrated network within the public sector'.[15] These submissions and releases all found their way, in some form, into the national press. 'Customers Unsure of Need for Change' (1.7.94), 'Post Office Watchdog Raps Sell-Off Plans' (30.9.94), 'Sub-Postmasters Seek Sale Pledge' (1.10.94) and 'Double Blow for Postal Sell-off' (3.10.94) were some of the headlines to emerge in the *FT*.

Reviewing the figures for organisational contributions (table 8.3), it transpires that many of the 'other organisations' (see tables 8.1 and 8.2), frequently presented as neutrals, are actually 'union allies'. These allies contributed substantially to press articles during the period. 'Rebels' were cited 68 times. Other cited 'allies', not already mentioned, included David Lane, the Liberal Democrats, the National Consumer Council (NCC), Lowe-Bell, and Age Concern. The contributions of these others amounted to 40 quotations and 59 organisational contributions. If the

Table 8.3 Organisations contributing to press coverage

	Pro-privatisation %	Anti-privatisation %	Others %
DTI/Heseltine	20.7		
Government			19.0
PO management	15.6		
Unions		12.6	
Labour		11.0	
Other union allies		10.5	
DTI allies (CBI, IoD)	0.9		
Rebels		8.5	
Public/postal workers			1.2
Total	37.2	42.6	20.2

Note: Sample, 564 contributions in 283 articles

15 Others included: the Ulster Unionist Party (submission, September 1994), the Periodical Publishers Association (submission, 30.9.94), and Reader's Digest (submission, 19.9.94).

totals for organisational contribution are re-evaluated, table 8.2 is reshaped as table 8.3 above. What transpires is that the media contributions of the unions and the Labour party could not alone match those arguing for privatisation. If union allies including rebels are added, media output is more constructed of anti-privatisers.

Significantly, most of the anti-privatisation contributions in fact came in the last five and a half weeks of the campaign – when media interest was consistently high and government legislation being finalised. During this period there thus occurred an unrelenting media barrage from supposedly neutral parties. This began with widespread coverage of the report by London Economics on 26 September[16] and ended in early November with stories focusing on the dissent of Conservative Party rebels. In total, assorted union allies made thirty-one contributions to articles in this period – just over half their input for the twenty-five weeks analysed. Labour Party (twenty-two) and Conservative party rebels (twenty-eight) added forty-nine contributions. The unions themselves only contributed to twenty-one articles. The total for anti-privatisation contributions then amounted to 112 in the last five and a half weeks – just under half (47 per cent) the total for the twenty-five week period. The effect was seemingly to isolate the government during its most important decision-making period – something that had been planned by the unions far in advance.[17] Ultimately the government's supply of institutional authority was effectively cancelled out, without the unions ever needing to gain a significant level of institutional legitimacy themselves.

---

16 This was followed by: David Lane, a former director for the Post Office, 'now a business consultant', attacking privatisation (29.9.94); an announcement that Lowe-Bell, 'the Conservative Party PR guru', was joining the unions to work against privatisation (29.9.94); POUNC, the industry's watchdog, arguing against splitting up and selling off parts of the Post Office (30.9.94); the PPS group of charities petitioning against privatisation (30.9.94); the NFSP criticising the government's Green Paper options (1.10.94); the publication of a MORI poll of Conservative Party chairmen in which 57 per cent supported the public sector option and only 39 per cent supported any form of privatisation (2.10.94); another MORI poll of Conservative voters in the constituencies of John Major and Michael Heseltine, which showed that 66 per cent were against the government's preferred option; John Taylor, Ulster Unionist MP, announced that he had had more recent letters on this subject than on any other in the previous ten years (3.10.94); the official submission on the Green Paper from the Ulster Unionists opposing the privatisation options (9.10.94); all polls were republished in full-page adverts on the day Heseltine addressed the Conservative Party conference (12.10.94); the National Consumer Council declared its opposition (18.10.94); an Early Day Motion, opposed to privatisation and supporting the London Economics alternative, signed by eight dissident Conservative MPs with more to follow (22.10.94); a leaked Post Office management report, which stated that the Treaty of Rome would force legislation on the government, threatening the future viability of the separate privatised Post Office companies (22.10.94); a MORI poll of Conservative MPs, which revealed that 77 per cent of mail on the issue was opposed to privatisation (24.10.94); between the 27 October and the 2 November, the press was dominated by stories of increases in rebel ranks and the London Economics alternative.

17 In early 1993, Connect Public Affairs Ltd had already predicted that the government would be attempting to announce legislation in the Queen's Speech in November 1994 (Connect Public Affairs Ltd correspondence, 16.4.93). All the consultants to the union campaign advised striking hard during the run-up to the November speech.

Setting news agendas, dividing oppositions and the creation of negative news

In spite of having less direct input into the news production process, union tactics did much to set agendas and interpretive frameworks. In addition to orchestrating a range of opposition voices, they continually pursued media-friendly lines of argument, encouraged divisions among the pro-privatisation lobbies and made each opposition proposition appear unworkable. Thus, in stark contrast to earlier decades, the unions managed simultaneously to avoid media scrutiny and to make their institutional opponents appear confused, untrustworthy and even illegal in their activities.

Presenting a positive union image

From the start, the unions worked hard to avoid the media pitfalls of earlier union campaigns by avoiding industrial action and minimising the issue of potential job losses. At the union annual conferences, each union passed motions condemning any moves towards privatisation but voted against strike action. As in several recent successful union campaigns (see chapter seven), the emphasis at all times was to protect public services and to protect the Post Office. The Post Office itself was promoted as a part of 'Britain's heritage' and an economically successful public service. The popularity of postmen and women were also played up, as was the importance of the local post office in rural communities. As Chris Proctor (interview, 2.6.97) explained:

> We didn't concentrate on traditional trade union interests. We lost 100,000 jobs in the BT privatisation and the job issue certainly worried our members. But we took the view that we lost that because demos and strikes were inherently bad news from a PR point of view. So the whole thing wasn't save our jobs but save your post office and protect your services ... We justified the fact that people liked the Royal Mail. Ideas really struck a chord. Just the issue of the Queen's head and the possibility that it wouldn't be on stamps anymore. It seemed almost unpatriotic to privatise the post office. Julia came up with the idea that people liked their local postman. We realised that we had 160,000 members; that we had 160,000 ambassadors that we could use.

To avoid accusations of intransigence, the unions campaigned, not against change, but for the positive alternative of greater commercial freedom within the public sector. Thus, the Economists Advisory Group (August 1993) and London Economics (September 1994) reports were compiled. Throughout, privatisation *per se* was not directly attacked. Rather the government's particular proposals for privatisation were. Returning to the media content analysis, it is similarly clear that the unions were rarely portrayed as defenders of union employment. Out of 285 articles, the jobs question is mentioned in the headline in only six pieces (less than 2 per cent). The jobs issue is only discussed in fourteen articles altogether – only 13 per cent of all stories in which the unions are mentioned and in less than 5 per cent in total.

Undermining Post Office management

It also becomes apparent that many of the difficulties of the DTI and Post Office management were compounded by, or arose directly out of, union activities. Around the start of September, the unions hit Post Office management hard. A UCW Sub-Group Committee circular (25.8.94) reports: 'As you will be aware the Post Office has launched a huge internal and external communications campaign. We aim to produce reliable figures to demonstrate how much this will cost them – it will be a good news story. Certainly it is unprecedented for public servants to act in this way during a privatisation debate.' An article about Post Office management expenditure duly appeared in the *Telegraph* (Goodman, 1994), to be repeated in *The Times* (Bassett and Pierce, 1994, p10) and other papers. The Post Office campaign was subsequently criticised by many papers, on grounds of expense and legality. As Ross Tieman of *The Times* asked (1994b, p21) 'And why have they broken the unwritten rule that says leading executives of state corporations never, repeat never, speak out on ownership issues?'

A MORI poll of post office managers, conducted for the CMA in August 1994, was also released to the press in September. This showed that 76 per cent of managers were actually in favour of the public sector option and that the higher levels of Post Office management were isolated: 'the results show' said Terry Degan of the CMA, 'that the Chairman and Chief Executive are not speaking for managers in their support for privatisation and break up of the Post Office'. At the same time, Post Office management were given the 'fat cat' tag and accused simply of seeking personal gain from any potential share sale.

The favourability profile of Post Office management consequently suffered a large dip in September. Management was now unsure of where the government stood and whether it should, or was legally able, to continue campaigning for the privatisation option. As a result of the union attacks they halted their media efforts and concentrated more on their lobbying campaign. After September, Post Office contributions to articles declined rapidly.

Dividing and conquering the Conservative Party

From an early stage, advice to the union was to put pressure on the government and exploit existing divisions.[18] Much of the union campaign was thus aimed at exploiting Conservative splits and complicating each new privatisation proposal. As Guy Black, at the time with Lowe-Bell, explained (interview, 18.6.97): 'There were three campaigns really … The third, to throw spanners in the wheels of the

---

18 As early as August 1992, Connect Public Affairs Ltd (correspondence, 21.8.92) was advising 'The object of the campaign is to make it politically difficult for the government to proceed with Post Office privatisation'; Lowe-Bell advised (presentation, 1994), 'THE CAMPAIGN MUST Focus the enormous support for the Post Office in a way that maximises the political opposition to privatisation on the government back benches … There are also government divisions to be exploited – The Conservative right could be mobilised to use the issue to undermine Heseltine's leadership ambitions'.

decision-making process – EU law, the commercialisation option was cheaper, etc. These were aimed at civil servants who advised ministers. A lot of articles appeared about the Post Office in which privatisation was not the issue – commercial freedom was.' First it was demonstrated that complete privatisation was unworkable because cross-subsidisation was essential for maintaining the rural network of offices and the other loss-making parts of the Post Office. When a 51 per cent privatisation was proposed, in order to safeguard these parts, the unions and their allies argued that it made more economic sense for the Post Office to be kept together, whether private or public. Eventually, when Heseltine made a last attempt to compromise with a 40 per cent privatisation, it was pointed out that this would bring in less revenue than three years' worth of the External Financing Limit (EFL) currently imposed on the Post Office (Lane, correspondence, 30.10.94) – thus making the option unpalatable for the Treasury. Ministers from the DTI were consequently forever forced on to the defensive. There were frequent 'assurances' and retreats by the DTI, all designed to allay public and Conservative backbench fears. But at each step, the unions changed their lines of attack again.

The unions did not only exploit confusions over policy, they targeted particular Conservatives with great accuracy. Lowe-Bell's ability to 'get behind enemy lines' and Connect's 'insider' access were used to good effect. These two sources gave the unions knowledge of the timing of government decision-making and of the personal divisions that existed in the cabinet and across the party. Thus, on 6 May 1994 (Connect Public Affairs Ltd, correspondence), Connect informed the UCW of the impending cabinet meeting on the issue that was to be held towards the end of the month. The UCW, following a Channel 4 news exclusive on the 17 May, was then ready to move into action. In addition to a number of dire warnings about the future of the Post Office, its press releases included a survey of Conservative backbenchers showing that 30 per cent wanted privatisation either slowed or stopped. Most of the press that day, most notably the *Telegraph*, included Alan Johnson's warnings about 'political and electoral suicide' and/or the survey results. The splurge of negative coverage, along with recently published opinion polls, might well have been enough to push an already wavering cabinet into announcing the delivery of a Green Paper – rather than the expected White one.

The UCW also diligently sought out the addresses of all local Conservative Party associations, Conservative councillors and MPs. This information was supplied to local branches so that extensive local mail campaigns could be organised.[19] Those especially targeted included Jeremy Hanley, David Hunt, Richard Ryder, John Major, Tony Newton and Douglas Hurd, all of whom were widely reported in the press as

---

19 As a UCW special branch circular (14.10.94) explained: 'The next two weeks will be crucial. We have identified a group of Cabinet Ministers and Government Whips upon whom we want to bring maximum pressure. The best way this can be done is for them to receive a large postbag from their own constituents. To this end we have produced a special leaflet for delivery in their constituency. IT IS VITAL THIS LEAFLET IS DELIVERED EARLY IN THE WEEK COMMENCING 17TH OCTOBER 1994.'

being either opposed to, or dubious about the prospects of, Post Office privatisation. Local Conservative MP doubts, often resulting from local campaigns, also found their way into the public domain. As Roland Rudd, then of the *FT*, recounted (interview, 23.11.98): 'The local campaigns were relentless and they frequently embarrassed local MPs into declaring themselves and potentially having to face the loss of their seats.' There were indeed several statements released to the press which spoke of Conservatives opposing privatisation on account of the mail they had received (e.g., Julian Critchley, 1994, p12, in *The Times*, Peter Emery in the *Telegraph*, on 8 September 1994, and John Taylor in the *FT* – Owen, 1994, p8). As one anonymous Conservative MP said (in Brown, 1994b, p6), 'I don't oppose privatisation but I have had a big mailbag of letters objecting. I think the government should pause.'

Polling was focused as much on Conservative voters, MPs, constituency chair(wo)men, and councillors, as it was on the general public. Many of these same people were polled after several months of being confronted with hostile correspondence and local press campaigns. Polls, press releases and opposition statements were then released and published on important decision-making days for the government and Conservative Party. A UCW special branch circular (26.10.94) revealed how the press had once again been deluged on the weekend before a Monday cabinet committee meeting on privatisation: 'The Cabinet Industry Sub Committee met on Monday, 24th October. This again was a crunch meeting. Colleagues would have seen the press reports over the preceding weekend … The next deadline will be Monday, 31st October when the Industry Committee meets again.' Once again, the *Sun*, *Times*, *FT* and *Independent* all carried stories about the likely collapse of the privatisation project that morning.

By the time of the Conservative Party conference in early October, Conservative Party divisions were being exploited to maximum effect. On the day Heseltine was to address the conference full-page adverts appeared in *The Times* and *Telegraph* (12.10.94) with the results of all the MORI polls, each demonstrating Heseltine's isolation from the public, Conservative grass roots activists, and Conservative voters. As Daniel Harris recounts, the unions and their supporters were out in force (interview, 18.6.97): 'During the Tory party conference we got the nicest, rosiest-faced postman to dish out blue stickers to save the Post Office. When Heseltine got up to talk he was met by this great sea of blue stickers.' In the weeks that remained before the final cabinet meeting, divisions continued, Heseltine remained isolated, and it thus became impossible to unite all parts of the party behind any single option.

Postscript

Since this case study was completed there have been several political discussions on the future of the Post Office. Although Post Office chief executives and chairmen have come and gone, New Labour has come to power, and Alan Johnson has become a Labour MP (in 1997), the same arguments have been played though several times. For much of 1998 the Labour government, pressed by Post Office management, came close to drawing up legislation for a 51 per cent privatisation.

This time the powerful Labour cabinet found itself split and divided under pressure. The arguments resulted in successive DTI ministers – Margaret Beckett and then Peter Mandelson – clashing with Gordon Brown and the Treasury, and contributed to the loss of their cabinet seats. The final result, pushed through by Mandelson shortly before his exit, was greater commercial freedom for the Post Office within the public sector – the option always promoted by the unions. According to several of the journalists interviewed (Roland Rudd, 23.11.98, Seamus Milne, 13.5.99, and Christine Buckley, 1.6.99) once again, the CWU (formerly the UCW) was largely responsible for halting the privatisation option at the discussion stage. As Christine Buckley recounted (interview, 1.6.99):

> At the Labour conference Derek Hodgson virtually eclipsed Peter Mandelson and the decision not to sell off half the Post Office went completely against the government's wishes. The government were privately scared of the power of the CWU and the threat of strike action. They were also scared of the threat to middle England – the threats to local post offices and the network in rural areas. Before Derek Hodgson took over the general secretary post he was seen as a bit of a radical firebrand. But he immediately became new union and followed the same lines of action taken by Alan Johnson.

Conclusion

While, the inadequacies of the DTI and Post Office figure strongly in the collapse of their campaigns, much of the evidence indicates that it was the UCW's campaign which tipped the scales. Opinion polls (NOP Market Research, Feb. 1987) showed that the privatisation of British Rail and the electricity and water utilities were as, if not more, unpopular with the public than Post Office privatisation.[20] Yet all were sold off by the same weakened Major government – something pointed out by several of the interviewees.[21] All but one of the seven journalists interviewed believed the union campaign was largely responsible for causing the Conservatives to back down. In Keith Harper's estimation (interview, 20.5.99):

> No other trade union campaign was as successful during the 80s and 90s. Compared to the miners – if they had kept intact rather than be divided by Scargill's actions, had tactics been different, they might have won. Also look at rail privatisation. The public were strongly against that as well but they lost. So yes, the UCW's campaign was unique and had much to do with the eventual outcome … Although the Conservatives were divided it was down to the campaign. Divisions didn't stop rail privatisation from proceeding.

---

20 In fact, polls of the general public, produced on the Post Office between 1987 and 1994, hint that the campaign strengthened public opinion in the unions' favour. In February 1987, NOP polls showed that 66 per cent preferred the Post Office to be kept public and 25 per cent preferred privatisation. In November 1992, 64 per cent opposed privatisation and 19 per cent supported it. By June 1994, 71 per cent opposed and 10 per cent supported it.
21 Including Keith Bill (19.6.97), Guy Black (18.6.97), Roland Rudd (23.11.98), Keith Harper (20.5.99).

That the Labour government, with an unchallengeable Commons majority and high levels of popular support, was also blocked by the unions, suggests that the collapse of government proposals in 1994 were not simply down to elite conflicts and weaknesses.

The success of the UCW campaign is notable in that it challenges both the pessimism of earlier radical work and the optimism of liberal arguments for journalistic autonomy. First, it clearly demonstrates the ability of 'resource-poor' and 'outsider' groups to gain productive access to the news production process and to those 'elite discourse networks' that tend otherwise to exclude them. The UCW combined its large membership resources with a few in-house experts and external consultants. Their bureaucracies were better co-ordinated and better suited to fighting a rapidly changing campaign. They also consistently managed to sidestep traditional media potholes and promote their campaign in media-friendly ways. In all of this, the UCW demonstrated that all the ploys of government and business PR are just as adaptable to union causes and can be used skilfully to overcome other deficiencies.

At the same time, as other parts of this study also argue, the liberal notions of independent journalism have also been severely undermined. The UCW demonstrated that professional PR methods can make a significant impact on the content of news articles. Government, Post Office and union statements, press conferences and news releases all found their way into the national press – frequently quoted word for word. Most of the time, third parties were presented as neutral representatives, with journalists seemingly unaware of the relationships that existed between the sources they were citing. Reports, polls and other statistics were often referred to without acknowledgement of their origins. Negative campaign material frequently set news agendas. In all of this it becomes clear that 'news values', journalist needs and routines, and news production in general, are not self-contained and independent processes. They are, in fact, observable and malleable procedures which sources can identify and use to gain advantage over other sources.

What also becomes clear is the methodological limitations of earlier content analysis and audience research. That organisations appear more often in the news and/or are cited more often does not necessarily mean they are setting agendas, being positively portrayed or winning arguments. As chapter six reveals, in the 1970s the unions had the greatest media access but were poorly represented next to government and management. In the 1994 dispute these positions were reversed, with government and management gaining most coverage but the poorest representation. That journalists and audience receptionists argue for a high level of autonomy in the reception process does not account for the fact that audiences and journalists are frequently unaware of where information comes from and its creation by partial sources. As Miller (1997) and Deacon et al. (1999) have both argued, there is an additional need for researchers to identify both the processes by which information comes to journalists, and what the final outcomes of campaigns are.

9
CONCLUSION

Public relations and the 'mediatisation' of politics

The rise of professional public relations

The first and most obvious conclusion is that there has been a major growth and spread of professional public relations in Britain. What was once seen as a minor employment area – outside of central government – has become increasingly professional and well resourced. The corporate sector generally, and the City in particular, took the lead in promoting professionalisation and expansion in the industry in the 1980s. Public relations was quickly adopted by the major political parties – first by the Conservatives and then by Labour and the Liberal Democrats. Two decades later, it is now the norm for all medium-sized organisations, be they businesses, institutions or voluntary groups, to have some form of public relations operation. It is very rare for large organisations to have no PR, and even the smallest businesses and associations are more likely to be instituting a communications policy if not hiring PR staff and/or consultants.

A steady expansion of the profession in all these and other areas suggests that organisational heads believe that the practice of PR has a significant use value for their organisations. Chapters three to eight gave a clear indication of just how important the practice has become for the corporate and trade union sectors. For businesses, public relations is, like marketing, advertising or information technology, another means for gaining a market edge. The uses generally include the enhancement of company images, brand management, the recruitment and retention of staff, the winning of contracts, the maintenance of relations with other businesses and the influence of regulatory or economic policy. For companies operating in the City, substantial PR investment has become necessary to sustain share prices (often making a difference of billions of pounds), reduce susceptibility to takeover, retain contracts, and influence financial regulators. For unions, public relations is proving to be equally valuable. In this sector it can be used to change union images, recruit and retain staff and members, place economic and social issues on the political agenda, and influence elite decision-makers in business and government.

In effect, professional public relations has come to operate as another form of modern conflict between organisations, interest groups and individuals, and is employed to achieve long-term and short-term objectives. Under the terms of engagement, audiences both narrow and wide are targeted, and attempts are made to control the communication channels between transmitting organisations and those audiences. Anything that may influence those communication channels is considered to be fair game – from high-profile individuals and journalists to institutions and experts. In such a way, the public relations strategies and information subsidies of one organisation (or, sometimes, individual) are pitted against another through the media and associated communication channels.

The influence of public relations on fourth estate journalism

Of considerable significance to media sociology is the degree to which public relations has worked to erode the autonomy of journalists at the micro level. The influence of public relations practitioners (or sources using PR techniques) was always much greater than scholars recorded, journalists admitted, or consumers were aware of. Many of the standard PR methods for gaining coverage, from manufactured 'diary events' to press conferences and press releases, became fully integrated into the news-gathering process decades ago. However, this working relationship, between PRPs and journalists, although never part of the media fourth estate ideal, was a less serious matter – as long as journalists retained a certain level of day-to-day autonomy, and public relations remained an underdeveloped and under-resourced profession. As chapter two points out, the conditions in both industries in Britain changed significantly during the 1980s and 1990s. Such changing conditions have clearly undermined the independence of journalists and left the ideals of fourth estate journalism more open to question.

In terms of the media industry, the most important change has been an overall decline in the level of news-gathering resources available to individual reporters. National journalists have continually been put under pressure to raise productivity by increasing news output without an equivalent rise in staff numbers or time. Market forces have been brought to bear so directly on journalists that their ability to produce independent, investigative and well researched pieces has been significantly eroded. Thus, national newspapers are going the way of regional papers and trade journals, in that they have developed an overdependence on external subsidies. Subsidies, in the form of newspaper price rises above inflation, cross-subsidisation of newspaper titles by multinational media empires, wire services, the Internet, and the PR industry in all its guises, are what have artificially sustained the national print media over the last decade.

In contrast, changes in the PR industry have been much more enabling for its practitioners. In this sector there has been a rise in both the levels of resources and professional expertise that are available to users of public relations. Public relations practitioners are therefore increasingly better resourced than their journalist counterparts. They also have become more effective by simply accumulating more detailed knowledge on how journalism works and on how particular journalists and publications operate. Public relations output is thus being skilfully adapted to integrate smoothly with the news production process.

Chapters two, five and eight all demonstrated that PR has become extremely successful in passing itself off as 'real news'. At the heart of effective public relations techniques lies a thorough understanding of news values and journalistic routines. If, for example, journalists seek out 'experts', institutions and statistics, in an effort to be objective, then professional PRPs attempt to use, or even create, such experts, institutions and statistics. If journalists tend to report negative news and scandals, then professional PRPs attempt to dig up negative stories that focus on their oppositions. If particular journalists favour certain types of story and format, and are likely to need to fill some space on a Monday, then PRPs will attempt to supply those types of story, in those formats, on a Sunday. Thus, a process that began with the press release and news conference has become much more sophisticated.

In effect, the liberal description of the fourth estate media, based on an image of independent autonomous journalists seeking out news, has been severely under-mined. While chapter two offered data that merely suggested that journalists are becoming overly reliant on PR output, chapters five and eight demonstrated that reliance quite significantly, and to a degree that many journalists would be unaware of. These trends look set to continue. Competition and proliferation in the media industries will result in further efficiency drives and a weakened media sphere. The obvious consequences will be a rise in the power of sources, owners and advertisers, and a greater reliance on public relations by the national media. At the same time, PR expansion will continue as journalist consumption rises and source needs increase. The dividing lines between news, PR, advertising and entertainment, will thus become further blurred.

Public relations and patterns of interest group/source access in Britain

While the dependence of journalists on PRPs appears to be increasing, is this dependence leading to significant changes in patterns of source access? Are certain sources gaining more access than others in the new public relations environment and, therefore, further undermining pluralist ideals of a media that gives voice to the broadest range of pubic concerns? The evidence of this study suggests two somewhat contradictory trends are taking place in Britain. Certain powerful sources are using PR to secure their long-term access advantages in sections of the national media. At the same time, however, 'resource-poor' and 'outsider' sources have also used public relations to gain more frequent and favourable coverage. How is this so and what are the factors involved in changing levels of source access?

Factors affecting access

This study has identified several factors that influence a source's capacity to gain access to news producers and obtain beneficial coverage. The first and second of these, already noted in several studies of sources, are the possession of *economic capital* and *media (or cultural) capital*. In this case media capital, in the form of legit-imate authority and expertise, is accumulated in the external responses of journal-ists and consumers and is also related to wider social influences. A third factor, one that has drawn less attention, is *human resources*. As this study has stressed, human resources are the main expense for any public relations work and their costs can vary considerably across different PR sectors. Good amateur PRPs and/or large groups of well-organised volunteers can potentially be just as effective as expensive professional communications operations.

A highly significant fourth factor, one repeatedly underlined in this book, is a *source's natural affinities with news producers*. Media–source affinity is affected by both *bureaucratic* considerations and by what journalists perceive to be *newsworthy*. Bureaucratic compatibility – referring to the ease with which journalists may practically report sources – is affected by such things as organisational structures, timetables, and the physical proximity of journalists to source organisations. 'Newsworthiness', a catch-all phrase for journalists and liberal media sociologists, equates to the belief of journalists that they should report sources because they judge them to be significant and/or on account of audience interest. Thus 'home news' journalists will report what consumer and environmental interest groups say, just as they will report decisions by powerful and authoritative sources – because of perceived 'public interest'. On the other side of the equation they will be reluctant to cover sources with large amounts of economic or cultural capital if they are not considered 'newsworthy' or are practically difficult to cover.

The fifth factor is *PR expertise, which also brings appropriate media contacts and strategies*. Chapters five, seven and eight offered examples of common PR strategies used by both corporations and unions. Essentially, PRPs bring a set of contacts and a level of knowledge about how journalists operate. Their main objectives are to (a) locate and exploit the PR resources available to an organisation, and (b) match up the requirements of that organisation with those of relevant news producers. In other words, PRPs develop strategies that uncover the potential affinities that exist between sources and journalists, and utilise the resources at their disposal to match up these affinities accordingly.

These factors are all related but are not inextricably linked. Media (or cultural) capital and human resources are more likely to be boosted by economic resources but they are not completely dependent on them. Public relations strategies are advantaged by cultural and economic capital but can operate with minimal amounts of either. Public relations strategies themselves can help to accumulate or lose all other types of resource and to develop new media–source affinities. This suggests that variously resourced groups can employ PR strategies that rely on alternative combinations of factors – each of which, if conditions are right, can result in a successful supply of information subsidies.

Government and corporate sources

Looking at this typology, the long-term access advantages of British government elites becomes clearer. Two particular factors appear to advantage those in government. The first of these is economic resource advantages. Chapter two demonstrates how PR resources and personnel are unequally distributed in favour of government and corporate interests. Thus, in addition to other forms of influence over media institutions (legal, ownership, advertising), government sources employ PR operations that are literally a hundred times larger than alternative sources acting in civil society. For simple economic reasons, therefore, elite institutional sources are likely to dominate as information subsidy suppliers over a long period. Second, the media also gravitate towards the reporting of government and institutional elites because of their higher levels of media capital. Because journalists, like their consumers, want to (a) get the opinion of experts and authorities, and (b) obtain the views of those considered powerful and influential, a natural affinity forms between journalists and government elites. Added to this is the fact that such sources provide regular 'beat' conditions for journalists – thus making institutional reporting a regular and simple means of producing journalist copy.

However, what is also important to note is that government elites benefit from each of the five factors outlined above, and they can therefore use their considerable advantages on all levels. They are thus becoming increasingly effective at managing routine access to the media. At times of national crisis (e.g., wars or large-scale industrial action), the concerted exploitation of all types of factor advantage results in a virtual monopoly of official source supply. The same is true when political elite consensus is reached on social and economic issues, and policies and messages are powerfully reinforced by concerted PR output from a number of elite sources (see Williams, 1977 and Hallin, 1994, for related discussions).

The play of these factors has been rather different for corporate sources. They have superior economic resources, human resources and PR expertise. However, such advantages are often negated by the fact that, for mainstream news at least, they have little media/cultural capital and weak affinities with news producers. As other studies in media sociology have already noted, they thus spend large sums on maintaining lower profiles and/or blocking journalist access. In numerous cases corporate elite debate and conflict do not even reach reporters. The real negotiation takes place in private face-to-face meetings and telephone calls.

But, more significantly, corporate sources have shifted their PR efforts towards areas of news production where such factors operate in harmony rather than conflict. The sector highlighted in this study is business and financial news in the national press. Here, business sources are also the main advertisers in, and consumers of, business news. Media–source affinities are good and the cultural capital of sources is high. In this case, journalists naturally gravitate towards City and business elites as the 'experts' and 'power brokers' in the field. In fact, the advantages of large corporate elites in business news, in terms of the five factors described, appear far greater than for political elites in mainstream news. As a result, journalists are left in the position of reporting outcomes or recording those conflicts that financial elites choose to play out in the media. With more public relations the media becomes increasingly focused on corporate elite concerns as elite sourcing of the media has become standardised. In the case of certain publications and national news sections the media has become almost entirely 'captured' by what I refer to as 'elite discourse networks'.

These networks, comparable to the 'policy communities' (Jordan and Richardson, 1982) identified in studies of political policy-making, are discursive spaces where elites, often in conflict, debate and attempt to influence key decisions. These conflicts and debates are severely skewed because they (a) only discuss issues relevant to corporate elites, and (b) discuss them according to the norms and values shared by those elites. As chapters four and five argue, in the case of the City, those concerns, norms and values have many areas of consensus that are not typical of the general population or even other elites. Thus, although elites may be in conflict, and journalists consciously assert their autonomy, such discourse networks are severely biased. The financial and business media have consequently become a means for publicising consensual corporate elite requirements, in the guise of economic norms, to decision-makers on all levels.

Unions, outsider and resource-poor sources

In spite of such trends, the number and range of interest groups gaining access to the media in the UK has appeared to increase and broaden. The opportunities for trade unions and pressure groups to gain favourable media coverage appear to have improved significantly with the dissemination of professional PR. How does the above typology of factors account for this?

Several explanations have been documented in this book. The first is that superior elite PR resources are not simply deployed for the benefit of cohesive elite communities. Research in politics (e.g., Grant, 1993, Richardson, 1993, Kavanagh, 1995) and media studies (e.g., Deacon and Golding, 1994, Hallin, 1994, Miller, 1994) has pointed out that corporate and government sources do not always act together and, indeed, are in frequent conflict with each other. As a result, economic and cultural resource advantages can often be cancelled out. Elite conflict can also result in negative publicity and/or journalists questioning the legitimacy of certain powerful sources. A related point is that elites sources may often actually be representing the views of non-elite constituencies. This may be because they are consciously acting as third-party endorsers, or because they are the victims of 'spin' themselves. The obvious conclusion to be drawn is that elite source advantages cannot be recorded on a simple balance sheet.

A second explanation, rarely noted in source literature, is that, although public relations efficacy can be loosely correlated with financial expenditure, PR is far from dependent on economic resources. As explained, the main costs of PR are human ones and, as chapters seven and eight demonstrate, voluntary labour combined with some PR expertise can do much to make up for a lack of economic resources and professional PRPs. As these chapters also observe, large unwieldy communications operations, operating within large corporate and government bureaucracies, can often be at a disadvantage in a fast-moving media campaign. Being smaller and more campaign focused, pressure group PRPs often have more specific knowledge and are quicker to respond to journalist needs than PRPs in government and corporate organisations. In effect, well organised pressure group sources can have a greater media affinity with journalists on the bureaucratic level.

Third, the affinity between unions/pressure groups and media producers can also be quite strong in terms of what is considered 'newsworthy'. News organisations clearly operate in a contradictory environment in which they tend to report elite interests and move in elite circles, but also have a *raison d'être* that includes maintaining a check on power and representing the general public. While they need to attract advertising and are owned by pro-capitalist patrons, they also need to attract wider audiences that are not necessarily happy with the effects of capitalism and can be cynical about business leaders. Media outlets, needing mass readerships, therefore need to appeal to large non-elite constituencies on a regular basis and often must be seen to be fulfilling some sort of fourth estate role. As chapter seven observes, union PR strategies have often attempted to exploit this potential affinity. Many have thus linked their campaigns with the needs of 'the public' and/or attacked 'greedy' and 'incompetent' corporate and government elites. Unions are less likely to argue about jobs and money. Instead the communications focus is on public safety, education levels, attacks on racial and sexual discrimination, social welfare and recruitment problems. In effect, unions have altered their agendas to become more media friendly and influential but, in the process, have also risked diluting some of their long-term political objectives.

Fourth, what source literature has also been slow to recognise is that forms of media (cultural) capital are far from dependent on, and are a lot more volatile than, accumulations of economic capital. This volatility is where public relations strategies and operations become vital – something that has become more apparent as alternative sources adopt professional PR. As chapter six argues, unions in the 1970s and 1980s had lots of media capital but non-existent PR strategies. As chapter seven suggests, and chapter eight demonstrates, union PRP strategies have proved to be fairly successful at accumulating all the forms of media capital outlined above. They have formed and maintained their own journalist contacts by improving media relations and supplying regular research and stories to them. They have worked hard to cultivate reputations associated with expertise, calm authority, forward thinking and public awareness. When lacking in cultural capital they have exploited that of others around them such as MPs, scientists and celebrities – using these figures to gain media access. Union PR strategies have thus been used to accumulate various forms of media capital as well as nullify that which is possessed by others.

Thus the ability to influence norms and values in the new public relations democracy is as uneven as the material distribution of political power and resources themselves. Outsider and resource-poor groups are making an impact in spite of resource inequalities. By making use of their human resources and applying strategies that integrate well with media requirements, they are getting more successful at accumulating their own media capital. On occasion they are therefore able to make a significant impact – especially when governments and businesses are unprepared or in conflict. However, the larger picture is not so optimistic. Many interest groups and individuals do not have the minimum resources necessary to mount even basic PR operations, while others inundate the media with their messages on a regular basis. The rise of professional public relations therefore means that institutions and corporations can further extend and institutionalise their media influence in the long term. It also means a greater media concentration on elite debates and/or the exclusion of non-elites from media access.

Public relations, policy-making and power relations

How are these changing patterns of media access and influence related to policy-making (not just at the level of government) and shifting power relations? Undoubtedly, policy-making in Britain over the last two decades, as with many other countries, has benefited the corporate sector. Power, in terms of the management of resources and influence of certain individuals over others, has shifted very definitely towards certain corporate elites – something recognised even by fomer advocates of liberal pluralism (e.g., Dahl, 1985, Grant, 2000). Transnational conglomerates have expanded. The burdens of regulation and taxation on business have, on balance, been steadily weakened. Company profits, as well as the personal wealth of the top 10 per cent of earners have increased. The burden of taxation has been loaded on to middle and low income earners and public services while national infrastructures have suffered long-term underinvestment. The state has only aided the transfer of power by (a) contracting out many of its management roles to quangos and the private sector, and (b) by presiding over legislation that has weakened the ability of consumer and trade union organisations to hold companies to account. Has increased public relations activity, coupled with a changing media environment, contributed to such shifts? If so, how have these two industries been implicated in a policy-making process that has so advantaged the corporate sector and the cause of neo-liberalism?

The obvious conclusion is that the arguments and ideas of corporate elites have gained privileged access to the mass media in a way that reflects their privileged access to the state. As such, a form of corporate-inspired 'dominant ideology' has been exported through the media to the mass of consumer citizens. Such ideological flows have resulted in media and public support for neo-liberal policy-making and pro-business political parties. That the majority of the press in the UK have supported such legislation and parties, coupled with the fact that most public relations expenditure has been by government and corporate sources, lends further support to this analysis. Such arguments concur with a range of critical media and politics literature.

However, certain findings in this thesis suggest that the role of public relations and the media in the policy-making process has been rather more complicated. To start, the studies of both the financial and union sectors revealed a complex mixture of alliances and conflicts that did not adhere to conventional models of top-down conflict. Conflict between rival corporate and/or state elites appear common – as do alliances between non-official/outsider groups with official/insider groups. Public relations conflicts and the media coverage that follows therefore defy simple corporate elite-versus-mass forms of analysis. In addition, the case studies indicated that public relations campaigning and media coverage appear to affect elite government and business decision-makers as much as the mass of consumer-citizens. This suggests support for a 'strong effects' model of media influence, but one in which policy-makers are also prone to being affected by media content influenced by multiple source/interest group PR.

Related to this, much of the opinion poll data cited in this study implies that the mass of consumer citizens are fairly antagonistic towards the excesses of neo-liberal policy-making and increasingly disillusioned with conventional politics and politicians. They might vote for pro-business parties, buy pro-business papers and support the capitalist system per se, but the majority of the UK population are rather more 'liberal' and society-oriented than those papers and parties. On the whole, they have very different views from corporate elites on taxation, privatisation, social welfare spending, the environment, trade unions, investment and employee rights. All of which suggests that, for much of the time outside electoral campaigns, the role of the media in policy-making is more connected to the manufacturing of elite rather than mass forms of consent.

Therefore, pro-business policy-making has been aided by corporate public relations in a number of more subtle ways. These ways have amounted generally to excluding the media, the general public and rival elites from knowledge of elite policy-making processes. Much corporate and government public relations activity (50 per cent or more according to many interviewees) serves the purpose of blocking media access to information. Thus a large proportion of policy and legislative negotiation, between corporate representatives and government policy-makers, goes unreported. An even larger proportion of business elite negotiation is not covered by journalists.

Conflict over policy-making, when it is reported, is still fairly restricted and limited by public relations activity in a number of ways. First, that which is reported becomes public largely because negotiations and conflict spill over and powerful interests resort to releasing information to the media. Second, those journalists which gain access are often fairly restricted in what they report and the lines of debate they pursue. They are highly dependent on small circles of PRPs and elite sources, and cannot afford to be excluded from such networks. The choice is thus continual exclusion or partial assimilation and, therefore, tacit support for existing relations, policy-making procedures, and governing structures.

Third, the information that does get reported, because it is aimed at particular decision-makers, is often exclusionary in its content and style. Only political insiders can really comprehend the meanings of certain shifts in policy and personnel in government and some of the terms bandied about on specific issues. Only corporate insiders can understand the jargon-ridden texts of financial and business reporting and the implications of statements by particular business personnel. Fourth, reporting patterns themselves mitigate against wider journalistic and public understanding. In general, reporting is driven by the immediate, the simple, the short term and the sensational. This makes the reporting of complex policy issues unpopular and has resulted in a decline of the reporting of policy matters in all news circles. When policy debates and decisions are reported this is often done without proper context or any general understanding of how such changes have contributed to larger patterns of change. Thus the general trends noted by critical researchers rarely result in more significant media campaigns or public outcries. Macro-level trends are lost in coverage of the isolated micro-level event.

Therefore, in several areas of reporting, most notably in economic and business news, the British print media has served to repeat the 'mobilisation of bias' (Bachrach and Baratz, 1962) identified in policy-making itself. The policy concerns of many interest groups, as well as the long-term effects of policy-making processes, have been frequently overlooked. Although journalists have occasionally attacked the excesses of the lobbying industry, cash for access/questions, and conflicts of ministerial interest, the general question of extensive business access to political policy-makers is not the subject of sustained media criticism. Similarly, journalists have attacked particular taxes but not the long-term shift to indirect taxation, high interest rates but not the influence of the City in setting such rates, and particular companies during a takeover bid but not the implications of the takeover for the workforce, consumers and the wider economy. Ultimately, public relations has aided the corporate sector not simply by the persuasion of large groups of consumer citizens but, additionally, by the exclusion of citizens and the persuasion of particular corporate and government elites.

The 1980s in Britain might be seen as a period in which corporate and government PR effectively privatised a number of policy debates and established several areas of unchallenged consensus. Thus, at the present time, privatisation and private enterprise are considered more beneficial than state control. Low inflation, engineered by interest rates and reduced public spending, are essential for the economy. Increased corporate regulation, taxation and accountability, as well as strong unions and interventionist government, are considered harmful. The strength of the economy is more important than social welfare because a strong economy supports better welfare. And so on. Such consensual frameworks have continued to drive decision-making in both government and business accordingly. As Abercrombie et al. (1984) argued previously, the development of any form of 'dominant ideology' appears to have played a more significant part in the evolution of powerful elite consensus than the persuasion of 'the masses'.

In contrast, the 1990s might be seen as a period in which alternative interest group PR began to break into established elite discourse networks and to use the media to bring policy debates more into the public sphere. Chapters seven and eight indicated that unions had achieved some notable successes over the decade. Undoubtedly, environmental and other pressure groups have also forced significant changes. Additionally, it should be noted that continued campaigning has managed to put issues such as welfare, education, health and the environment back on the front-line agendas of the main political parties. Such campaigns are likely to have contributed to the support gained by the Labour Party at the 1997 election – a party seen to be stronger on each of these issues.

However, despite such developments, pluralist optimism should remain muted. Dramatic victories by pressure groups and unions using public relations have been irregular. It takes concerted efforts for media-inspired campaigns, carried out by 'outsider' groups, to affect major policy decisions. Such instances cannot in any way be compared to the multiple daily decision-making processes that fail to find coverage or that are dominated by government and/or business sources. Of additional concern to outsider groups in particular (although of equal concern to politics generally) are the ideological shifts required to gain regular favourable coverage. As different groups develop media-oriented strategies, so policy agendas get altered and risk being trivialised. A focus on personal corruption or company ineptitude comes to replace discussion of the effects of privatisation or global warming. Just as pressure groups risk incorporation, the more established they become, so campaigning organisations risk assimilation into the media politics of middle England.

Appendices

APPENDIX I
LIST OF INTERVIEWEES

One hundred and three interviews were conducted with ninety-seven individuals. The majority of the interviews took place 'on the record' and most citations are referenced. However, a proportion of interviewees, as well as particular parts of on-the-record interviews, were recorded 'off the record'. All interviewees, bar two senior civil servants in the DTI, are listed here.

Trade union public relations

Keith Bill, Director of Union Communications – 19.6.97
Tristan Evans, PR/Communications Officer at the Musicians' Union (MU) – 2.10.97
Olive Forsythe, Head of Press/PR at NUT – 19.5.97
Lawrie Harries, Head of Press/PR at RMT – 7.10.97
Daniel Harris, previously Campaigns and Media Officer at UCW – 18.6.97
Noel Howell, Head of Press/PR at BIFU – 2.9.97
Hannah Jeffries, Head of Press/PR at the Association of Electrical Engineers' Union (AEEU) – 31.7.97
Karen Livingstone, Media Officer at GMB – 21.5.97
John Monks, Head of Communications at UNISON – 16.10.97
Andrew Murray, Head of Communications at TGWU – 9.10.97
Mike Power, Campaigns and Press Officer at TUC – 28.4.97
Chris Proctor, Campaigns and Media Officer at CWU – 2.6.97
John Richards, Media Officer and Journal Editor at ASLEF – 20.5.97
Craig Ryan, Chief Press Officer and Journal Editor at FDA – 30.7.97
Miles Weber, Head of Campaigns and Communications at MSF – 13.10.97

Other union

Stephen Charkham, General Secretary of the Hospital Consultants and Specialists' Association (HCSA) – 10.10.97
Chris Darke, General Secretary of BALPA – 3.10.97
Rosie Eagleson, General Secretary of AMO – 1.8.97
David Evans, General Secretary of POA – 1.8.96 and 3.10.96
Harry Fletcher, Assistant General Secretary of NAPO – 13.10.97
Joe Marino, General Secretary at BFAWU – 14.10.97

Corporate public relations – consultants and in-house

John Aarons, Director of Corporate Communications Division at the Communications Group – 5.7.96
Martin Adeney, Managing Director of Group Public Relations at ICI – 17.12.98

Paul Barber, Group Corporate Affairs Director of Inchcape – 20.8.98

John Bates, Public Relations Co-ordinator for Group 4 – 11.7.96 and 22.4.96

Simon Bryceson MBE, Director of Government and Public Affairs at Burson-Marsteller (Previous work for Media Natura, Friends of the Earth and the Liberal Democrats) – 17.7.96

Tim Blythe, Director of Corporate Affairs at WH Smith – 15.9.98

Nick Boakes, Managing Director of Grandfield – 18.8.98

Nick Chaloner, Director of Corporate Affairs at Abbey National – 16.9.98

Jonathan Clare, Deputy Managing Director at Citigate Communications – 16.9.98

Gerald Clark, Senior Consultant at Shandwick – 15.9.98

Bob Cowell, Founding Partner of Makinson Cowell – 3.3.99

Jonny Elwes, Account Manager at Infopress – 23.7.96 and 31.7.98

Gary Freemantle, Director of Consumer Division at the Communications Group – 5.7.96

Bob Gregory, Director at Bell Pottinger – 21.8.98

Alison Hogan, Partner at Brunswick – 20.10.98

Chris Hopson, Director of Corporate Affairs at Granada Media Group – 13.10.98 and 25.1.99

Tim Jackaman, Chairman of Square Mile – 8.10.98

Martin Jackson, Director at Dewe-Rogerson – 11.9.98

Peter Jones, Director of Corporate Communications at BUPA/Previously Head of Public Relations at British Airways – 9.9.98

Ellis Kopel, Director of Ellis Kopel PR Consultants – 23.7.96 and 23.6.98

James Lindsey, Corporate Public Relations Manager for the Post Office – 24.6.97

Angus Maitland, Chairman of the Maitland Consultancy – 17.9.98

Nick Miles, Chief Executive of Financial Dynamics – 17.8.98

Lisa Newman, Account Director Financial Division, at the Communications Group – 5.7.96

David Nolder, Director at Citigate – 22.12.98

Richard Oldworth, Chief Executive of Buchanan – 26.8.98

Stuart Prosser, Head of the City and Financial Section of the IPR and Head of Public Relations for the Royal Bank of Scotland – 22.6.98

John Reynolds, Managing Director of the Financial Division of Shandwick – 15.9.98

Simon Rigby, Director at Citigate – 20.11.98

Roland Rudd, Founding Partner of Finsbury – 15.10.98 and 23.11.98

Jonathan Russell, Director of Corporate Affairs at Thames Water – 14.1.99

Michael Sandler, Chairman of Hudsen-Sandler – 19.10.98

Jan Shawe, Director of Corporate Affairs at the Prudential – 7.10.98

Maureen Smith, Chairwoman of The Communications Group – 5.7.96

Will Whitehorn, Corporate Affairs Director of Virgin – 23.10.98

Nigel Whittaker, UK Chairman of Burson-Marsteller – 14.10.98

Journalists

David Blackwell, Business Correspondent for the *FT* – 17.5.99

Alex Brummer, Financial Editor of the *Guardian* – 16.6.99

Christine Buckley, Industrial Correspondent for *The Times* – 1.6.99

John Carvell, Education Editor the *Guardian* – 30.1.97

Barrie Clement, Industrial Correspondent of the *Independent* – 25.5.99

Neville Davis, Editor and Freelance Trade Journalist – 29.1.97

Melanie Essex, Chief Assistant to the Head of Political Programmes (Tony Hall) at the BBC – 5.2.97

Stephen Farish, Editor of *PR Week* – 25.7.96 and 16.8.96

Roland Gribben, Business Editor of the *Telegraph* – 21.5.99

Keith Harper, Transport Editor (former Labour) for the *Guardian* – 20.5.99

John Jay, Business Editor of the *Sunday Times* – 8.6.99

Joy Johnson, Freelance Journalist and ex Labour Director of Campaigns, Elections and Media – 23.1.97

Nicholas Jones, Political Correspondent at BBC, formerly Industrial Relations Correspondent – 5.3.97

Stephen Kahn, Associate Business Editor of the *Daily Express* – 24.5.99

Seamus Milne, Labour Editor of the *Guardian* – 13.5.99

Richard Northedge, Deputy Editor of *Sunday Business* – 25.5.99

Raymond Snoddy, Media Correspondent of *The Times* – 17.5.99

Jon Snow, Channel 4 News Anchor – 22.1.97

Robert Taylor, Industrial Correspondent of the *FT* – 20.5.99

Michael Walters, Deputy City Editor of the *Daily Mail* – 19.10.98

Others

Richard Abbott, Account Manager for CARMA International – 24.7.96

Guy Black, Director of the Press Complaints Commission – previously at Lowe-Bell – 18.6.97

Alistair Defriez, Director General of the Takeover Panel – 11.11.98 and 22.12.98

Department of Trade and Industry, interviews with two anonymous sources 16.6.97 and 24.6.97

Mario Dunn, Head of Research for UCW in 1994 – 23.6.97

Keith Hamill, Financial Director at WH Smith – 17.2.99

Ian King, Communications Officer for the Liberal Democrats – 17.6.96

Bill Leaske, Marketing Development Manager for Two-Ten Communications – 14.1.97

Chris McDowall, Executive Director of the PRCA – 13.8.96

Paul McFarland, Managing Director of Two-Ten Communications – 14.2.97

Sandra Macleod, Managing Director Europe of CARMA International – 24.7.96

Richard Power, Commercial Director at RF Hotels (previously Director of Corporate Affairs at Forte) – 30.11.98

Linda Rogers, National Organiser at NUJ – 7.1.97

John Rose, Institute of Public Relations – 6.1.97

Steven Shaw, Director of the Prison Reform Trust – 16.7.96

Tim Weller, Group Financial Controller at Granada, 19.1.99

Graham Williams, Director of External Affairs at the Investor Relations Society – 26.10.98

TABLE PRINTOUTS FOR TRADE UNION SURVEY

Table A.1 Degree of union contact with the media

Value label	Frequency	Valid percentage	Cumulative percentage
Daily	24	45.3	45.3
Weekly	12	22.6	67.9
Monthly	3	5.7	73.6
Several times/year	13	24.5	98.1
Never	1	1.9	100.0
Missing	1		
Total	54	100.0	

Table A.2 How PR/communications dealt with in unions

Value label	Frequency	Valid percentage	Cumulative percentage
General Sec Only	10	18.5	18.5
PR Individual	1	1.9	20.4
PR Department	20	37.0	57.4
Part-timer	9	16.7	74.1
General Sec with other	6	11.1	85.2
No PR function	5	9.3	94.4
Consultancy only	3	5.6	100.0
Total	54	100.0	

Table A.3 Numbers of people involved

Value label	Frequency	Valid percentage	Cumulative percentage
No PR	5	9.3	9.3
General Secretary	13	24.1	33.3
Part-timer	15	27.8	61.1
1-2 people	10	18.5	79.6
2.5–8 people	10	18.5	98.1
More than 8	1	1.9	100.0
Total	54	100.0	100.0

Notes: Mean 2.125 (people/union) median 0.500 (part-time person) mode 0.500 (part-time person); sum 114.75 (total people employed in union communications for sample)

Table A.4: 'During the 1980s, PR/communications resources have …'

Value label	Frequency	Valid percentage	Cumulative percentage
Increased greatly	6	13.0	13.0
Increased moderately	16	34.8	47.8
Stayed the same	15	32.6	80.4
Decreased moderately	5	10.9	91.3
Decreased greatly	0	0.0	91.3
Don't know	4	8.7	100.0
Missing	8	14.8	
Total	54	100.0	

Table A.5 'In the 1990s, PR/communications resources have …'

Value label	Frequency	Valid percentage	Cumulative percentage
Increased greatly	18	38.3	38.3
Increased moderately	18	38.3	76.6
Stayed the same	8	17.0	93.6
Decreased moderately	3	6.4	100.0
Decreased greatly	0	0.0	100.0
Missing	7		
Total	54	100.0	

Table A.6 'Over the next five years do you expect your PR/communications resources to …'

Value label	Frequency	Valid percentage	Cumulative percentage
Increase greatly	13	28.3	28.3
Increase moderately	18	39.1	67.4
Stay the same	14	30.4	97.8
Decrease moderately	1	2.2	100.0
Decrease greatly	0	0.0	100.0
Missing	8		
Total	54	100.0	

Table A.7 Background experience of staff dealing with PR/communications

Value label	Frequency	Valid percentage	Cumulative percentage
PR only	3	6.5	6.5
Journalism only	11	23.9	30.4
PR and journalism	15	32.6	63.0
Neither	17	37.0	100.0
Missing	8		
Total	54	100.0	

Table A.8 'Good communications/PR is now essential for winning strikes/pursuing industrial action'

Value label	Frequency	Valid percentage	Cumulative percentage
Strongly agree	14	29.2	29.2
Agree	18	37.5	66.7
Don't know	7	14.6	81.3
Disagree	9	18.8	100.0
Strongly disagree	0	0.0	100.0
Missing	6		
Total	54	100.0	

Table A.9 'PR/communications is becoming the key union method for achieving political and industrial goals'

Value label	Frequency	Valid percentage	Cumulative percentage
Strongly agree	11	22.9	22.9
Agree	25	52.1	75.0
Don't know	4	8.3	83.3
Disagree	8	16.7	100.0
Strongly disagree	0	0.0	100.0
Missing	6		
Total	54	100.0	

Table A.10 The first communications priority of unions

Value label	Frequency	Valid percentage	Cumulative percentage
Membership recruitment	11	26.2	26.2
Campaigns/lobbying	3	7.1	33.3
Union profile	2	4.8	38.1
General media relations	1	2.4	40.5
Journal/other publications	7	16.7	57.1
Internal/member communic	18	42.9	100.0
Missing	12		
Total	54	100.0	

Table A.11 Top communications priorities of unions overall (sum of top three communications selections)

Value label	Frequency	Percentage	Percentage of unions prioritising
Membership recruitment	18	15.3	33.3
Campaigns/lobbying	20	16.9	37.0
Union profile	11	9.3	20.4
General media relations	22	19.5	42.6
Journal/other publications	13	11.0	24.1
Internal/member communic	33	28.0	61.1
Total	118	100.0	

Table A.12 Top communications priorities for campaigns overall (sum of top three campaigns selections)

Value label	Frequency	Percentage	Percentage of unions prioritising
Industrial Action	10	12.7	18.5
National employment issues	8	10.1	14.8
Union image	14	17.7	25.9
National indust campaigns	12	15.1	22.2
Local empt/ind campaigns	7	8.9	13.0
Influence members/recruit	12	15.2	22.2
Influence politics/legislation	14	17.7	25.9
Other	2	2.5	3.7
Total	79	100.0	

Table A.13 Individual union relations with the media, 1970s–1990s

Value Label	1970s frequency	1970s percentage	1980s frequency	1980s percentage	1990s frequency	1990s percentage
Very good	2	5.6	1	2.4	4	8.0
Good	10	27.8	7	16.7	24	48.0
Neutral	14	38.9	15	35.7	17	34.0
Bad	9	25.0	13	31.0	4	8.0
Very bad	1	2.8	6	14.3	1	2.0
Don't know/missing	18		12		4	
Total	54	100.0	54	100.0	54	100.0

Table A.14 'Compared to the 1980s, has union access
to the media in the 1990s …'

Value label	Frequency	Valid percentage	Cumulative percentage
Increased greatly	9	19.6	19.6
Increased moderately	21	45.7	65.2
Stayed the same	8	17.4	82.6
Decreased moderately	6	13.0	95.7
Decreased greatly	2	4.3	100.0
Don't know/missing	8		
Total	54	100.0	

Table A.15 'Compared to the 1980s, has favourable media
coverage of unions in the 1990s …'

Value label	Frequency	Valid percentage	Cumulative percentage
Increased greatly	4	8.3	8.3
Increased moderately	34	70.8	79.2
Stayed the same	9	18.8	97.9
Decreased moderately	0	0.0	97.9
Decreased greatly	1	2.1	100.0
Don't know/missing	6		
Total	54	100.0	

Table A.16 'Improved public opinion of unions is due more to unpopular government and a decrease in strike activity – *NOT* public relations'

Value label	Frequency	Valid percentage	Cumulative percentage
Strongly agree	2	4.3	4.3
Agree	17	37.0	41.3
Don't know	8	17.4	58.7
Disagree	18	39.1	97.8
Strongly disagree	1	2.2	100.0
Missing	8		
Total	54	100.0	

Table A.17 'PR/communications tactics are limited and will never really replace other union strategies and campaigning forms'

Value label	Frequency	Valid percentage	Cumulative percentage
Strongly agree	1	2.1	2.1
Agree	16	33.3	35.4
Don't know	9	18.8	54.2
Disagree	18	37.5	91.7
Strongly disagree	4	8.3	100.0
Missing	6		
Total	54	100.0	

Table A.18 'Money spent on public relations is better spent on other union priorities'

Value label	Frequency	Valid percentage	Cumulative percentage
Strongly agree	0	0.0	0.0
Agree	4	8.5	8.5
Don't know	10	21.3	29.8
Disagree	24	51.1	80.9
Strongly disagree	9	19.1	100.0
Missing	7		
Total	54	100.0	

BIBLIOGRAPHY

Primary research material

ABN AMRO Hoare Govett (Granada Broker) Internal Documents/Correspondence: 'Notes From Forte Presentation at UBS', 14.12.95, 18.12.95, 'Notes From Forte Presentation at UBS', 20.12.95, 'Suggestions for Day 39 Document', 20.12.95

Access Opinions Ltd (May 1994) 'Post Office Privatisation – A Survey of MPs'

Advertising Association (15.6.98) press release

Annan Report (1977) *Report of the Committee on the Future of Broadcasting*, London, HMSO

BDO Stoy Hayward Management Consultants (1994) *The Public Relations Sector – An Analysis for the Department of Trade and Industry*, London, BDO Stoy Hayward Management Consultants

Bernstein, A. (18.1.96) letter 'To Forte Shareholders and Holders of Forte Convertible Bonds and, for Information Only, to Holders Under the Forte Options Schemes'

BZW internal documents/correspondence (20.12.95)

BZW Securities (21.12.95) press releases

CARMA International (1996) company and promotional material

Citigate Communications Ltd Internal Documents
(1996) 'Granada's Bid for Forte Plc – PR Week Public Relations Awards 1996', submission to *PR Week*
'Re: Trade Press Interviews', 18.12.95
'Granada – Performance Against Competitors', 20.12.95
'Forte Comparison with Competitors', 21.12.95
Internal memos: 3.1.96, 4.1.96a, 15.1.96
'Granada Group Plc – Offer for Forte – Advertising Rational, 4.1.96b
'Granada – Unattributable Analysts Research', 4.1.96c
Correspondence with Henley Management College, 9.1.96
Correspondence with London Business School, 10.1.96
Correspondence with LSE, undated
'Re: Interview with Don Davenport', 11.1.96
'Academic Articles and Other Features', 16.1.96
'Re: Don Davenport Interview with Caterer and Hotel Keeper', 18.1.96

Communication Managers Association (CMA) (Sept. 1994) press releases

Communication Workers' Union (CWU, formerly UCW) Research document, 28.6.96, 'The Proposed Privatisation of the Post Office: How We Beat It'

Confederation of British Industry (CBI) (1990) 'A Nation of Shareholders – Report of the CBI Wider Share Ownership Task Force', London, CBI

Confederation of British Industry (CBI) and Abbey Life Assurance Co. Ltd (1981) 'The Headline Business: A Businessman's Guide to Working with the Media', London, CBI

Connect Public Affairs Ltd correspondence with UCW, 21.8.92, 26.11.92, 30.11.92, 2.12.92, 9.2.93, 22.2.93, 29.3.93, 16.4.93, 6.5.94, 21.4.94, 10.6.94, 31.5.94

Consumers' Association (October 1994) 'The Future of Postal Services – Consumers' Association Response to the Green Paper'

Cook, R. (Labour Shadow Trade and Industry), press releases, 27.7.94, 23.8.94

Davis, A. (1998) *Trade Union Communications in the 1990s – A Report for the TUC and its Affiliate Unions*, London, TUC

Department of Trade and Industry (DTI) (June 1994) *The Future of Postal Services – A Consultative Document*, Green Paper, London, HMSO

DHL International (UK) Ltd (September 1994) 'Response to the "Future of Postal Services – A Consultative Document"'

Direct Marketing Association (September 1994) 'Response to the Green Paper'

Economists Advisory Group (EAG) (August 1993) 'Commercialisation of the Post Office: How to Secure Financial Independence without Risking Service Quality'

Emery, P. (Conservative MP for Honiton), press release, 8.9.94

Forte Documents

    Forte Annual Report and Accounts, 1995

    'Creating Value', 8.12.95

    Defence Document, untitled, 15.12.95

    'For Hotels, For Profits, For Quality, For Growth, For Shareholder Value', 2.1.96a

    'For Value – A Premium Rated International Hotel Company – Forte', 15.1.96

    'Forte – Disposal of the Roadside Business', 16.1.96

    Forte, R, 'Letter to Shareholders', 3.1.96

    Forte press releases, 15.12.95, 1.1.96, 2.1.96b

Gallup Polls

    Gallup (1991) 'The Media and the PR Industry: A Partnership or a Marriage of Convenience?' Gallup survey for Two-Ten Communications, London, Social Surveys

    Gallup (September 1991) *Gallup Political and Economic Index*, London, Social Surveys

    Gallup (September 1995) *Gallup Political and Economic Index* London, Social Surveys

Granada Documents

    Analyst Presentations (undated), 'Offer for Forte', 'Granada', 'Granada – Delivering the Promise'

    Granada Annual Report and Accounts, 1995, 1996, 1998

    'Granada Group Plc – Offer for Forte Plc', 24.11.95a

    'Granada Group Plc – Listing Particulars Relating the Offer for Forte Plc', 24.11.95b

    'Creating More Value', 14.12.95

    'Granada Final Offer for Forte', 9.1.96

    'The Choice', 16.1.96

    Press releases, 27.12.95, 10.1.96, 12.1.96, 12.1.96, 14.1.96, 14.1.96, 15.1.96, 15.1.96, 15.1.96, 17.1.96, 18.1.96, 19.1.96, 23.1.96, 24.1.96

    Granada/Citigate Internal Research Documents: 'Forte Hotels Inc', undated, 'Forte Demerger Proposals', undated, 'Stakis', undated, 'Granada/Forte: The Management Issue', undated, 'Communications programme – Granada Response to Forte Defence Document', undated, 'Granada Group Plc – An Alternative Media Schedule', 5.12.95, 'Journalists Round Ups and Analysts Comments', 18.1.96

    'Granada Bid for Forte – Evidence of Success', 1996

Hansard, 15.7.92 (p1138), 19.5.94 (pp967–80), 12.7.94 (pp840–925), 19.10.94 (Motion No.143), 21.11.94 (p352), 12.2.97 (pp223–4)

HMSO (1980–98) *Financial Statement and Budget Reports' 1979/80–1997/98*, London, HMSO

Institute of Directors (1994) *The Future of Postal Services – the IoD's response to a DTI Consultation Document*, London, IoD

Institute of Public Relations (IPR) (1983a–1998a) *Sword of Excellence Awards*, London, IPR

Institute of Public Relations (IPR) (1991, 1994, 1998b) *Membership Surveys*, London, IPR

Investor Relations Society Reports

    Investor Relations Society (IRS) (1994) *Trends and Developments in Investor Relations*, London, IRS

    Investor Relations Society (IRS) (1997) *Annual Report and Accounts*, London, IRS

    Investor Relations Society (IRS) (1998) *Investor Relations in the UK: Current Practices and Key Issues*, London, Business Planning and Research

Kleinwort Benson Securities Ltd press release (on behalf of Forte and Whitbread), 27.12.95

Labour Party Campaign Pack Against Post Office Privatisation (1994), London

Labour Party Documents

    Labour Research Department (1923) *The Press*, London, LRD

    Labour Research Department (1946) *The Millionaire Press*, London, LRD

    Labour Research Department (August 1991) *New Times for Union Journals*, London, LRD

    Labour Research Department (August 1993) *Union Journals in Transformation*, London, LRD

Lane, D. correspondence with UCW and MPs, 10.7.94, 12.7.94, 12.7.94, 14.8.94, 17.8.94, 9.9.94, 30.10.94

Lazard Brothers and Co. Ltd (financial adviser to Granada) press releases: 22.11.95, 22.11.95, 4.12.95, 9.12.95, 15.12.95, 21.12.95, 29.12.95, 29.12.95, 29.12.95, 30.12.95, 2.1.96, 5.1.96, 9.1.96, 16.1.96, 7.2.96, 29.12.95

Lazard Brothers internal documents/correspondence: 15.12.95, 'Conglomerate?', 29.12.95

London Economics, correspondence with UCW, 1.8.94, 30.9.94

London Economics (September 1994) *The Future of Postal Services – A Critique of the Government's Green Paper*, London, London Economics

London Stock Exchange

    London Stock Exchange (1994) *Stock Exchange Quarterly*, London, London Stock Exchange

    London Stock Exchange, (1994–98), *London Stock Exchange Fact File*, London, London Stock Exchange

    London Stock Exchange, (1996) *Report on the Committee on Private Share Ownership*, London, London Stock Exchange

Lowe-Bell Political, correspondence with UCW, 19.5.94, 26.7.94

Lowe-Bell Political, presentation (1994) 'The Freedom to Deliver – Enterprise and Efficiency for the Post Office in the Public Sector'

McCarthy, C. (1984) *The Feasibility of Establishing a New Labour Movement Newspaper*, London, TUC

McQuail, D. (1977) *Analysis of Newspaper Content, Report for the Royal Commission on the Press*, London, HMSO

Mintel Marketing Intelligence (1995) *Financial Public Relations*

MORI polls and other material

    (1979) 'The Role of Public Relations in Business and Government – A Qualitative Study Among Users of PR' MORI research report for the PRCA

    (1987) *British Public Opinion: General Election 1987*

    (October 1991) Attitudes to the Postal Service

    (December 1992) Attitudes to the Postal Service

    (March 1994) Attitudes to the Post Office

    (April 1994) Attitudes to the Post Office

(August 1994) Post Office Managers Survey
(August 1994) Sub Post Offices Survey
(October 1994) Tory Backbenchers
Poll Data in *British Public Opinion*, 1992–98, produced monthly
Company and promotional material (1997)
Mail Users Association (June 1994) 'Response to the Green Paper "Future of Postal Services"'
Mail Users Association press releases: 17.6.94, 20.7.94
National Consumer Council (October 1994) 'Privatising Postal Services – The Consumer View'
National Consumer Council press release, 19.10.94
National Federation of Sub-Postmasters (NFSP) (30.9.94) 'Response to the Consultative Document on the Future of Postal Services'
National Federation of Sub-Postmasters press release, 30.9.94
National Opinion Poll (NOP) Poll (Aug. 1991)
National Opinion Poll (NOP) Market Research (Feb. 1987) 'Attitudes to Privatisation'
National Union of Journalists (NUJ) (1994, 1996, 1998) *National Union of Journalists Surveys of Members*, London, NUJ
Neill, Lord (1998) *Neill Report: 5th Report of the Committee on Standards in Public Life: The Funding of Political Parties in the United Kingdom*, London, HMSO Cm 4057–1
Nolder, D. (15.1.96) letter to journalists
Panel on Takeovers and Mergers, Reports (1975/76–1996/97), London, Takeover Panel
Periodical Publishers Association (30.9.94) 'The Future of Postal Services – a Submission to the Department of Trade and Industry'
Post Office Documents
    Post Office (Feb 1997a) 'The Post Office Communications Directory'
    Post Office (Feb 1997b) 'The Post Office Business Briefs'
    Post Office (1994) 'The Future of Postal Services – The Need for Change …'
    Post Office press releases: 18.10.94, 14.12.94
Post Office Unions Council (POUC) (March 1994) 'Submission to the Department of Trade and Industry Review of the Future of the Post Office', POUC
Post Office Unions Council (POUC) (1994) 'The Future of Postal Services – POUC Report on Government's Green Paper', 29 September POUC
Post Office Users National Council (POUNC) press release 30.9.94
PR Week Publications (25.3.93 to present), London, Haymarket Publications
    'PR Week – The First 10 years 1984–1994'
    'The Rise of Consultancy – 25 Years of the PRCA'
    'PR Week Salary Survey' (1993–99)
    'PR Week In-House Survey' (1993 and 1995)
    'Top 150 PR Consultancies' (1993–99)
    'PR Week Public Relations Awards' (1992–99)
    PR Week (1998) *Contact – The Press and Public Relations Handbook*, London, Haymarket Press
PRCA Publications, London
    (1979) 'The Role of Public Relations in Business and Government – A Qualitative Study Among Users of PR', MORI
    The Public Relations Year Book (edns 1978–98)
    (1990) 'Key Note Report – An Industry Sector Overview – Public Relations Consultancies' (2nd edn)
    (1994) *Public Relations in Practice – Case Studies*, Vol. I

'Inter-firm Comparisons 1995 – An Independent Survey by William Shackleman Ltd'

Protect Your Postal Services Documents

Protect Your Postal Services press releases 27.7.94a, 27.7.94b

Protect Your Postal Services (September 1994) 'PPS Submission on the Government's Green Paper on the future of Postal Services'

Protect Your Postal Services publication (1994) 'Freedom to Deliver – Commercial Freedom for the Post Office in the Public Sector'

Protect Your Postal Services correspondence with UCW and draft documents, 11.3.93, 8.4.93, 17.6.93, 30.6.93, 19.7.94.

Reader's Digest (19.9.94) 'Readers Digest Response to the Green Paper on the Future of Postal Services'

Rees-Mogg, W. (1992) 'The Financial and Business Press', in Englefield, D. (ed.) *Getting the Message Across – The Media, Business and Government*, London, Industry and Parliamentary Trust, pp7–9

Research and Marketing Ltd (March 1993) 'PR Week-Two-Ten Industry Barometer', London, PR Week-Two-Ten

Rice, C. (1984) *Trade Union Communications: A Suitable Case for Treatment?*, London, Trade Union Resource Centre

Robinson, G. (9.1.96) speech 'Forte: Speech for Analysts and Press', City Presentation Centre

Takeover Panel, (1987–98), *Takeover Panel Annual Reports*, London, London Stock Exchange

Trade and Industry Committee (1994) '*First Report – The Future of the Post Office*', 16 February, London, HMSO

TUC Publications and Conference Papers, London

TUC Congress Reports (1950–96)

1973, 'Fourth Meeting on Communication' (assorted documents)

1977a, 'Trades Councils and the Media: Notes for Officers of Trades Councils and County Associations of Trade Councils'

1977b, 'TUC Policy Proposals on the Media' (from TUC, February 1977 conference on the media, reproduced in Beharrell and Philo, 1977)

1979a, 'How to Handle the Media: A Guide for Trade Unionists'

1979b, 'Media Coverage of Industrial Disputes January and February 1979: A Cause for Concern'

1980a, 'Behind the Headlines: TUC Discussion Documents on the Media'

1980b, 'The Organisation, Structure and Services of the TUC – A TUC Consultative Document'

1982, 'A Guide for Trade Unionists to Critical Viewing and Listening'

1983, 'The Other Side of the Story: A TUC Report on Redress Against Abuses By the Media'

1985, 'Guidelines for Trade Unions on Use of Advertising'

1986, 'Guidelines for Trade Unions on Use of Video'

1989, 'The Role of the Media in a Democracy: A One Day TUC Conference'

1994a, 'The New TUC: New Unionism'

1994b, 'Campaigning for Change: A New Era for the TUC'

1996, 'Trade Unions: The Popular Verdict'

1997, 'Campaign Pack on Employee Rights'

1997, 'TUC Directory'

Touche Ross correspondence 19.12.95

Two–Ten Communications (1993) 'Press Attitudes to 'News Sources' and the Role of PR', Two–Ten Communications Research Report.

Two–Ten Communications (1997) company and promotional material

Ulster Unionist Party, September 1994, 'Comments on the Green Paper "The Future of Postal Services"'

Union Communications correspondence with UCW, undated

Union of Communication Workers Internal Documents and Campaign Materials
  Correspondence with NFSP and Sub-Postmasters, 12.8.94, September 1994
  'Stand By Your Post – Campaign Brief', undated
  Strategy Documents and Minutes of 'UCW Sub-Group Committee' Meetings on Privatisation Issue: 21.1.92, 27.10.92, 29.10.92, 21.6.93, 19.7.93, 20.9.93, 18.10.93, 20.12.93, 2.2.94, 21.2.94, 16.5.94, 22.5.94, 19.6.94, 29.6.94, 1.7.94, 25.8.94, 14.9.94
  Special Branch Circulars: 2.2.94, 24.3.94, 28.3.94, 20.4.94, 29.4.94, 18.5.94, 19.5.94, 15.6.94, 29.6.94, 4.7.94, 3.8.94, 11.8.94, 30.8.94, 15.9.94, 12.10.94, 14.10.94, 26.10.94, 2.11.94, 30.11.94
  Union of Communication Workers Campaign Materials, undated
  'Post Office Review – The Effects on Northern Ireland', July 1994
  letter to Northern Irish MPs, 2.8.94
  Press releases:18.5.94, 19.5.94, 16.6.94, 12.9.94, 12.10.94, 2.11.94.14.12.94

Weber, J. (1979) *Television Coverage of Industrial Conflict: Viewers Perception of any Bias in Main News Coverage of Industrial Disputes in the Early Months of 1979*, London, Independent Broadcasting Authority

Whitbread press release, 27.12.95

William Shackleman Ltd (1996) *Inter-Firm Comparisons 1995 – An Independent Survey*, London, PRCA

Books and articles

Abercrombie, A., Hill, S. and Turner, B. (1980) *The Dominant Ideology Thesis*, London, Allen and Unwin

Abercrombie, A., Hill, S. and Turner, B. (1990) *Dominant Ideologies*, London, Unwin Hyman

Abercrombie, N. (1990) 'Popular Culture and Ideological Effects', in Abercrombie, A., Hill, S. and Turner, B. *Dominant Ideologies*, London, Unwin Hyman, pp199–228

Adeney, M. and Lloyd, J. (1986) *The Miners' Strike: Loss Without Limit*, London, Routledge Kegan Paul

Advertising Statistics Yearbook (1991, 1998), Lincolnwood, IL, NTC Publications

Alexander, J.C. (1981) 'The Mass News Media in Systemic, Historical and Comparative Perspective', in Katz, E. and Szesco, T. (eds) *Mass Media and Social Change*, Beverly Hills, CA, Sage, pp17–51

Althusser, L. (1984) *Essays on Ideology*, London, Verso

Anderson, A. (1991) 'Source Strategies and the Communication of Environmental Affairs', *Media, Culture and Society*, Vol. 13, No. 4, pp459–76

Anderson, A. (1993) 'Source-Media Relations: The Production of the Environmental Agenda', in Hansen, A. (ed.) *The Mass Media and Environmental Issues*, Leicester, Leicester University Press, pp51–68

Anderson, A. (1997) *Media, Culture and the Environment*, London, UCL Press

Andrew, J. (1995) *How to Understand the Financial Press* (2nd edn.), London, Kogan Press

Andrew, K. (1990) *The Financial Public Relations Handbook*, Cambridge, Woodhead Faulkner

Ang, I. (1985) *Watching Dallas*, London, Methuen

Bachrach, P. and Baratz, M. (1962) 'Two Faces of Power', *American Political Science Review*, Vol. 56, No. 4, pp947–52

Bagdikian, B. (1992) *The Media Monopoly* (4th edn), Boston, MA, Beacon Press

Bagdikian, B. (1997) *The Media Monopoly* (5th edn), Boston, MA, Beacon Press

Ball, A. and Millard, F. (1986) *Pressure Politics in Industrial Societies*, London, Macmillan

Barnett, S. and Curry, A. (1994) *The Battle for the BBC*, London, Aurum Press,

Bassett, P. and Cave, A. (1993) 'All for One: The Future of the Unions', pamphlet, London, Fabian Society

Bassett, P. and Pierce, A. (1994) 'PO Faces Test on Spending', *The Times*, 8 September, p10

Bates, S. (1994) 'Poll Shows Local Tory Chiefs Oppose PO Sell-Off', *Guardian*, p4

Baudrillard, J. (1988) *Selected Writings* (ed. by Poster, M.), Cambridge, Polity Press

Beck, U. (1992 [1986]) *Risk Society: Towards a New Modernity*, London, Sage

Beckett, F. (1977) 'Press and Prejudice', in Beharrell, P. and Philo, G. (eds) *Trade Unions and the Media*, London, Macmillan, pp32–49

Beharrell, P. and Philo, G. (eds) (1977) *Trade Unions and the Media*, London, Macmillan

Bennett, N. (1996) 'Forte Fantasia', *Sunday Telegraph*, Business Section, 14 January, p2

Berkman, R. and Kitch, W. (1986) *Politics in the Media Age*, New York, McGraw-Hill

Bernays, E. (1923) *Crystallizing Public Opinion*, New York, Bani and Liveright

Billig, M., Deacon, D., Golding, P. and Middleton, S. (1993) 'In the Hands of the Spin Doctors: TV, Politics, and the 1992 General Election', in Miller, N. and Allen, R. (eds) *Its Live But is it Real?*, London, John Libby Press, pp111–21

Black, S. (ed.) (1995) *The Practice of Public Relations* (4th edn), Oxford, Butterworth-Heinemann

Blumler, J. (1990) 'Elections, the Media and the Modern Publicity Process', in Ferguson, M. (ed.) *Public Communication – The New Imperative*, London, Sage, pp101–13

Blumler, J.G. and Gurevitch, M. (1986) 'Journalists' Orientations to Political Institutions: the Case of Parliamentary Broadcasting', in Golding, P., Murdoch, G. and Schlesinger, P. (eds) *Communicating Politics: Mass Communication and the Political Process*, Leicester, Leicester University Press, pp67–92

Blumler, J.G. and Gurevitch, M. (1995) *The Crisis of Public Communication*, London, Routledge

Boorstein, D. (1962) *The Image*, London, Weidenfeld and Nicolson

Boswell, J. and Peters, J. (1997) *Capitalism in Contention – Business Leaders and Political Economy in Modern Britain*, Cambridge, Cambridge University Press

Bottomore, T. (1993) *Political Sociology*, London, Pluto Press

Bourdieu, P. (1979) *Distinction*, London, Routledge

Bourdieu, P. (1993) *The Field of Cultural Production*, Cambridge, Polity Press.

Bourdieu, P. and Wacquant, L. J. D. (1992) *An Invitation to Reflexive Sociology*, Cambridge, Polity Press

Bourne, C. (1995–96) 'Papers Before Profit', *Journalist*, December–January, pp18–19

Bowman, P. (ed.) (1989) *Handbook of Financial Public Relations*, London, Heinemann Professional

Brown, C. (1994a) 'Defeat on Royal Mail a New Blow for Heseltine', *Independent*, 3 November, p19

Brown, C. (1994b) 'Rebels Threaten Post Office Sale', *Independent*, 28 October, p6

Brummer, A. (1996) 'Lots of Stakes but Few Holders', *Guardian*, 16 January, p15

Buckingham, L. and Atkinson, D. (1999) 'Whisper it … Takeovers Don't Pay', *Guardian*, 30 November, p27

Budge, I. and McKay, D. (1993) *The Developing British Political System: The 1990s* (3rd edn), Harlow, Longman

Burson-Marsteller (1996) *Doing Business with Blair – An Analysis of the Impact of a Labour Government on Industry*, London, Burson-Marsteller

Button, M. and Bolton, S. (1998) A. *Practitioners Guide to the City Code on Takeovers and Mergers*, London, City and Financial Publishing

Cairncross, A. (1992) *The British Economy Since 1945*, Oxford, Blackwell

Calhoun, C. (ed.) (1992) *Habermas and the Public Sphere*, Cambridge, MA, MIT Press

Central Office of Information (COI) (1970–99) *The IPO Directory: Information and Press Officers in Government Departments and Public Corporations*, London, COI

Clegg, S. (1989) *Frameworks of Power*, London, Sage

Coates, D. (1984) *The Context of British Politics*, London, Hutchinson

Cockerell, M. (1988) *Live from Number Ten*, London, Faber and Faber

Cockerell, M. (1997) *A Word in the Right Ear*, BBC2 documentary, 9 January

Cockerell, M., Hennessey, P. and Walker, D. (1984) *Sources Close to the Prime Minister: Inside the Hidden World of the News Manipulators*, London, Macmillan

Commission on Social Justice (1994) *Social Justice: Strategies for National Renewal*, London, Vintage

Corner, J. and Schlesinger, P. (1993) 'Editorial', *Media, Culture and Society*, Vol. 15, No. 3, pp339–44

Cracknell, J. (1993) 'Issue Arenas, Pressure Groups and Environmental Issues' in Hansen, A. (ed.) *The Mass Media and Environmental Issues*, Leicester, Leicester University Press, pp3–21

Crawford's Directory of City Connections (1981/82, 1990, 1994, 1998), London, Directory Publishers Association

Crewe, I., and Gosschalk, B. (eds) (1995) *Political Communications: The General Election Campaign of 1992*, Cambridge, Cambridge University Press

Crewe, I., and Harrop, M. (eds) (1986) *Political Communications: The General Election Campaign of 1983*, Cambridge, Cambridge University Press

Crewe, I., and Harrop, M. (eds) (1989) *Political Communications: The General Election Campaign of 1987*, Cambridge, Cambridge University Press

Crewe, I., Gosschalk, B. and Bartle, J. (eds) (1998) *Political Communications: Why Labour Won the General Election of 1997*, London, Frank Cass

Critchley, J. (1994) 'The Last Post for the Tory Left', *The Times*, 24 August, p12

Crouch, C. and Dore, R. (eds) (1990) *Corporatism and Accountability: Organised Interests in British Public Life*, Oxford, Clarendon Press

Curran, J. (1978) 'Advertising and the Press', in Curran, J. (ed.) *The British Press: A Manifesto*, London, Macmillan, pp229–67

Curran, J. (1986) 'The Impact of Advertising on the British Mass Media', in Collins, R., Curran, J., Garnham, N., Scannell, P., Schlesinger, P. and Sparks, C. (eds) *Media, Culture and Society: A Critical Reader*, London, Sage

Curran, J. (1990a) 'Cultural Perspectives of News Organisations: A Reappraisal and a Case Study', in Ferguson, M. (ed.) *Public Communication – The New Imperative*, London, Sage, pp114–34

Curran, J. (1990b) 'The New Revisionism in Mass Communications Research: A Reappraisal', *European Journal of Communication*, Vol. 5, June, pp130–64

Curran, J. (1996) 'Rethinking Mass Communications', in Curran, J., Morley, D. and Walkerdine, V. (eds) *Cultural Studies and Communications*, London, Arnold, pp119–65

Curran, J., Ecclestone, J., Oakley, G. and Richardson, A. (eds) (1986) *Bending Reality*, London, Pluto Press

Curran, J. and Gurevitch, M. (eds) (1991) *Mass Media and Society*, London, Arnold

Curran, J. and Seaton, J. (1997) *Power Without Responsibility* (5th edn), London, Routledge

Curtice, J. and Semetko, H. (1994) 'Does it Matter What the Papers Say?', in Heath, A., Jowell, R. and Curtice, J. (eds) *Labour's Last Chance?* Aldershot, Dartmouth

Cutlip, S., Center, A. and Broom, G. (1985) *Effective Public Relations* (6th edn), Englewood Cliffs, NJ, Prentice-Hall

Cutlip, S., Center, A. and Broom, G. (1994) *Effective Public Relations* (7th edn), Englewood Cliffs, NJ, Prentice-Hall

Cutlip, S., Center, A. and Broom, G. (2000) *Effective Public Relations* (8th edn), Englewood Cliffs, NJ, Prentice-Hall

Dahl, R. (1961) *Who Governs? Democracy and Power in an American City*, New Haven, CT, Yale University Press

Dahl, R. (1985) *A Preface to Political Economy*, Cambridge, Polity Press

Dahlgren, P. and Sparks, C. (eds) (1991) *Communication and Citizenship*, London, Routledge

Davies, M. (1985) *Politics of Pressure: The Art of Lobbying*, London, BBC Books

Davis, A. (2000a) 'Public Relations Campaigning and News Production: The Case of New Unionism in Britain', in Curran, J. (ed.) *Media Organisations in Society*, London, Arnold, pp173–92

Davis, A. (2000b) 'Public Relations, News Production and Changing Patterns of Source Access in the British National Press', *Media, Culture and Society*, Vol. 22, No. 1, pp33–59

Davis, A. (2000c) 'Public Relations, Business News and the Reproduction of Corporate Elite Power', *Journalism, Theory, Practice and Criticism*, Vol. 1, No. 3, pp282–304

Davis, A. (2000d) 'Public Relations, Political Communications and National News Production in Britain 1979–99', unpublished PhD thesis, University of London

Dayan, D. and Katz, E. (1992) *Media Events*, Cambridge, MA, Harvard University Press

Deacon, D. (1996) 'The Voluntary Sector in a Changing Communication Environment', *European Journal of Communication*, Vol. 11, No. 2, pp173–99

Deacon, D. (1999) 'Charitable Images: The Construction of Voluntary Sector News', in Franklin, B. (ed.), *Social Policy, the Media and Misrepresentation*, New York, Routledge, pp51–68

Deacon, D. and Golding, P. (1994) *Taxation and Representation*, London, John Libby Press

Deacon, D, Fenton, N. and Bryman, A. (1999) 'From Inception to Reception: the Natural History of a News Item', *Media, Culture and Society*, Vol. 21, No. 1, pp5–32

Dreier, P. (1982) 'Capitalists Versus the Media: An Analysis of an Ideological Mobilization Among Business Leaders', *Media, Culture and Society*, Vol. 4, No. 2, pp111–32

Dreier, P. (1988) 'The Corporate Complaint Against the Media', in Hiebert, R. and Reuss, C. (eds) *Impacts of Mass Media*, (2nd edn), New York, Longman, pp425–43

Douglas, D. (1985) *The Role of the Media in the Great Coal Strike of 1984/1985*, Doncaster, D. Douglas

Douglas, L. (1998) 'Newsrooms with no Typewriters', *British Journalism Review*, Vol. 9, No. 3, pp43–8

Douglas, S. (1986) *Labor's New Voice: Unions and the Mass Media*, Norwood, NJ, Ablex

Dunleavy, P. and O'Leary, B. (1987) *Theories of the State*, London, Macmillan

Dunleavy, P., Gamble, A., Holliday, I. and Peele, G. (eds) (1997) *Developments in British Politics 5*, London, Macmillan

Edwards, P. and Bain, S. (1988) 'Why are Trade Unions Becoming More Popular? Trade Unions and Public Opinion in Britain', *British Journal of Industrial Relations*, Vol. 26. No. 3, pp311–26

Eldridge, J. (1995) *Glasgow Media Group Reader, Vol. 1: News Content, Language and Visuals*, London, Routledge

Elliot, P., Murdock, G. and Schlesinger, P. (1986) '"Terrorism" and the State: A Case Study of the Discourses of Television', in Collins, R., Curran, J., Garnham, N., Scannell, P., Schlesinger, P. and Sparks, C. (eds) *Media, Culture and Society*, London, Sage, pp264–86

Englefield, D. (ed.) (1992) *Getting the Message Across – The Media, Business and Government*, London, Industry and Parliamentary Trust

Ericson, R.V., Baranek, P.M. and Chan J.B.L. (1989) *Negotiating Control: A Study of News Sources*, Milton Keynes, Open University Press

Ericson, R.V., Baranek, P.M. and Chan J.B.L. (1991) *Representing Order – Crime, Law and Justice in the News Media*, Milton Keynes, Open University Press

Evans, H. (1983) *Good Times, Bad Times*, London, Weidenfeld and Nicolson

Ewen, S. (1996) *PR! A Social History of Spin*, New York, Basic Books

Fallows, J. (1996) *Breaking the News: How the Media Undermine American Democracy*, New York, Pantheon

Farrelly, P. (1999) 'The Short Arm of the Law', *Observer*, 7 November, p2

Fidler, J. (1981) *The British Business Elite – Its Attitudes to Class, Status and Power*, London, Routledge and Kegan Paul

Financial Times (FT) (1996) 'Shedding Light on Bid Fees', *Financial Times*, 23 January, p8

Fildes, C. (1996) 'It's a Great War for the City's Army of Mercenaries', *Daily Telegraph*, 22 January, p23

Finn, D. (1981) *The Business–Media Relationship: Countering Misconceptions and Distrust*, New York, AMACOM

Fishman, M. (1980) *Manufacturing News*, Austin, TX, University of Texas

Fiske, J. (1989) *Understanding Popular Culture*, London, Routledge

Forgacs, D. (ed.) (1988) *An Antonio Gramsci Reader: Selected Writings 1916–1935*, London, Lawrence and Wishart

Forte, C. (1997) *Forte: The Autobiography of Charles Forte*, (2nd edn), London, Pan Books

Foucault, M. (1975) *Discipline and Punish: The Birth of the Prison* (trans. Sheridan, A.), London, Penguin

Foucault, M. (1980) *Power/Knowledge: Selected Interviews and Other Writings 1972–1977* (ed. Gordon, C.), Hemel Hempstead, Harvester Wheatsheaf

Franklin, B. (1994) *Packaging Politics: Political Communications in Britain's Media Democracy*, London, Arnold

Franklin, B. (1997) *Newzak and News Media*, London, Arnold

Franklin, B. (ed.) (1999a) *Social Policy, the Media and Misrepresentation*, New York, Routledge

Franklin, B. (1999b) 'Soft-Soaping the Public?: The Government and Media Promotion of Social Policy', in Franklin, B. (ed.) *Social Policy, the Media and Misrepresentation*, New York, Routledge

FT500 (1997) *Financial Times 500*, London, FT Partnership Publications

FT500 (1998) *Financial Times 500*, London, FT Partnership Publications

Gaber, I. (1995) 'Driving the News or Spinning Out of Control: Politicians, the Media and the Battle for the News Agenda', inaugural lecture, London, Goldsmiths College.

Gaber, I. (1998) 'The Media and Politics', in Briggs, A. and Cobley, P. (eds) *The Media: An Introduction*, Harlow, Longman, pp392–411

Gandy, O. (1980) 'Information in Health: Subsidised News', *Media Culture and Society*, Vol. 2, No. 2, pp103–15

Gandy, O. (1982) *Beyond Agenda Setting: Information Subsidies and Public Policy*, NJ, Ablex

Gans, H.J. (1979) *Deciding What's News: A Study of CBS Evening News, NBC Nightly News, Newsweek and Time*, New York, Vintage Books

Garnham, N. (1990) *Capitalism and Communication: Global Culture and the Economics of Information*, London, Sage

Gavin, N. (ed.) (1998) *Economy, Media and Public Knowledge*, London, Cassells/University of Leicester Press

Gerth, H.H. and Wright Mills, C. (eds) (1991) *From Max Weber: Essays in Sociology* (2nd edn), London, Routledge

Gibbon, H. (ed.) (1997) *Privatisation Yearbook 1997*, London, Privatisation International

Gitlin, T. (1980) *The Whole World is Watching*, Berkeley, CA, University of California Press

Gitlin, T. (1994) *Inside Prime Time* (2nd edn), London, Routledge

Glasgow University Media Group (GUMG) (1976) *Bad News*, London, Routledge

Glasgow University Media Group (GUMG) (1980) *More Bad News*, London, Routledge

Glasgow University Media Group (GUMG) (1982) *Really Bad News*, London, Routledge

Glasgow University Media Group (GUMG) (1985) *War and Peace News*, Milton Keynes, Open University Press

Glasgow University Media Group (GUMG) (1993) *Getting the Message*, London, Routledge

Goldenberg, E. (1975) *Making the Papers: The Access of Resource-Poor Groups to the Metropolitan Press*, Lexington, MA, D.C. Heath

Golding, P. and Middleton, S. (1982) *Images of Welfare – Press and Public Attitudes to Poverty*, Oxford, Martin Robinson

Golding, P. and Murdock, G. (1996) 'Culture, Communications and Political Economy', in Curran, J. and Gurevitch, M. (eds) *Mass Media and Society*, London, Arnold, pp11–30

Goldsmiths Media Group (2000) 'Media Organisations in Society: Central Issues', in Curran, J. (ed.) *Media Organisations in Society*, London, Arnold, pp19–65

Goodman, G. (1995) *UK Press Gazette*, 18 December

Goodman, A., Johnson, P. and Webb, S. (1997) *Inequality in the UK*, Oxford, Oxford University Press

Goodman, P. (1994) 'Fury as PO Spends £2m to Push Sell-Off', *Telegraph*, 12 August

Gould, P. (1998) *The Unfinished Revolution: How the Modernisers Saved the Labour Party*, London, Abacus

Grant, W. (1993) *Business and Politics in Britain* (2nd edn), London, Macmillan

Grant, W. (1995) *Pressure Groups, Politics and Democracy in Britain*, New York, Harvester Wheatsheaf

Grant, W. (2000) *Pressure Groups and British Politics*, London, Macmillan

Greenslade, R. (1994) 'The Slick and the Dead', *Media Guardian*, 20 June, pp4–5

Greenslade, R. (1996) 'Big Rush, No Breakthrough', *Guardian*, 15 July, p25

Griffiths, T. (1977) 'The Production of Television News', in Beharrell, P. and Philo, G. (eds), *Trade Unions and the Media*, London, Macmillan, pp60–72

Grunig, J.E. and Hunt, T. (1984) *Managing Public Relations*, New York, Holt, Rinehart and Winston

Habermas, J. (1988 [1973]) *Legitimation Crisis* (trans. McCarthy, T.) Cambridge, Polity Press

Habermas, J. (1989 [1962]) *The Structural Transformation of the Public Sphere: An Inquiry into a Category of Bourgeois Society* (trans. Burger, T.), Cambridge, Polity Press

Habermas, J. (1997) *Between Facts and Norms*, Cambridge, Polity Press

Hackett, R. (1992) 'The Depiction of Labour and Business on National Television News', in Grenier, M. (ed.) *Critical Studies of Canadian Mass Media*, Markham, Ontario, Butterworth, pp59–82

Hall, S. (1986) 'Media Power and Class Power', in Curran, J., Ecclestone, J., Oakley, G. and Richardson, A. (eds), *Bending Reality – The State of the Media*, London, Pluto Press, pp5–14

Hall, S. and Jacques, M. (1989) *New Times: The Changing Face of British Politics in the 1990s*, London, Lawrence and Wishart

Hall, S., Critcher, C., Jefferson, T., Clarke, J. and Roberts, B. (1978) *Policing the Crisis – Mugging, the State, and Law and Order*, London, Macmillan

Hall Jamieson, K. (1996) *Packaging the Presidency: A History and Criticism of Presidential Campaign Adversiting* (3rd edn), Oxford, Oxford University Press

Hallin, D. (1994) *We Keep America on Top of the World – Television Journalism and the Public Sphere*, London, Routledge

The Hambro Company Guide (1995) London, Hemmington Scott

The Hambro Company Guide (1998) London, Hemmington Scott

Hammond, J. (1995) 'Public Relations in the Non–Commercial Sector', in Black, S., (ed.) *The Practice of Public Relations*, London, IPR

Hanrahan, G. (1997) 'Financial and Investor Public Relations', in Kitchen, P. (ed.) *Public Relations – Principles and Practice*, London, International Thomson Business Press

Hansen, A. (1993) 'Greenpeace and Press Coverage of Environmental Issues' in Hansen, A., (ed.) *The Mass Media and Environmental Issues*, Leicester, Leicester University Press, pp150–78

Hansen, A. (2000) 'Claims-Making and Framing in British Newspaper Coverage of the "Brent Spar" Controversy', in Allan, S., Adam, B. and Carter, C. (eds) *Environmental Risks and the Media*, London, Routledge, pp55–72

Harding, T. (1998) '"Viva Camcordistas" – Video Activism and the Protest Movement', in McKay, G. (ed.) *DIY Culture: Party and Protest in 90s Britain*, London, Verso

Harper, K. (1994) 'Revolt Stamps Out Sale of Post Office', *Guardian*, 3 November, p5

Harris, R. (1990) *Good and Faithful Servant*, London, Faber and Faber

Harrison, M. (1985) *Television News: Whose Bias?*, Reading, Policy Journals Publication

Harrop, M. (1986) 'The Press and Post-War Elections', in Crewe, I. and Harrop, M. (eds) *Political Communications: The General Election Campaign of 1983*, Cambridge, Cambridge University Press, pp137–49

Held, D. (1989) *Political Theory and the Modern State*, Cambridge, Polity Press

Held, D. (1995) *Democracy and the Global Order: From the Modern State to Cosmopolitan Governance*, Cambridge, Polity Press

Held, D. (1996) *Models of Democracy* (2nd edn), Cambridge, Polity Press

Herman, E. (1982) 'The Institutionalisation of Bias in Economics', *Media, Culture and Society*, Vol. 4, No. 3, pp275–92

Herman, E. and Chomsky, N. (1988) *Manufacturing Consent*, New York, Pantheon

Herman, E. and McChesney, R. (1997) *The Global Media: The New Missionaries of Global Capitalism*, London, Cassell

Hetherington, A. (1985) *News, Newspapers and Television*, London, Macmillan

Hill, B. (1990) 'Britain: The Dominant Ideology Thesis After a Decade', in Abercrombie, A., Hill, S. and Turner, B. (eds), *Dominant Ideologies*, London, Unwin Hyman, pp1–37

Hills, J. (ed.) (1996) *New Inequalities: The Changing Distribution of Income and Wealth in the United Kingdom*, Cambridge, Cambridge University Press

Hoge, J. (1988) 'Business and the Media: Stereotyping Each Other', in Hiebert, R. and
    Reuss, C. (eds) *Impacts of Mass Media* (2nd edn), New York, Longman, pp422–5
Hollingsworth, M. (1986) *The Press and Political Dissent*, London, Pluto Press
Hollis, (1998) *UK Press and Public Relations Annual 1997–98* (29th edn), Sunbury on
    Thames, Middlesex, Directory Publishers Association
Horseman, M. and Shepherd, J. (1996) 'Granada Details £100 million savings', *Independent*,
    4 January
Hutton, W. (1995) 'No Jab to Halt the Takeover Virus', *Guardian*, 6 December, p17
Hutton, W. (1996) *The State We're In*, London, Vintage
Hutton, W. (1998) 'The Power 300', *Observer*, supplement, 1 November, pp1–15
Independent Labour Party Information Committee (1923) *The Capitalist Press: Who Owns It
    and Why*, London, ILP
Ingham, B. (1991) *Kill the Messenger*, London, Fontana
Ingham, B. (1996), 'It's the Message that Matters', *British Journalism Review*, Vol. 7, No. 3,
    pp6–10
Investors Chronicle (1996) 'It's Time to Make up Your Mind', *Investors Chronicle*,
    19 January
Jhally, S. (1987) *The Codes of Advertising – Fetishism and the Political Economy of Meaning in
    Consumer Society*, London, Routledge
Jim Conway Foundation (1993) *Trade Unions: The Thatcher Years*, Stockton-on-Tees, Jim
    Conway Foundation
Jones, N. (1986) *Strikes and the Media: Communication and Conflict*, Oxford, Blackwell
Jones, N. (1987) *The Media and Industrial Relations: The Changing Relationship*, Warwick
    Papers in Industrial Relations, No. 18, Warwick University
Jones, N. (1995) *Soundbites and Spin Doctors – How Politicians Manipulate the Media and Vice
    Versa*, London, Cassell
Jones, N. (1997) *Campaign 1997: How the General Election was Won and Lost*, London, Indigo
    Press
Jones, N. (1999) *Sultans of Spin: The Media and the New Labour Government*, London, Orion
Jordan, G. (ed.) (1990) *The Commercial Lobbyists: Politics and Profit in Britain*, Aberdeen,
    Aberdeen University Press
Jordan, G., and Richardson, J. (1982) 'The British Policy Style or the Logics of Negotiation',
    in Richardson, J. (ed.) *Policy Styles in Western Europe*, London, Allen and Unwin,
    pp80–110
Jordan, G. and Richardson, J. (1987) *Government and Pressure Groups in Britain*, Oxford,
    Clarendon Press
Jowell, R., Brook, L. and Davids, L. (eds) (1992) *International Social Attitudes: The 9th BSA
    Report*, Aldershot, Dartmouth
Jowell, R., Brook, L. and Davids, L. (eds) (1993) *International Social Attitudes: The 10th
    BSA Report*, Aldershot, Dartmouth
Joyce, J. (1996) 'Granada Triumphs in Classic City Struggle', *PR Week*, 26 January, p1
Kavanagh, D. (1990) *British Politics – Continuities and Change*, Oxford, Oxford University
    Press
Kavanagh, D. (1995) *Election Campaigning: The New Marketing of Politics*, Oxford,
    Blackwell
Kavanagh, D. and Gosschalk, B. (1995) 'Failing to Set the Agenda: The Role of the Election
    Press Conferences in 1992', in Crewe, I. and Gosschalk, B. (eds), *Political
    Communications: The General Election Campaign of 1992*, Cambridge, Cambridge
    University Press, pp160–74

Kavanagh, D. and Seldon, A. (eds) (1989) *The Thatcher Effect: A Decade of Change*, Oxford, Clarendon Press

Keane, J. (1988) *Civil Society and the State: New European Perspectives*, London, Verso

Keane, J. (1991) *The Media and Democracy*, Cambridge, Polity Press

Kelley, S. (1956) *Professional Public Relations and Political Power*, Baltimore, MD, Johns Hopkins University Press

Kerr, A. and Sachdev, S. (1992) 'Third Among Equals: An Analysis of the 1989 Ambulance Dispute', *British Journal of Industrial Relations* Vol. 30, No. 1, pp127–43

Kimball, P. (1994) *Downsizing the News: Network Cutbacks in the Nation's Capital*, Baltimore, MD, Johns Hopkins University Press

King, A. (ed.) (1998) *New Labour Triumphs: Britain at the Polls*, Chatham, NJ, Chatham House

Kitchen, P. (ed.) (1997) *Public Relations – Principles and Practices*, London, International Thomson Business Press

Klamer, A., McClosky, D. and Solow, R. (eds) (1988) *The Consequences of Rhetoric*, Cambridge, Cambridge University Press

Knight, G. (1992) 'Strike Talk: A Case Study of News', in Grenier, M. (ed.), *Critical Studies of Canadian Mass Media*, Markham, Ontario, Butterworth, pp47–58

Kopel, E. (1982) *Financial and Corporate Public Relations: The Integrated Approach*, London, McGraw-Hill

Koss, S. (1984) *The Rise and Fall of the Political Press in Britain*, London, Hamish Hamilton

Lash, S. and Urry, J. (1994) *Economies of Signs and Spaces*, London, Sage

L'Etang, J. (1996) 'Corporate Responsibility and Public Relations Ethics', in L'Etang, J. and Pieczka, M. (eds) *Critical Perspectives in Public Relations*, London, International Thomson Business Press, pp82–105

L'Etang, J. (1998) 'State Propaganda and Bureaucratic Intelligence: The Creation of Public Relations in 20th Century Britain', *Public Relations Review*, Vol. 24, No. 4, pp413–41

L'Etang, J. and Pieczka, M. (eds) (1996) *Critical Perspectives in Public Relations*, London, International Thomson Business Press

Letwin, S.R. (1992) *The Anatomy of Thatcherism*, London, Fontana

Lichter, S. and Rothman, S. (1988) 'Media and Business Elites', in Hiebert, R. and Reuss, C. (eds), *Impacts of Mass Media*, New York, Longman, pp448–62

Lindblom, C. (1977) *Politics and Markets: The World's Political Economic Systems*, New York, Basic Books

Lippmann, W. (1922) *Public Opinion*, New York, Macmillan

Lowe, R. (1993) *The Welfare State in Britain Since 1945*, London, Macmillan

Lowe, P. and Goyder, J. (1983) *Environmental Groups in Politics*, London, George Allen and Unwin

Maloney, K. (1997) 'Teaching Organisational Communications as Public Relations in UK Universities', *Corporate Communications*, Vol. 2, No. 1

Manners, N. (1992) 'The Company and the Media', in Englefield, D. (ed.), *Getting the Message Across – The Media, Business and Government*, London, Industry and Parliamentary Trust, pp10–13

Manning, P. (1998) *Spinning For Labour, Trade Unions and the New Media Environment*, Aldershot, Ashgate

Manning, P. (1999) 'Categories of Knowledge and Information Flows: Reasons for the Decline of the British Labour and Industrial Correspondents Group', *Media, Culture and Society*, Vol. 21, No. 3 pp313–36

Marchand, R. (1998) *Creating the Corporate Soul: The Rise of Public Relations and Corporate Imagery in American Big Business*, Berkeley, CA, University of California Press

Marsh, A. and Gillies (1983) 'Trade Union Journals Revisited', *Industrial Relations Journal*, Vol. 14, No. 2, pp52–9

Marsh, A. and Locksley, G. (1983) 'Capital in Britain: Its Structural Power and Influence Over Policy', *Western European Politics*, Vol. 6, No. 2, pp36–60

Marsh, D. (1990) 'Public Opinion, Trade Unions and Mrs Thatcher', *British Journal of Industrial Relations*, Vol. 28, No. 1, pp57–65

McChesney, R. (1997) *Corporate Media and the Threat to Democracy*, New York, Seven Stories Press

McIlroy, J. (1995) *Trade Unions in Britain Today*, Manchester, Manchester University Press

McKay, G. (ed.), (1998) *DIY Culture: Party and Protest in 90s Britain*, London, Verso

McNair, B. (1994) *News and Journalism in the UK*, London, Routledge

McNair, B. (1995) *An Introduction to Political Communication*, London, Routledge

McNair, B. (1996) 'Performance in Politics and the Politics of Performance: Public Relations, the Public Sphere and Democracy', in L'Etang, J. and Pieczka, M. (eds), *Critical Perspectives in Public Relations*, London, International Thomson Business Press, pp35–53

McShane, D. (1983) *Using the Media* (2nd edn), London, Pluto Press

McSmith, A. (1996) *Faces of Labour: The Inside Story*, London, Verso

Media Expenditure Analysis Ltd (MEAL) (1980–96) *MEAL Digest*, monthly digest

Meech, P. (1996) 'Corporate Identity and Corporate Image', in L'Etang, J. and Pieczka, M. (eds) *Critical Perspectives in Public Relations*, London, International Thomson Business Press, pp65–81

Michael Bland Communications Consultancy (1989) *Financial PR Opportunities in the National Press*, Colchester, MBCC

Michael Bland Communications Consultancy (1990) *PR Opportunities in the National Press*, Colchester, MBCC

Michie, D. (1998) *The Invisible Persuaders: How Britain's Spin Doctors Manipulate the Media*, London, Bantam Press

Middlemas, K. (1979) *Politics in Industrial Society: The Experience of the British System Since 1911*, London, Andre Deutsch

Middlemas, K. (1991) *Power, Competition and the State, Vol 3: The End of the Post-War Era*, London, Macmillan

Miller, D. (1993) 'Official Sources and "Primary Definition": The Case of Northern Ireland', *Media, Culture and Society*, Vol. 15, No. 3, pp385–406

Miller, D. (1994) *Don't Mention the War: Northern Ireland, Propaganda and the Media*, London, Pluto Press

Miller, D. (1997) 'Dominant Ideologies and Media Power: The Case of Northern Ireland', in Kelly, M.J. and Connor, B.O. (eds) *Media Audiences in Ireland*, Dublin, University of Dublin Press, pp126–45

Miller, D. (1998) 'Promotional Strategies and Media Power', in Briggs, A. and Cobley, P. (eds) *The Media: An Introduction*, Harlow, Longman, pp65–80

Miller, D. and Dinan, W. (2000) 'The Rise of the PR Industry in Britain, 1979–98', *European Journal of Communication*, Vol. 15, No. 1, pp5–35

Miller, D. and Williams, K. (1993) 'Negotiating HIV/AIDS Information: Agendas, Media Strategies and the News', in Eldridge, J. (ed.), *Getting the Message*, London, Routledge, pp126–42

Miller, D. and Williams, K. (1998) 'Sourcing AIDS News', in Miller, D., Kitzenger, J., Williams, K. and Beharrell, P. *The Circuits of Mass Communication*, London, Sage, pp123–46

Milliband, R. (1969) *The State in Capitalist Society*, London, Weidenfeld and Nicolson

Millward, N. (1994) *The New Industrial Relations? Based on the ED/ESRC/PSI/ACAS Survey*, London, Policy Studies Institute

Minkin, L. (1991) *The Contentious Alliance: Trade Unions and the Labour Party*, Edinburgh, Edinburgh University Press

Mirsky, N. (producer) (1999) *Blood on the Carpet*, BBC2 documentary, 13 February

Mitchell, N. (1997) *The Conspicuous Corporation – Business, Publicity, and Representative Democracy*, Ann Arbor, MI, University of Michigan Press

Morley, D. (1980) *The Nationwide Audience*, London, BFI

Morley, D. (1992) *Television Audiences and Cultural Studies*, London, Routledge

Murdock, G. (1982) 'Large Corporations and the Control of the Communications Industries', in Gurevitch, M., Bennett, T., Curran, J. and Woollacott, J. (eds) *Culture, Society and the Media*, London, Methuen, pp118–50

Myers, N. (1986) 'Union World', in Curran, J., Ecclestone, J., Oakley, G. and Richardson, A. (eds) *Bending Reality*, London, Pluto Press, pp72–5

Nacos, B. (1990) *The Press, Presidents, and Crises*, New York, Columbia University Press

Negrine, R. (1994) *Politics and the Mass Media in Britain* (2nd edn), London, Routledge

Negrine, R. (1996) *The Communication of Politics*, London, Sage

Negroponte, N. (1995) *Being Digital*, London, Hodder and Stoughton

Nelson, J. (1989) *Sultans of Sleaze – Public Relations and the Media*, Toronto, Between the Lines

Newman, K. (1984) *Financial Marketing and Communications*, London, Holt, Rinehart and Winston

Nicholson, E. and Trundle, E. (1986) *PR in a Changing City*, London, London Business School

Norris, P. and Gavin, N. (eds) (1997) *Britain Votes 1997*, Oxford, Oxford University Press

Norris, P., Curtice, J., Sanders, D., Scammell, M. and Semetko, H. (1999) *On Message: Communicating the Campaign*, London, Sage

Offe, C. (1984) *Contradictions of the Welfare State* (ed. Keane, J.), Cambridge, MA, MIT Press

Offe, C. (1985) *Disorganised Capitalism: Contemporary Transformations of Work and Politics* (ed. Keane, J.), Cambridge, Polity Press

Offe, C. and Wiesenthal, H. (1985) 'Two Logics of Collective Action', in Offe, C. *Disorganised Capitalism: Contemporary Transformations of Work and Politics*, Cambridge, Polity Press, pp170–220

Olasky, M. (1987) *Corporate Public Relations – A New Historical Perspective*, Hillsdale, NJ, Lawrence Erlbaum Associates

Olson, M. (1965) *The Logic of Collective Action*, Cambridge, MA, Harvard University Press

O'Shaughnessy, H. (1998) 'Maybe We Have a Future After all', *British Journalism Review*, Vol. 9, No. 4, pp56–9

Owen, D. (1994) 'Double Blow for the Postal Sell-Off', *Financial Times*, 3 October, p8

Page, B., Shapiro, R., Dempsey, G. (1987) 'What Makes Public Opinion', *American Political Science Review*, Vol. 81, No. 1, pp23–44

Parenti, M. (1992) *Make Believe Media – The Politics of Entertainment*, New York, St. Martins Press

Parenti, M. (1993) *Inventing Reality: The Politics of News Media* (2nd edn), New York, St Martins Press

Parsons, W. (1989) *The Power of the Financial Press: Journalism and Economic Opinion in Britain and America*, London, Edward Elgar

Pavlik, J. (1996) *New Media and the Information Superhighway*, Boston, MA, Allen and Bacon

Phillimore, P. and Moffatt, S. (2000) '"Industry Causes Lung Cancer": Would You be Happy with that Headline? Environmental Health and Local Politics', in Allan, S., Adam, B. and Carter, C. (eds), *Environmental Risks and the Media*, London, Routledge, pp105–16

Philo, G. (ed.) (1995) *Glasgow Media Group Reader, Vol. 2: Industry, Economy, War and Politics*, London, Routledge

Philo, G., Beharell, P. and Hewitt, J. (1977) 'Strategies and Policies', in Beharrell, P. and Philo, G. (eds), *Trade Unions and the Media*, London, Macmillan, pp135–42

PMS (1997) *Guide to Pressure Groups*, London, PMS Publications

Poster, M. (ed.) (1988) *Jean Baudrillard: Selected Writings*, Cambridge, Polity Press

Piore, M. and Sabel, C. (1984) *The Second Industrial Divide*, New York, Basic Books

Pollard, S. (1992) *The Development of the British Economy 1914–90* (4th edn), London, Edward Arnold

Pool, M., Mansfield, R., Blyton, P. and Frost, P. (1981) *Managers in Focus: The British Manager in the Early 1980s*, Aldershot, Gower

Porter, H. (1994) 'Respectable … Remote', *Media Guardian*, 20 June, p4

Poulantzas, N. (1975) *Classes in Contemporary Capitalism*, London, New Left Books

Power, M. and Sheridan, G. (1984) *Labour Daily? Ins and Outs of a New Labour Daily and Other Media Alternatives*, London, TUC

Pratten, C. (1993) *The Stock Market*, Cambridge, Cambridge University Press

Puette, W. (1992) *Through Jaundiced Eyes: How the Media View Organised Labor*, Ithaca, NY, ILR Press

Ramanadham, V. (1993) *Privatisation – A Global Perspective*, London, Routledge

Richardson, J. (1993) *Pressure Groups*, Oxford, Oxford University Press

Richardson, J. and Jordan, G. (1979) *Governing Under Pressure*, Oxford, Martin Robertson

Rosenbaum, M. (1997) *From Soapbox to Soundbite: Party Political Campaigning in Britain Since 1945*, London, Macmillan

Rubin, B. (1977) *Big Business and the Mass Media*, Lexington, MA, Lexington Books

Rubinstein, W.D. (1993) *Capitalism, Culture, and Decline in Britain 1750–1990*, London, Routledge

Rudd, R. (1994) 'Lobbyists Deliver First-Class Service', *Financial Times*, 20 May, p10

Rusbridger, Alan (1996) 'Serious Newspapers Cost Money', *Press Gazette*, 22 March, p15

Sampson, A. (1996) 'The Crisis at the Heart of our Media', *British Journalism Review*, Vol. 7, No. 3, pp42–51

Scammell, M. (1995) *Designer Politics: How Elections are Won*, London, Macmillan

Schiller, H. (1989) *Culture Inc. – The Corporate Takeover of Public Expression*, Oxford, Oxford University Press

Schiller, H. (1992) *Mass Communication and the American Empire* (2nd edn), Boulder, CO, Westview Press

Schlesinger, P. (1990) 'Rethinking the Sociology of Journalism: Source Strategies and the Limits of Media-Centrism', in Ferguson, M. (ed.) *Public Communication – The New Imperative*, London, Sage, pp61–83

Schlesinger, P. and Tumber, H. (1994) *Reporting Crime: The Media Politics of Criminal Justice*, Oxford, Clarendon Press

Schlesinger, P., Murdock, G. and Elliott, P. (1983) *Televising Terrorism*, London, Comedia

Schudson, M. (1996) 'The Sociology of News Production Revisited', in Curran, J. and Gurevitch, M. (eds), *Mass Media and Society* (2nd edn), London, Arnold, pp141–59

Scott, J. (1991) *Who Rules Britain*, Cambridge, Polity Press

Scott, J. and Griff, C. (1984) *Directors of Industry: The British Corporate Network 1904–76*, Cambridge, Polity Press

Searjant, G. (1996) 'Granada's Forte Takeover to Cost Tax Payers £450 million', *The Times*, 22 January, p1

Seaton, J. (1991) 'Trade Unions and the Media', in Pimlott, B. and Cook, C. (eds), *Trade Unions in British Politics: The First 250 Years*, Harlow, Longman, pp272–90

Serra, S. (2000) 'The Killing of Brazilian Street Children and the Rise of the International Public Sphere', in Curran, J. (ed.), *Media Organisations in Society*, London, Arnold

Seymour-Ure, C. (1996) *The British Press and Broadcasting Since 1945* (2nd edn), Oxford, Blackwell

Shoemaker, P. (1989) 'Public Relations Versus Journalism – Comments on Turrow', *American Behavioural Scientist*, Vol. 33, No. 2, pp213–15

Sigal, L.V. (1973) *Reporters and Officials – The Organisation and Politics of Newsmaking*, Lexington, MA, Lexington Books

Smith, P. (1989) 'Investor Relations – Professionals and Institutions', in Bowman, P. (ed.) *Handbook of Financial Public Relations*, London, Heinemann Professional

Smith, W. (1988) 'Business and the Media: Sometimes Partners, Sometimes Adversaries', in Hiebert, R. and Reuss, C. (eds), *Impacts of Mass Media*, New York, Longman, pp444–7

Snow, J. (1996) *Press Gazette*, 20 September, p5

Sola Pool, I. de (1983) *Technologies of Freedom*, Cambridge, MA, Harvard University Press

Spillius, A. (1996) 'Friend or Foe?', *Media Guardian*, 13 May, p10

Stauber, J. and Rampton, S. (1995) *Toxic Sludge is Good For You – Lies, Damn Lies and the Public Relations Industry*, Monroe, ME, Common Courage Press

Sudarsanam, P. (1995) *The Essence of Mergers and Acquisitions*, London, Prentice Hall

Taylor, R. (1994) *The Future of the Trade Unions*, London, Andre Deutsch

Taylor, R. (1994a) 'Battle Fought from Behind Enemy Lines', *Financial Times*, 3 November, p8

Thomas, R. (1996) 'Cheap Labourers Pawns in the Takeover Game', *Guardian*, 10 January, p16

Thomson, S., Stanich, L. and Dickson, L. (1998) 'Gun Control and Snowdrop', *Parliamentary Affairs*, Vol. 51, No. 51, pp329–44

Tieman, R. (1994a) 'Plea to Privatise the Post Office Quickly', *The Times*, 12 August, p19

Tieman, R. (1994b) 'Waiting for the Government's Postal Orders', *The Times*, 3 September, p21

Tiffen, R. (1989) *News and Power*, Sydney, Allen and Unwin

The Times 1000: 1995 (1996), London, Times Books

Timmins, N. (1994) 'Sub-Postmasters Oppose Sell-Off', *Independent*, 15 August, p2

Truman, D. (1951) *The Governmental Process*, New York, Alfred A. Knopf

Tuchman, D. (1978) *Making News*, New York, Free Press

Tulloch, J. (1993) 'Policing the Public Sphere – the British machinery of News Management', *Media, Culture and Society*, Vol. 15, No. 3, pp363–84

Tumber, H. (1993) ''Selling Scandal': Business and the Media', *Media, Culture and Society*, Vol. 15, No. 3, pp345–61

Tunstall, J. (1971) *Journalists at Work*, London, Sage

Tunstall, J. (1996) *Newspaper Power: The National Press in Britain*, Oxford, Oxford University Press

Tunstall, J. and Palmer, M. (1991) *Media Moguls*, London, Routledge

Turner, B. (1990a) 'Australia: The Debate about Hegemonic Culture', in Abercrombie, A., Hill, S. and Turner, B. *Dominant Ideologies*, London, Unwin Hyman, pp158–81

Turner, B. (1990b) 'Peroration on Ideology', in Abercrombie, A., Hill, S. and Turner, B. *Dominant Ideologies*, London, Unwin Hyman, pp229–56

Turrow, J. (1989) 'Public Relations and Newswork: A Neglected Relationship', *American Behavioural Scientist*, Vol. 33, No. 2, pp206–12

Tye, L. (1998) *The Father of Spin: Edward L. Bernays and the Birth of Public Relations*, New York, Crown

Useem, M. (1984) *The Inner Circle: Large Corporations and the Rise of Business Political Activity in the US and the UK*, Oxford, Oxford University Press

Veljanovski, C. (ed.) (1989) *Freedom in Broadcasting*, London, Institute of Economic Affairs

Verzuh, R. (1990) 'Changing Images: British Trade Union Communication Under Thatcherism', unpublished postgraduate thesis, Warwick University and TUC Library

Vogel, D. (1983) 'The Power of Business in America: A Reappraisal', *British Journal of Political Science*, Vol. 13, No. 1, pp19–44

Walton, P. and Davis, H. (1977) 'Bad News for Trade Unionists', in Beharrell, P. and Philo, G. (eds) *Trade Unions and the Media*, London, Macmillan, pp118–34

Warner, R. and Silk, L. (1979) *Ideals in Collision – The Relationship Between Business and the News Media*, New York, Carnegie-Mellon University Press

Watts, D. (1997) *Political Communications Today*, Manchester, Manchester University Press

Wernick, A. (1991) *Promotional Culture – Advertising, Ideology and Symbolic Expression*, London, Sage

White, J. and Mazur, L. (1995) *Strategic Communications Management: Making Public Relations Work*, Wokingham, Addison-Wesley

Whitfield, M. (1994) 'Post Office Managers Reject Sale', *Independent*, 8 September, p7

Williams, G. (1996) *Britain's Media – How They Are Related*, London, Campaign for Press and Broadcasting Freedom

Williams, R. (1977) *Marxism and Literature*, Milton Keynes, Open University Press

Wilson, D. (1984) *Pressure: The A to Z of campaigning in Britain*, London, Heinemann

Wilson, K.M. (2000) 'Communicating Climate Change Through the Media: Predictions, Politics and Perceptions of Risk', in Allan, S., Adam, B. and Carter, C. (eds) *Environmental Risks and the Media*, London, Routledge, pp201–17

Winter, J. (1990) *The Silent Revolution – Media, Democracy and the Free Trade Debate*, Ottawa, University of Ottawa Press

Wright Mills, C. (1956) *The Power Elite*, Oxford, Oxford University Press

Wykes, M. (2000) 'The Burrowers: News About Bodies, Tunnels and Green Guerillas', in Allan, S., Adam, B. and Carter, C. (eds) *Environmental Risks and the Media*, London, Routledge, pp73–89

Wynn-Davies, P. (1994) 'Tory MPs "Oppose Sell-Off of Royal Mail"', *Independent*, 24 October, p6

Young, H. (1989) *One of Us*, London, Macmillan

INDEX